GIVE THE FANS SWEET FA © Peter Farrell 2015

In memory of the **167** oil rig workers who sadly perished on **Piper Alpha** on **6**[th] **July 1988.**

Gone, but never forgotten.

Acknowledgements

I have always had this image of somebody writing a book and living like a recluse, tucked away in a log cabin up in the mountains for months on end.

My log cabin was an oil rig in the North Sea where I did my other job for two or three weeks at a time. So if you're ever thinking of writing a book, it would certainly be worth considering working on an oil platform... and if you already work on one, then I would definitely recommend writing a book. Either way, I would like to say a special thank you to everybody in the oil and gas industry for providing the perfect environment for me to write this book.

Meeting so many different people in various locations on these rigs, in many countries around the world, has also given me the opportunity to meet supporters from football clubs everywhere. This, more than anything else, has helped me to appreciate their views and opinions, which is why, no matter which football team they may support, my respect for my fellow fans will always remain equal.

I would like to thank all my friends and colleagues that I have loved working with, including my tiger feet mates. Yes, that's right, that's right. My Indian colleagues, who I converted into Evertonians, my friends from Scotland, Wales, Ireland (North & South), Denmark, Norway, Germany, Holland, Cyprus, Saudi Arabia as well as Port Elizabeth, South Africa, and not forgetting the beautiful people I met in Toronto, Canada and those passionate New York City FC fans.

A very special thank you must go to Valerie Ball, my editor. When I first spoke to Val a few years ago, she informed me she had no real interest in football. Once she told me that, I knew then that this was the person I wanted to edit my book. I explained to her that this was not a book about football, but football fans and there were no offside rules in this book, only broken rules.

Fortunately for me, Val accepted my invitation. During the writing of this book, she has always been there for me and I would very much welcome the opportunity to work with her again.

Finally, I would like to thank my old friend Michael, my wife and all my family for their continued support and everybody else who has helped make this book possible.

INTRODUCTION

Dear Man in the Suit,

When I look back, I realise I've had a most unusual and extraordinary life as a football fan and there have been many times when I've asked myself how different it would have been if I hadn't queued up that day and met you. Although you don't know me, you obviously have no inkling of how much you changed my perception of football, or that you actually altered the course of my whole life. That much I can say with my hand on my heart and without any exaggeration.

For many years, I have desperately wanted to contact you and let you know how you opened my eyes into what really goes on in football, as well as sending me on an incredible journey, a journey I could never have imagined possible.

Had it not been for you, I would never have met all those interesting and wonderful people and I certainly wouldn't have written this book.

You may think that I have a lot to thank you for, but the undeniable truth is that I will never be able to forgive what you did to me. Although you may not have intended to do so, I hold you fully responsible for ruining the beautiful game I once loved as much as life itself.

You see, ignorance really is bliss. Up until the day I met you, I belonged to a totally different world where I was living the dream as an innocent and naive, loyal supporter, a life that only a football fan could possibly understand. It was without doubt the happiest period of my life, travelling the length and breadth of the country supporting the team I loved, even if it meant me parting with every single penny I had. I loved, lived and breathed football and I really believed it when they called me the twelfth man.

When I see football fans today at the match, jumping up and down, screaming when their team scores, I feel so envious of them and would give anything to be one of those passionate, excited fans once again. But you took away all of that passion; it felt exactly like the day when I discovered there was no Father Christmas - and what a huge disappointment that was to me as a young lad. Well, my feelings were exactly the same that day when we met.

You not only gave me an insight to a world I never knew existed, but you also took away in an instant the innocent, naive love I had for football. Just as with Santa, I now know that the game I grew up loving isn't real any more.

I don't feel that I benefited in any way, either, or that I was educated by having my eyes opened. To me it feels more as if I was hypnotised or brainwashed and there have been many times when I felt like screaming all the way down Wembley Way, "What right did you have to do that to me?"

If there were any possible way of being hypnotised back into that football fanatic tomorrow, believe me, I would pay anything. But thanks to you, I know that's never going to happen to me again.

I really hope you read this book because, like me, you belong in another world as well, but yours is a totally different world, a world where people like yourself cannot see how wrong it is to be disrespectful to genuine football fans.

You certainly opened my eyes; it's now my turn to open yours.

Yours sincerely,

Peter Farrell.

CONTENTS

One
A Fan's Baptism

I didn't know how many hours I'd been lying there, eyes wide open, staring up into the darkness, my imagination working overtime. The silence was broken only by the barking of a distant dog and although I strained my ears, there were no sounds of any human activity at all. If I could only hear the chink of milk bottles then at least then I would know this interminable night was nearing the end.

Unconsciousness must have overcome me at some stage because the next thing I knew, I was being jolted awake by my own screaming voice. My mother was shaking me by the shoulder.

"Do you know what the time is? I thought you couldn't wait for today to come and you've gone and missed it?"

"What do you mean? What time is it then?"

It was when she replied it was nearly four o'clock in the afternoon that the screaming started. I couldn't believe it… how could they have let me sleep all day? I had obviously slept in due to the fact that I'd had very little sleep all night. But what were they thinking of when they knew how much today meant to me?

When I opened my eyes, though, it was still dark and Mum was actually still in bed. She'd been shaking me awake in my dream which of course had turned into a nightmare.

Anyway, after what had to be the longest night ever, I was up, dressed and ready at 6am, to be taken to watch my team playing live for the very first time in my life, even though the game wasn't due to kick off until

3pm that afternoon. After the long night, I still had another eight or nine hours to fill somehow.

Visiting the club you support for the very first time is an unforgettable experience for any football fan and mine was no exception. The year was 1970 and I was ten years old.

I watched *The Double Deckers* and *The Banana Splits* on TV and after hours of nagging my dad, he eventually took me and my older brother, Anthony, on what would be the first of a lifetime of journeys to Goodison Park, the home of Everton Football Club. I'll never forget the excitement of sitting in my dad's Ford Anglia with its distinctive interior smell and seeing this magnificent stadium for the very first time… and we were still a couple of miles away.

The enormous royal blue arena, draped in flags and banners, could easily be seen from a distance and there must have been thousands of people, as if summoned in some kind of hypnotic trance, all slowly walking like Zombies in one direction and drawn towards this huge stadium.

Outside the ground, I couldn't believe the size of those police horses and to be standing right up alongside them for the very first time was amazing. There was that warm aroma of hot dogs that you never forget; another being the smell of the freshly printed match-day programmes. But as any fan will testify, going through the turnstile and seeing that green turf in real life for the very first time is just… Wow! An unbelievable sight and one that stays with you forever.

We were amongst the first in the ground and kick-off was still almost two hours away. We paid to get into the Paddock (standing area in those days). I couldn't see over the wall separating the fans from the pitch and if the truth be known, I would still struggle to see over it today. Some kids were standing on beer crates, whilst others were sitting on their dads' shoulders and some were lucky enough to perch on the barriers.

When Everton and Derby County walked out onto the pitch, the noise was deafening and the atmosphere was something I had never before experienced in my life and from that moment on, the only thing I ever wanted to do when I grew up was to play for Everton. Seeing my hero, Alan Ball, in real life, running with the ball and wearing his famous white boots was an unforgettable and pivotal moment and without even realising what had happened, I had just been baptised an Evertonian.

Another thing that will always stick in my mind was hearing my dad swear and although this seemed strange at first, it somehow didn't sound vulgar or offensive. Some of the one-liners I heard were brilliant as this non-stop barrage of insults was hurled at the referee, the opposing players, as well as one or two of our own players and this was just from my dad. I couldn't help wondering if he'd have sworn like that if my mum had been there. I'm not sure whether it was the euphoria or excitement of the match occasion, but it wasn't like sitting next to my old fella, he was more like a brother or one of my mates. Perhaps that explains why our kid and I began calling him by his first name, Jimmy.

Isn't it funny, growing up and being at very special occasions, how the stories seem to remain in your head for the rest of your life? I can still vividly remember Jimmy telling us on that day how, years ago, clubs used to let women in free of charge to stop the men swearing.

I'm not sure though if it would have had that much of an impact as I could see quite a few women standing near us and the men were still swearing. In fact, some of the women were swearing more than the men.

Although the match ended in a 1-1 draw, it didn't matter. I was hooked. After the game, we made Jimmy wait with us for a couple of hours for the players to leave in their cars, hoping to get a glimpse and possibly even an autograph. I can remember running over to Alan Ball's car with a million other kids, only to end up at the back and missing out. When Alan Ball had driven away, I was heartbroken and although I couldn't have known it at the time, there were to be plenty more heartbreaking moments supporting my team, Everton.

Alan Ball, my hero, wearing his unique white boots

The following season, our Anthony decided to go to the other side of Stanley Park, to Anfield, and watch our closest rivals, Liverpool, with his mates. Although Jimmy was at first a little disappointed, he eventually forgave him, especially when he realised he only had to pay for two season tickets instead of three.

My younger brother, Jeggsy, followed me and Jimmy to Everton, with my youngest brother, Joey, and younger sister, Julie deciding to follow our Anthony over to the forbidden land.

So there we were, at the start of a family divide, not unusual for football fans on Merseyside. As you can imagine, our family life was very competitive and there was certainly never a dull moment in our gaff. But that's the way it was and still is on Merseyside, families split in two, and do you know what? I wouldn't like to see it any other way. In a funny kind of way, I would prefer to see families divided rather than communities and certain city regions. At least you knew it was more of a friendly rivalry, if you know what I mean, and I suppose that's what makes Merseyside such a special place.

A Derby match - when two clubs from the same city play against each other is always special, but whenever Everton and Liverpool meet, it's even more special. The Merseyside Derby is actually quite unique, seeing supporters from both teams sitting next to each other, wearing different colours. It's something I've always been very proud of and Derby days as we grew up were brilliant in our house, especially if it was our team that won.

Eventually, after a few years, I did what a lot of other young people did and started going to the game with my mates. This was the time when I started venturing further afield and travelling around the country; suddenly my knowledge of English geography was second to none.

I was fourteen years of age in 1974 and I can vividly remember one weekend when Everton had to play one of their FA cup games on a Sunday, which at the time was absolutely unheard of. Because of the miners' strike and an oil embargo by OPEC members, there was an energy crisis in the UK at the time. These were difficult times with people having to work a three-day week to save fuel and football clubs were even banned from using their floodlights. Liverpool were also drawn to play at home in an FA cup match, so permission was granted by the FA for Everton to play their cup tie against West Bromwich Albion on the Sunday, with Liverpool playing their match twenty four hours earlier on the Saturday, as there wouldn't have been enough energy to supply both grounds in the same city on the same day.

This was all well and good and sounded like problem solved. However, because of a very old by-law which had been in force since 1780 that prohibited charging for any kind of entertainment in a public place on Sundays, football clubs and Everton in particular had a bit of a problem on their hands.

Now there was no way that clubs were going to allow thousands of people into their grounds free of charge, so a way was devised to bypass this archaic law. To stay within the law, admission into the game was made free, but instead of fans paying to gain entry, they had to buy a programme or a team sheet for the normal cost of getting into the ground. So, in effect, fans were still paying to get in, but it was just under a different guise. The price of a programme would vary, depending on where you sat in the ground.

But there was another twist to this quite unusual problem. To make absolutely sure the clubs didn't get into trouble for bypassing this law, it was decided they would have to leave one gate open, free to enter. That way, they really did appear to be allowing people into a public place to be entertained free of charge.

This was manna from heaven for me and my mates, until we discovered the club would not be revealing which was the free gate.

"Never mind," we said to ourselves. "We'll just walk round every single gate until we find out which one it is."

So on the day of the match, we made sure we arrived early and began walking round to find the free gate.

"Sorry, boys, not this one," was something we were sick of hearing as we made our way round every single turnstile, looking for the Holy Grail. We didn't for one minute realise how long this would take, but with a very large crowd of people and many probably trying exactly the same thing, it was a lot more difficult than we had expected.

After about two hours of getting nowhere, we were now starting to get cheesed off and with only fifteen minutes to kick off, we knew we were running out of time. We asked one of the stewards where this free gate was.

"Oh, you're on the wrong side of the ground," he said. "It's round by the Park End."

"You're joking. We already tried every one of them," I told him.

"You must have skipped the free one."

"Well, which gate is it in the Park End?"

"I'm not sure which one exactly, but it's definitely round there," he insisted.

"Thanks very much," I said.

We ran round as quickly as we could and tried every turnstile once again.

"Lying bastard! He must support Liverpool," my mate said.

By now we could hear the teams coming out onto the pitch and panic began to set in. I walked over to one of the other stewards.

"Okay, we give in. Which is the free gate, please?"

I couldn't believe his reply.

"Oh, you're on the wrong side of the ground, it's round by the Gwladys Street."

"Listen, mate," I said. "We've just come from there and have been sent round on a wild goose chase for the past three hours. We've spent all our money, as we thought we would be allowed in free, we're just about to miss the kick off and you wanna send us back round there. You don't happen to support Liverpool by any chance, do you mate?

"I do, actually," he said.

We all knew there were a few stewards at Everton who supported Liverpool, as it was a chance for them to earn a few quid when their team played away. These Liverpool fans must have had a great laugh, sending us Evertonians on a wild goose chase. We then started walking round again, but this time, instead of looking for the free turnstile, we were now looking for a steward who supported Everton.

Eventually one of my mates shouted, "This steward supports Everton!"

We ran over to him quickly and asked him

which was the free gate?

"I don't know," he said.

By now we could hear the teams' names being announced on the public address system and we were starting to lose it.

"You don't fucking know," my mate said, "and you fucking work here."

"We're asking you for the last time, which one is the fucking free gate? Or shall we go to the office to register a complaint and then straight to the newspapers?"

"Listen, boys... I'm not lying to you, honestly. I'm not even sure if there is a free gate open, but seeing as you're having such a bad day, if you follow me, I'll escort you inside the ground, free of charge."

Why we never met this beautiful man in the first place, I'll never know. He brought us straight through one of the gates and just in time for the kick off.

I then apologised. "Thanks, I said, "and we're sorry for swearing at you, especially on a Sunday."

At around fifteen years of age, my love for Everton football club was so great that school was just something that happened in between Everton's next game and the weekends couldn't come quickly enough. Friday afternoon's science lesson would be spent secretly planning our route to Newcastle, Tottenham and many other grounds around the country.

But when the letters from school began arriving at our house regarding my lack of interest and attendance, I used to pay our Anthony to forge my parents' signatures and send them straight back.

I've never been able to figure out why schools

right across Merseyside seem to produce so many celebrities and our school, St John's in Bebington was no exception. Pete Burns, the singer from Dead or Alive was a year above me and had a top hit with *You Spin Me Right Round*. Paul Usher, who was a year younger and in our junior school, played Barry Grant in Brookside. Oh... and there's even this bloke that's become a football author.

When the teachers eventually cottoned on to me intercepting their letters, the Head called at our house personally to inform my parents and I was suspended with immediate effect. As you can imagine, Jimmy and Josie were not too pleased and they knew there was only one punishment. The timing couldn't have been worse for me, as it was the Merseyside Derby that weekend when Everton were playing Liverpool at Anfield.

When they took my ticket off me I was devastated. If it had been any other match, fair enough, but there was no way I could miss the Derby. My mates and I had been very lucky to get hold of tickets for this match as they were like gold dust. We had spoken about nothing else for weeks leading up to this game and in those days, the matches were not screened live on TV like they are today, which made my punishment even harder.

With my Derby ticket confiscated and languishing upon my parents' dressing table in their bedroom (they knew full well I wouldn't dare go into their room and take it), my mates kept asking me what I was going to do, constantly reminding me that this wasn't any old football match, it was the *Merseyside Derby*.

I suppose this could be an appropriate moment

to finally confess to my own four children that your dad never really got all those qualifications or did brilliantly in school after all. Sorry, kids, but you know how it is…

I lost count of the number of apologies I made. I even cried and begged Jimmy and Josie to choose another punishment. But I'd already exhausted every one of those and they obviously hadn't worked. Being a father today, I must admit I would have to do the same thing but, for me at the time, they were both bang out of order for taking my Derby ticket.

Anyway, the night before the game and after countless more rejected apologies, I'm still not sure for how many days I promised to clean our Anthony's room, but I bribed him to go in and get me the ticket, as they would never have suspected him of entering their room.

The next morning, our kid came into my room quite early with the ticket as the match was kicking off earlier, at eleven-thirty in the morning, due to the Grand National horse race taking place at nearby Aintree. I can still proudly remember thinking, another huge sporting event and the world's greatest horse race, also staged in Liverpool, yeah, we've got the lot on Merseyside. Even though the National wasn't run until the afternoon, in those days the police and everybody else made sure it wouldn't clash with a football match, especially a Derby, as the whole of Merseyside would have come to a standstill. I always used to think it was so that the footballers could go and watch their horses run in the National later that day (and I meant the horses that they owned). In fact, I still do.

I once heard somebody say, 'Always buy a good pair of shoes or a good bed, because you're either in one or the other.' But on this particular day, I made sure I was in neither, as I lay there pretending to be asleep, wearing my Doc Martens boots and waiting for our kid to come into my room with my ticket. Before Anthony gave me the ticket, he made me promise not to grass him up for getting it. He also told me I was wasting my time as Everton were going to get hammered. I knew he would also be at the match, but he would be in the Kop end shouting for Liverpool with his mates.

"We'll see about that," I said, as I climbed out of my bedroom window so that Jimmy, who was downstairs, didn't notice me leaving, but not before I left a brilliant effigy of me lying in bed, just in case my parents checked my room.

My mates were waiting for me at the bottom of our road and I was on my way to the Merseyside Derby.

When we reached Anfield the atmosphere was electric and you could feel the pre-match Derby nerves setting in. The stakes were so high that both Everton and Liverpool knew they couldn't contemplate losing this match. Any other match, maybe, but not to your neighbours and dearest rivals. There were hordes of fans outside the ground without tickets asking if anybody had any spares and my mates and I knew how lucky we were to have ours, especially me managing to get hold of mine at the eleventh hour.

As we walked up to the turnstile, I pulled out my ticket when suddenly one of my mates grabbed my arm.

"Peter, quick, look who's standing at the turnstile!"

"Oh shit!" A profanity escaped my young lips as I looked up. I couldn't believe it… it was Jimmy. He knew which turnstile I had to go through and had travelled to the game to catch me before I could go in. He hadn't spotted any of us yet and we all stood back out of the way, deciding what to do. My mates were laughing their heads off, but I didn't find it at all funny and by the look on his face, Jimmy seemed pretty determined I would serve my punishment and miss this match.

Knowing that Jimmy was also a big Everton fan, one of my mates, Simon, joked and said, "He's not really that bothered about you getting into trouble in school, Peter. He just wants your Derby ticket, mate."

I appealed to my mates to help me. What the hell was I going to do? I even asked a steward if I could go in through another gate. No, I couldn't. How was I going to get past my dad who was standing like some kind of sentry, arms folded and just waiting for me to arrive?

There was only one thing for it.

"I'm going to have to go up close to him and let him chase me so I can get him away from that gate," I told my mates.

So, bold as brass, I walked right up to him and said, "Hello, Jim, what you doing here?"

"Come here, you!" he shouted as I began my escape. It must have been hilarious for my mates, watching my dad chasing me up the Anfield Road, then all the way along the Main Stand, up along the back of the Kop and then back around the old Kemlyn Road. Having completed almost 360 degrees of the stadium, poor Jimmy was lagging quite a distance behind and all that swearing couldn't have helped his breathing much.

I played in the school team and was quite fit at the time so it was fair to assume I would get back to the turnstile first. I quickly produced my ticket to the gateman and slipped safely inside the ground.

My mates were laughing like mad and everybody watching must have wondered what was going on. When Jimmy eventually reached the turnstile, still swearing and seriously out of breath, he tried to get in, but was stopped by a policeman, who must have thought he was a bit long in the tooth to be a football hooligan. I could just pick up snatches of his breathless response.

"...suspended from school, the little bug... ticket off him... punishment... ejected from the ground immediately..."

It was too late; I was safely inside and making myself scarce in the crowd. Unfortunately, though, like many other Derby games in my childhood, we lost to Liverpool and I was beginning to regret ever taking the ticket in the first place, as I now had to return home and face the music.

"Was it really worth it?" I kept asking myself on the way home. Now I was in even more trouble and because Jimmy was also an Evertonian, he wouldn't be in the best of moods either, with us losing to Liverpool.

This experience may well have been my first lesson in the injustice of fans always getting the bum deal. It didn't seem fair that I'd just put myself in all kinds of trouble with my parents by supporting and worshipping these very fortunate footballers, who were now on their way to having a nice day out at the Grand National. I was in no hurry to return home and I even made sure I didn't get back until after the Grand National, hoping Jimmy might have just landed a 100/1 winner.

I'll always remember Josie answering my knock

on the door when I eventually arrived home, trying her best not to laugh as I walked in. What I quickly detected from my mum was a situation where she was trying to be serious with me but finding it difficult. I could just imagine Jimmy telling her the tale of how he chased me around Anfield when he got back. Knowing Josie as I do, it must have been almost impossible for her to keep a straight face.

She said to me, loud enough for Jimmy to hear and obviously trying to defuse and calm down an angry parent, "You know what you did was wrong, Peter, but we've decided not to talk about it until we've all had a chance to calm down."

"Thank God for that," I thought. She was brilliant at defusing situations and still is today. I think mothers must possess that innate quality, as my wife's pretty good at it as well. Anyway, I quickly stole a glance at Jimmy who was sitting down watching *World of Sport* or *Grandstand* and by the look on his face he obviously hadn't landed that 100/1 winner on the National either. To this day, I'm still not sure if he was more upset with me, his horse, or Everton getting beaten. Either way, we'd both seen better days.

A few years later when my lovely dad passed away, the priest asked our family if there were any memories we would like to share at his funeral. Without telling anybody in my family, I wrote a little note and the following is what the priest read out to a packed church:

"A few years ago, when Peter was late for a Derby match and Jimmy being the lovely, kind dad that he was, got up early as the Grand National was on and gave his son a lift over to Anfield."

So that my mum and the rest of the family

would really get the joke, I had also written:

"Because Peter had done so very well at school, Jimmy said to him, "Jump in son, I'll take you and your mates to the game."

To be quite honest, I wasn't sure how Josie was going to react, or the rest of the family for that matter, as I was risking upsetting them all on this very sad day. But I needn't have worried. As the priest was speaking, Josie looked over at me, laughing with the rest of the family and I could also hear my mates behind me laughing along with everybody else who knew the real story.

The priest must have wondered what was so funny about a father giving his son a lift to a football match. I am one hundred percent certain my dad would have loved what the priest read out as well. I would like to think I inherited a tiny bit of his great sense of humour and it really did put a smile on all our faces on what was otherwise a very sad day for our family.

Outside the church Josie said, "I want to tell you something that I've never told you before, because it would have undermined our authority as parents, but to be perfectly honest, when your dad returned home from Anfield that day, we laughed our heads off. But of course, I somehow had to keep a straight face when you knocked at the door."

It was so heart-warming to hear that from my mum, but also rather poignant as I could just imagine the two of them laughing together at the time, as they so often did.

Two
Blue Peter

For me personally, growing up as a football fan was absolutely brilliant. My old head school teacher, or even Jimmy and Josie would never have believed how much football actually helped me with my education. Some of the new words I learnt, I'd never heard in school. Words like innocuous, penultimate, aggregate, crescendo, partisan, nostalgia, tenacity and trepidation were all picked up from commentators in football. Not to mention all the funny clichés, like a potential banana skin. My Geography also improved with all that travelling and being an Evertonian, as the old song goes... *And if you know your history...* I certainly did. Transfer fees and match attendances were great for my maths. I was even picking up some Latin with Everton's motto, *nil satis nisi optimum,* which translates as 'nothing but the best is good enough' and I would never in my wildest dreams have written a book if it hadn't been for football.

However, it wasn't all roses. As everybody is no doubt aware, football also had its dark side and the 1970's and 80's were undeniably an extremely dangerous time to be a football fan. With the hooligan problem probably at its peak it didn't matter who you supported, travelling to watch your team involved many daring risks, as fans where no longer making the back pages of newspapers, but many of the front ones. If you kept your head down in those days and were aware of the dangers, you learned how to avoid certain situations, but your safety was by no means guaranteed.

I'll never forget my very first away game which was at Manchester City's old ground, Maine Road, as a naive fifteen-year-old. I can still recall getting off the train with my mates, Simon and Dave, at Victoria station in Manchester and thinking what a great welcoming reception the police had given us Everton fans. They even escorted us on to the many buses waiting to take us up to the ground! It sounds daft now, I know, but I can honestly remember thinking, surely it didn't need this many police to show us where Manchester City's ground was? It was only when the bus turned the corner that I realised the significance of the massive police presence.

Unfortunately for us, the police weren't the only ones welcoming us to Manchester that day. Hundreds of Man City fans were waiting round the corner and began showering our bus with bricks and bottles. Without a word of exaggeration, we were all lying on the floor fearing for our lives as the windows were coming through all around us and there was glass everywhere. I can remember lying there, frightened out of my wits and praying, "Jesus, Mary and Joseph, if we manage to survive this, I swear I'll never go to another away match ever again." It really was a terrifying experience. The police appeared to be absolutely powerless to stop what was happening and we genuinely feared for our lives.

I'll never know how the driver managed to manoeuvre us to safety that day, but it was a terrifying introduction to away games. I can remember a strange and eerie silence as we drove up to the football ground with hardly any windows left on the bus, as well as it being cold and draughty.

When we eventually arrived at the game, there were a few people looking over at our bus but not appearing overly concerned, maybe because this type of thing did seem to be a regular occurrence. They must have thought, there goes another Everton bus that's just been bricked. Could you imagine something like that happening today? It would definitely be on the main news, as well as being plastered across every social media website.

I travel quite a lot nowadays in my job as a welder and even after all those years, whenever I pass through Manchester, I still get butterflies in my stomach. Visiting new places with my job can still seem a bit strange and even though I've been doing this for many years now, I can't help thinking back to what it was like for an innocent fifteen-year-old who'd never been anywhere before in his life. That's one side of football I certainly don't miss.

Although Everton lost the game, we got to listen to the famous Man City fan, Helen, ringing her bell and even though our trip to Manchester was a scary experience, it didn't stop us travelling to follow our team, but I swore I would never take that Manchester train ever again.

I should have learned my lesson at Manchester City, but if Everton had been playing in Beirut or even Baghdad, it still wouldn't have stopped me following my team. Every single away game was fraught with danger and you really needed to have your wits about you.

When I travelled to The City Ground, Nottingham Forest, and still as daft as a brush, I don't know what the hell I was thinking whilst waiting to be served in a chip shop with a load of Forest fans standing behind me in the queue. The penny only dropped when I heard some of them saying, 'lets go and beat up the Scouse bastards.' When it was my turn to be served and the lady asked me what I wanted, I just froze, unable to speak.

I couldn't believe how stupid I had been and I knew once they heard me speak, it wouldn't just be the fish getting battered. I thought of just walking out, but they would have known straight away I was an Evertonian and I had to try and remain calm.

She asked me once again what I wanted. Panic can do very strange things to people and to this day, I still can't explain why I asked for a portion of chips in a very broad Irish accent.

I looked around slowly at the Forest fans, as they all said together, 'Ay up, Scouser... he's a fucking Scouser.'

"Would you like vinegar?" she asked.

"No tanks," I said.

I don't know why I was still putting on what I thought was an Irish accent, as they had all sussed me anyway. It must have been my nerves.

I heard one of them say, 'Let's do him in.' Not surprisingly, I suddenly lost my appetite and decided there were more important things in this life than a bag of chips and without further ado, I did what Usain Bolt does for a living. I may not have been quite as fast, but I can say for certain I wasn't far off.

"No tanks... I mean thanks!" I shouted as I made my escape down the street. Fortunately, I ran into a load of Scousers and I mean loads of them and when the chips are down, you can always rely on your own fans to come to the rescue.

Nothing, though, could compare to the most terrifying football experience of them all, when I travelled to Charlton to watch Everton with my mate, Dennis. Everything seemed like a normal Saturday afternoon, apart from the journey being a bit quiet from Euston station to the Valley Stadium. I was doing what I always did, talking to fellow fans, on this occasion a Charlton dad with his young boy, as we exchanged some banter with our teams about to do battle. They were the ones who told me that Rodney Charlton Trotter from *Only Fools and Horses* was named after their team.

I asked why there were not many Charlton fans on the train, considering we weren't that far from the ground. I was also wondering why they weren't wearing their red Charlton colours to the match.

He gave me an incredulous look. "You have to be very careful on these trains, mate."

"You're joking aren't you? The train's almost empty," I said.

I couldn't put my finger on it, but something didn't seem right. The journey was far too peaceful and lacked that normal footie match atmosphere.

Talk about the calm before the storm. We pulled into the next station and as I looked through the window, I was absolutely shocked and couldn't believe my eyes. Standing on the platform waiting to board our train was a sight, I swear, I will take to my grave.

There were hundreds and hundreds of football fans and just like me and Dennis, they were all wearing blue. At last it now felt like we were on our way to a football match and I smiled at Dennis.

"Here's all the Everton fans, mate. We must have got the wrong train connection."

I was looking out for friends or anybody I knew, but I couldn't recognise any of them.

Suddenly, Dennis grabbed hold of me. "Peter," he said very seriously, "these aren't Evertonians, mate."

The man with his son gave me a very scared look and told us to zip our shell suits up to hide our Everton shirts. "Quick!" he urged and put a finger to his lips, warning us to keep quiet. He looked very concerned and it now became very clear why there were not many Charlton fans on this train and even more so, why this guy and his boy were not wearing their red Charlton colours.

These fans swarmed onto the train, jumping up and down squeezing past each other into each compartment, including ours, chanting... The Millwall, clap, clap, clap! The Millwall, bang, bang, bang! As they knocked on the trains doors, walls and even the windows.

Like all football supporters they chanted in unison, but Dennis and I were more than aware that these were not like all football supporters. With all due respect to the good Millwall supporters, these fans held the worst reputation in the land for hooliganism and violence and Dennis and I had somehow managed to find ourselves stuck right in the middle of them, with no way out. This was another one of those rare moments in my life when I was speechless.

Just to compound our fears even further, one of the Millwall fans said, 'Hey, the facking scousers are in town today, aren't they?

'S'right,' another said, 'they're playing Charlton. Wouldn't it be facking great if we bumped into those facking Scouse bastards today and kick the shit out of them?'

Dennis and I just looked at each other, knowing full well if they heard our accents, the chances of getting off this train alive would be almost nil. I had absolutely no worries about Dennis opening his mouth, as he must have been as scared as I was. My biggest fear was the little boy with his dad asking me in front of the Millwall fans, who my favourite Everton player was.

I was literally praying, please don't talk to me now, son. I looked at his dad, who could see the fear in my face and realised how dangerous this situation had become. He was trying to keep his young son distracted from talking to me.

The Millwall fans then started singing, 'If you all hate the scousers, all hate the scousers, all hate the scousers, clap your hands.' I'm not sure who was clapping the loudest, me or Dennis.

I could no longer make eye contact with this little boy or his dad and I was becoming worried in case they noticed that my hands and legs were now shaking uncontrollably, or if one of them made conversation with me or Dennis. No Irish, Welsh or even a Timbuktu accent would get us out of this one. When I put on my Irish accent in Nottingham, I was young, daft and probably felt safer in a chip shop. But trapped and surrounded by these fans with the most dangerous reputation in the country on a train, with no way off, was a very frightening situation. I was also older now and a little bit wiser and therefore more aware of the danger we faced.

Another burst of *The Millwall*... broke out and I was now joining in and banging on the glass as well. When Dennis saw what I was doing, he started banging too, as we looked at each other, fearing for our lives.

I remember thinking, as long as these cockneys keep singing and banging on the glass, we're safe as houses and I was praying they wouldn't stop in case this little kid asked me why I had suddenly become a Millwall fan.

Although it was only two or three stations, it seemed like the longest train journey of my life and the horrible thing about it was that there was nowhere to run. As we pulled into the next station, my prayers were answered and much to our relief, the Millwall fans started getting off the train. We even had to look as if we were getting off with them, in case they sussed us at the last minute. It was without question the closest shave I'd ever encountered in football and it was brought home to me all the more by the little boy who said to me when they'd all got off the train, "I thought you supported Everton?" Phew!

There was another time, when the shoe was on the other foot. I was at Anfield one week with our Anthony and some of our mates who supported Liverpool. Everton were not playing on that particular day and in those days that's what we used to do. We loved football and we could afford to go as well. It was also a bit ironic, as Liverpool just happened to be playing Man City. As we were leaving the ground after the match we noticed a young lad of about fifteen years of age, who looked lost and absolutely terrified. He was on his own, making his way back towards the coach parking area and although he didn't want anybody to know, it was very noticeable that he was a City fan. He wasn't wearing any football scarf, which in those days was a big give-away and made him stand out even more. I remember thinking at the time, if he stood out to us, looking scared, what must he have looked like to the scallies, waiting to beat up any City fans they could find?

We walked over to him and asked him if he was okay. He didn't want to talk to us, as that would have revealed his Manchester accent and he must have thought we were going to attack him.

"Listen, mate," I said, "we know you're a City fan, but you've got nothing to fear from us." I also told him he wouldn't make it to the coach park on his own, as there were loads of scallies waiting to do him in. I told him we would walk him to his coach and he would be okay. Although he was still unsure about us, his options were rapidly disappearing as many of his fellow City fans were being attacked alongside us. The police were trying to intervene, but as they stopped one skirmish, another broke out straight away. He didn't have much choice but to trust us.

I tried my best to reassure him that we were not football hooligans. It was just as well we went to his aid, because as we turned the corner a load of scallies came over to us and asked me and my mates if we had the time. This was a ruse to find out how we spoke, as they were looking for anybody with a Mancunian accent.

"Five to five la," I answered, in my best scouse accent. I looked at our friend from Manchester who, by this stage, hung his head down and was turning a funny colour.

"It's okay," one of the scallies said, "they're Scousers."

There was no way he would have got past this gang on his own and it still disturbs me all these years later to think what would have happened to him if we hadn't helped him.

When we reached his coach, the colour began to return to his face and he gave me and my mates a big hug and thanked us for our help.

I said to him, "I hope you're not a hooligan," and it was nice to hear him regain his voice as he told us he used to throw bricks and bottles at buses outside

Victoria Station in Manchester but that he would never ever do it again, after seeing today how nice some fans really were. I think a couple of my mates wanted to walk him back to the scallies when he told us that, but I thought it was nice for him to see how wrong it was and he could now start helping other fans in the way that we helped him.

On another occasion, I can remember helping a Tottenham fan who'd lost his mates at Goodison. We took him on the bus to Lime Street train station to get his train back to London and like the Man City fan, he didn't open his mouth once on the journey in case anybody heard his cockney accent.

I'm not looking for any medals, but helping away fans get back safely somehow became a regular feature of going to the match and I lost count of the number of times my mates and I did this. On the rare occasions when I couldn't make it to the match, it got to the point where I'd be worrying about whether fans were getting home safely.

I had mates from many different clubs around England and the funny thing was, I didn't have to be at the match to meet them. No matter where you went you just couldn't get away from football. Whilst on holiday, our Anthony and I became good mates with a Man Utd fan we had met at Butlins holiday camp in Pwllheli, North Wales. If I remember rightly, his name was Johnny Gunter. During that great week, we also met Micky Petts, from Dagenham. Micky was a big West Ham fan, who became a regular visitor to Merseyside and my mum saw him as an adopted member of the family.

I couldn't then and still can't understand now how anybody could attack another human being for

26

simply supporting a different football team.

Although it was dangerous, travelling to away grounds was so much more exciting in those days as the visiting teams could and would bring as many as ten thousand fans, who always used to be allocated the whole area behind one of the goals, unlike today when they're only allowed to bring about two thousand. The atmosphere today is nowhere near the same, though...

The old section originally reserved for away fans has now been sold off to home supporters, which appears to have been put in place to make clubs more money. I'm also a bit concerned that some of the weaker referees may be influenced by the larger home support. Personally, I don't think it's fair to stop fans travelling to watch their teams play away and that choice has most definitely been taken away from us.

On a lighter note, I can also remember some funny moments back then, like the time Queens Park Rangers came to Goodison and their star player, Stan Bowles, who enjoyed a flutter in the bookies, was all over the papers during that week, when his wife had apparently left him due to his gambling. When QPR arrived at Everton the following Saturday, the Everton fans were singing, "Stanley, Stanley, where's your wife? Stanley, where's your wife?" Stan Bowles promptly marched right behind the Gwyladys Street goal, where the singing was coming from and stretched out his arms in an exaggerated shrug as if to say, 'I haven't got a clue.' He received a resounding cheer for that and I think the Evertonians took Stan Bowles to their hearts afterwards, as it was the perfect reply for giving him stick all afternoon.

One particular occasion wasn't so funny, though. Well, not for me, anyway. This huge police officer, who was built like the proverbial outhouse came into the Gwyladys Street End where we Everton fans used to stand behind the goal. I'm not sure why he came in but it was probably to stop some kind of disturbance and I do remember a lot of fans shouting, swearing and spitting at him.

I can truthfully say I never once shouted, swore or spat at this policemen as I was too busy, as always, watching the match. However, he turned around and threw a right haymaker that Mike Tyson would have been proud of... and guess who caught it right on the chin? The next thing I remembered was waking up with a crowd around me and some people helping me up off the floor, asking if I was okay.

A few of them were shouting at the policeman that this young lad didn't do anything wrong. I can't remember much of the game after that and as Everton were playing in a cup match, I wasn't to know when getting out of bed that morning that we'd both get knocked out.

Growing up on Merseyside in the seventies, my mates and I were regulars at Goodison Park, the home of Everton Football Club, but as I said, that didn't stop us occasionally going to watch our fierce rivals, Liverpool, the following Saturday or even our other Merseyside neighbours, Tranmere Rovers, on a Friday night. We were all football daft and the great thing was in those days, as kids, we could all afford to go.

With the price of tickets today, not to mention travel and refreshments, kids and the elderly simply can't afford to go any more. What was once a favourite pastime for working class people has somehow evolved into a day out for the rich and middle classes, as well as being a venue for businessmen to entertain their clients.

Looking back, I can remember hordes of kids and elderly people going to football grounds up and down the country, truly excited by the beautiful game.

Today, TV companies try to seduce us into subscribing to their channels by portraying happy family scenes in and outside football grounds on match days, but that's not what I see at football matches today. What I see are mostly men, some of them bare-chested, spending extortionate amounts of money following their teams. I've lost count of the number of dads I know personally who can no longer afford to take their kids to the game, or even bother going themselves, myself included.

The next time you go to the match or if you're just watching *Match of the Day*, have a closer look. You may be surprised by what you see.

And there is also more to it than just being unable to afford inflated prices. If you dig a little deeper, you begin to wonder if there are other sinister forces at work here. Even if we were to have the money, I don't believe our custom is as welcome as we would like to think, as it seems to me that some clubs today are targeting a different kind of audience.

Putting it bluntly, it appears certain clubs would prefer to sell as many tickets as possible to corporate companies in the executive suites now installed in many of our grounds, as this has become very big money for them. Also, I've noticed that a lot of our bigger clubs are now making more tickets available to fans from out of town and even abroad. Some of these are not proper fans, but actually tourists and the clubs know full well that these tourists will spend large amounts of money in their souvenir shops, unlike the local fans who simply go to watch the game and then go straight home.

Our big football clubs have obviously done their market research and from a business point of view, it appears very profitable for them to provide tickets not only to fans and tourists from different areas of the UK, but also other parts of the world. How gratifying it must be to watch them queuing up in their droves at their souvenir shops.

Another thing that saddens me is how alienated players and clubs are from their fans now. What I am about to tell you wouldn't happen today.

A few years ago, when we were playing Aston Villa, our Jeggsy and a couple of mates and I travelled down to Birmingham to watch the game and stayed overnight in the Copthorne Hotel. The Everton team were also staying there and they were quite openly mixing with the fans and talking to them before the match. There didn't seem to be the wide gap that exists today when, for some reason, fans are not allowed anywhere near the players.

We were talking to the Everton goalkeeper, Neville Southall, and he spent quite a bit of time talking to me and Jeggsy.

Incidentally, whenever we travelled away to watch our team, we always used to dare each other to do some really daft things. Some fans liked fighting, but we always treated it as a day out and to have a good laugh. Some of the things we used to do were quite mad and on this particular occasion, our Jeggsy dared me to ask if we could have a lift up to Villa Park on the team coach.

So I walked over and asked Mike Walker who had just taken over as manager of Everton if we could have a lift to the ground on the players' coach.

He stood there looking at us very seriously and said, "Are you joking?"

"No," I said, "we're going up to Villa Park to watch the game and with you and the players going there as well, it saves us having to get a taxi."

Honestly, you should have seen Mike Walker's face, it was a picture. We never thought for one single second he would turn round and say, 'Yeah, hop on the bus, boys,' but it was worth asking, just to see his face.

We were trying not to laugh, and it was dead funny watching him stand there, shaking his head. If any part of him was possibly considering agreeing to our request, my next question most certainly put paid to this.

With the straightest face I could hold, I said, "You see, if we know we have a lift from you, Mike, we won't have to worry about having to leave too early for Villa Park and we can have another couple of pints here in the hotel while we wait for you and the players to get ready."

Jeggsy whispered, "If he says yes, I'm going to ask him if we can play as well."

As I say, the funny bit was the expression on his face, looking at us and hardly believing what he was hearing. He must have thought to himself, '*While we wait for you and the players… a couple more pints… who are these dickheads?*'

"Sorry boys," Mike said. "Insurance wouldn't allow it, red tape, etc… blah, blah, blah."

"Never mind," I said. "We understand. You didn't mind us asking, did you?"

"No," he said, but he was still shaking his head as he walked away and must have thought, 'cheeky buggers.'

After we left, we asked each other if we could think of any other manager who may just have said yes to this request. I said Terry Venables and Tommy Docherty; Harry Redknapp was also mentioned and I think somebody said Sir Alf Ramsey, but I think that one was more of a joke.

At our next home game I was walking into the Everton ground with our Jeggsy and my mates when, by sheer coincidence, who did we notice about to walk in through the reception area? Yes, it was Mike Walker.

I shouted over to him, "Hey, Mike! Any chance of a lift home on the coach after the match, mate?"

"I recognise that voice," he said as he turned round. "Oh, not you lot again!" and he smiled, shaking his head at us.

You wouldn't believe it, but about four weeks later, we were walking into Prenton Park to watch a Tranmere Rovers match when who was walking in right behind us in the queue? You've guessed it... Mike Walker.

I said to our Jeggsy, "Oh my God, I don't believe it! Look who's standing right behind us."

Jeggsy remarked, "Oh shit. What's he doing here?"

He said, "Quick, we're going to have to hide or he'll think we're stalking him!"

We were laughing our heads off and trying to get out of the way, but it was too late and there was nowhere to hide. Then he noticed us and he just stood there for what seemed like an eternity, staring at us. It was one of the strangest feelings I've ever had in my life, as he just stood there looking at us as if we were indeed stalking him.

I don't think anybody knew what to say,

including Mike Walker himself, until I just impulsively blurted out, "Hey, Mike, are you going to let us on this fucking coach or what?" We all burst out laughing.

His face, once again was a picture but this time, he burst out laughing as well. Goodness knows what he must have thought. He asked us what we were doing at Tranmere Rovers. After we convinced him we were not stalking him and explained we didn't live far from Tranmere, he saw the funny side. Well done, Mike, good sport and top man.

I also used to live for cup final day years ago and watching the build-up all morning to the actual match. The teams leaving their hotels, *It's a Knockout*, all those celebrities cashing in and jumping on the bandwagon, pre-match entertainment... all of it was brilliant. We used to close the curtains in our house to stop the sun bleaching out the TV screen. In fact, if I'm being totally honest, we closed them anyway even if it wasn't sunny because it all added to the occasion.

If you were looking out of the window and spotted somebody walking along the road that was otherwise deserted, you couldn't help thinking how very strange these people were... didn't they know the cup final was on? How odd.

We used to send our mum to the shop for sweets, pop, crisps and loads more goodies and when the final eventually kicked off, our front room resembled a mini football terrace, being packed full of family and friends. My mum used to come and pop her head round the door like Mrs Doyle from *Father Ted* and ask if anyone wanted a cup of tea and she would often walk back out without even getting an answer as nobody could hear her. (Sorry, Mum).

You'd be sitting there, supporting a new team

for that day, but deep down really wishing it was your team. It was just a brilliant day. After the game, we had the annual ritual of a kick about on the street and relived the cup final.

Another thing we used to do to our mum was to pretend when the rugby results came on the TV that they were football scores and we'd ask her to be quiet while we listened to them, trying desperately to hold in our giggles. Because it was rugby, which we knew absolutely nothing about, we never had a clue when the reporter would say, 'Wakefield Trinity 33 points, Saint Helens 66.' As if any football teams would ever score that many goals. As she never followed rugby or football, our mum used to fall for it every time, would say, 'Sorry, love,' in her beautiful soft Irish accent and remain quiet, believing they were football scores. It was a bit mean, I know. Sorry again, Mum.

I still become very emotional when I see TV footage of those great finals in the sixties and seventies. You often see players who are sadly no longer with us and even more upsetting from a personal point of view, there were much loved family members who watched those games with me who are also no longer around. Just writing about this is very emotional for me; I miss those finals days so much. To be truthful, I can't bring myself to watch some of those great games any more, as much as I love them; they bring back so many great memories, but some terribly sad ones as well.

Most of my childhood memories involve and relate to FA cup finals. If somebody were to ask me what I was doing when I was seven years of age, I would think back to Tottenham beating Chelsea 2-1 in the 1967 FA cup final. Or if I was nine, then I wouldn't think that was when I started in that class at school or got a new bike. I would simply recall seeing Neil Young scoring for Man City when they beat Leicester in the 1969 FA cup final.

The first time we got a colour TV involved an FA cup final. In 1970 we watched Leeds and Chelsea draw 2-2 at Wembley on the Saturday in black and white and for the replay at Old Trafford on the Wednesday night, my dad came in with a colour TV. Wow! It was unbelievable as we stayed up late to watch David Webb score Chelsea's winner in extra time.

In the same way that people remember particular places by a certain song, I remember times in my childhood relating to football and FA cup finals. It sounds daft I know, but that's how much the event meant to me.

Sadly, today I can take it or leave it and I would struggle to remember who won the FA Cup last season, or the season before, yet I can tell you the two teams in every single final from the early sixties right up until the nineties. The FA Cup was a one-off in those days with every club dreaming of reaching Wembley, unlike today, when a lot of clubs now see it more as a headache and not as important as their league survival.

Another thing I've noticed and don't like seeing today is that the losing fans in the final have already left the ground when the winners are picking up their trophy and that empty section of Wembley Stadium looks just awful to me.

And don't get me started on Wembley tickets, or should I say the lack of. When Everton got to the cup final in 2010 against Chelsea, they received an allocation of 25,000 tickets from the FA. With about 37,000 fans attending Everton's home games, you wouldn't need my old maths teacher to tell you there would be about 12,000 disappointed fans. This problem has existed since I was a child and to me it is so disrespectful to those fans who have travelled to watch their team all season in all kinds of weather and then when they get to the final, their custom isn't welcome. This is one of the top issues that we fans need to address.

Sometimes, you feel no matter which way you look at it, we fans just can't win. If your team plays rubbish and you don't make Wembley, you're naturally disappointed. And even if they play superbly and do make it, you then have the huge disappointment of not being able to get a ticket. You just can't win and either way, being a fan, the chances are you're going to end up being let down, one way or the other.

But I already knew and accepted this. I'd put up with it for many years as a downtrodden football fan and had always thought, unfortunately, that's just the way it was; it had always been that way and I didn't really think anybody could do anything to change things. Until, that is, one remarkable and very strange incident that was about to take me completely by surprise and would dramatically alter my whole life. Little did I know that this incident would make me realise that it wasn't just about fans being ripped off. As you will discover, it was much more serious than that.

Three
Man in a suit

It was the early nineties and football was experiencing some serious changes as the English Premier League had just begun. With its new name, live televised matches and money flooding in from everywhere, how could the beautiful game ever be the same again? And with these changes came the money people, including the rich owners, the sponsors, TV companies and agents. Even the ticket touts were rubbing their hands with glee and must have thought all their birthdays had come at once as this newly created huge market handed them another license to exploit us fans.

Although the players were also benefiting from this financial bonanza, who could really blame them, as all they ever wanted to do from a very early age was to play football? If the opportunity had come my way, I'd have jumped at it as well.

But there were many other people boarding the gravy train who had never shown any interest in football – until now, that is – and it seemed everybody was getting a slice of the cake. However, as always, there was one group of people not included in this deal... we fans. Not only were we not receiving a crumb, but it was now actually going to cost us a hell of a lot more money to watch our football, whether we went to the game or stayed at home to watch it on TV. Either way, there were people who wanted to relieve us of our money and they knew exactly how to do that.

There was no doubting that this new and exciting league caught the imagination of everybody and to a lot of people it looked like the best thing since sliced bread. Deep down, I knew it wasn't going to be fair, but then when has it ever been any other way for us football aficionados?

A football revolution was taking place and the game was definitely transforming, but I could never in my wildest dreams have imagined to what extent, until one pivotal moment not only changed my whole perception of the beautiful game forever, but was also about to re-shape and alter my entire life.

What started out like any other morning, turned into one of those days in life, which I can only describe as a bit like people remembering where they were when news broke about the Twin Towers attack, or the shootings of President Kennedy and John Lennon. Well, that's certainly how it felt for me.

It was a bitterly cold, wet and windy morning when I was queuing up with my younger brother, Jeggsy, outside a very well-known Premier league club. We were waiting to purchase two tickets to watch our team, Everton. Although the weather was horrible, these tickets were in very short supply and we would have stood there for hours in a full scale hurricane if necessary, just to get hold of our tickets. After being moved along by the stewards, waiting for over a couple of hours and soaked through to the skin (nothing unusual for us footie fans) we felt so relieved to find ourselves near the front and close to the ticket window at long last.

The tickets we were hoping to buy were for a very important cup match. They were like gold dust and there were certain restrictions which meant we were only allowed to purchase two tickets each – again, nothing out of the ordinary. But something very unusual was about to happen and without actually realising it then, my whole future, not just as a football fan but as a person, would dramatically change as a direct result of what took place in the next few minutes.

A tall, well-built man dressed in a suit suddenly appeared from nowhere and asked me and our kid if he could jump in front of us in the queue as he was in a big hurry. We told him we didn't mind, but a few hundred people standing behind us and dripping wet may have something to say about it. His pushy demeanour assured us he would only be a few seconds so we kind of agreed to let him in. After all, he could only purchase two tickets anyway and there would be enough left.

He then introduced himself and whispered something to the ticket lady, who couldn't quite hear him, as she asked him to speak up and repeat himself. We were immediately intrigued and couldn't resist moving a step closer to see what was going on. What we were about to hear next left us absolutely gobsmacked, as he then asked for a staggering twenty complimentary tickets… yes, *twenty* free tickets. He told the lady he was collecting these tickets on behalf of some football authority administrative department and pulled out a piece of paper and handed it to her. We couldn't believe it when she suddenly turned around and produced a box marked 'complimentary tickets' which must have contained hundreds.

We both stood there and watched, open-mouthed, as she counted out twenty tickets and handed them over to the man. She then asked him if he was looking forward to the match. If I was surprised by witnessing all this, I was absolutely shell-shocked by his reply when he told her he didn't really like football, but was obligated to attend the game.

"God bless him," our Jeggsy said. "Fancy

making the poor bloke attend this really massive cup match and free of charge as well."

"Yeah, you're right, but at least he didn't have to wait in the queue and get soaked like the rest of us," I said.

He simply thanked the lady and walked away without paying one single penny. I turned round to our kid and the people queuing behind me, shaking my head in disbelief.

"Did you see that?" I asked.

One guy said, "She just handed over twenty complimentary tickets, didn't she?"

"Yeah. She flippin' did." Only I don't think I said flippin.

All of us in the queue were absolutely astounded, unable to take in what we had just seen.

Our kid said, "He doesn't even like football... no wonder he was bloody whispering."

I looked down at my hands, which were now numb and turning blue with the cold. The rain had penetrated my shoes and socks to the point where I could no longer feel my feet and each drop that slid off my nose compounded the bitter taste in my mouth. I looked to the faces around me, every one of them etched with misery from the sheer cold and wet. My thoughts were racing now; there was a nagging, anxious feeling in my gut and I shuddered.

What was happening to me?

This defining moment was to shake me to the core and for the very first time in the whole of my life as a devoted football fan, I heard myself utter the words, 'What the hell am I doing here?' Yes, that's exactly what I said to myself, 'What the hell am I doing here?' repeating the phrase, just to confirm the suspicions of my own mind.

As a fan I'd experienced just about every emotion that could be thrown at me... the euphoria of cheering my beloved team to victory in cup finals, the heartbreak of seeing them lose in cup finals, the disappointment of being unable to get a ticket, frustration at queuing for hours in all weathers and spending every last penny I had to ensure I got any tickets that were available and travelling to every away game to further demonstrate my passion. But now, in this surreal moment, it wasn't just the bittersweet taste of rain in my mouth that discomfited me. Serious elements of doubt were beginning to question my loyalty and I didn't like it. Of course this wasn't just about twenty complimentary tickets. I was well aware that some of the rich and famous obtained free tickets with ease while we had to queue up and pay full price with what little money we had; as football fans, it was just a sad fact of life that we accepted. But this bloke from the football authorities didn't even like football and for some reason that day, to witness it first-hand brought home the injustice of it all.

I never knew why I hadn't noticed prior to this; standing in a queue, rigid with cold and soaked through to the skin had never bothered me before. But suddenly and although he didn't realise it, this man in a suit had somehow planted the first negative seeds, reminding me of the many disappointments such as being unable to even get a ticket or, like this particular occasion, having to borrow the money and then queue for hours, shivering in the pouring rain.

"Next please!" came the call from the ticket lady, which brought me out of my trance.

Back in the present moment, I asked if I could

have twenty tickets and could she make them all complimentary as well, please. She looked at me and started laughing and asked me once again how many tickets I really wanted. "Oh, sorry," I said, "could you make that thirty, please, before any more privileged people turn up and take the lot?"

"I'm sorry," she said, "but you're only allowed two and you have to pay for them."

I asked her how anybody was allowed to obtain twenty tickets just like that and free of charge as well.

"I know," she said, "it's not right and I agree with you, but I'm only doing my job."

The fact that the ticket lady wasn't happy confirmed to me how wrong this was. I told her I understood she was only doing her job and I certainly wasn't having a go at her, but I asked her how many other privileged people had these arrangements. She just shrugged her shoulders and as we walked away with our two tickets (which we paid for) I could hear the person behind me sarcastically asking for forty tickets, please, and all complimentary.

When Jeggsy and I arrived home we told our family and friends what had happened. They couldn't believe it either and we were now all wondering if this went on regularly... and how many freebies were our clubs actually giving away? I wasn't so naive as to think that complimentaries never existed, but getting twenty tickets completely free and for a major cup match was, in my opinion, absolutely disgusting and taking the proverbial. I also considered it extremely disrespectful to us fans and bang out of order. As I said, we fans were only allowed two tickets each, which we naturally had to pay for. The people at this club would also have known that.

You may have detected that I was just a bit cheesed off with this very disrespectful arrangement. My other concern, though, was that these tickets may have been going to ticket touts, and that had me really wound up. So much so, in fact, that I telephoned the club in question, who simply told me they didn't discuss their private ticket arrangements.

"What you really mean," I said, "is you won't discuss these ticket arrangements with us fans unless we're in the know and part of the clique." I'm not sure what happened at that point, but there must have been some fault with the telephone because I could no longer hear the person on the other end of the line, as I was repeatedly saying, "Hello, can you hear me? Is there anybody there?" All that money these clubs must be making and their phones didn't even work properly! Oh well, I thought, I'll try the Football Association.

So I phoned and asked them if they were aware of certain clubs handing out complimentary tickets like confetti to so-called important people in suits, whilst we fans were not only paying extortionate prices but also having to queue for hours to purchase only two tickets for big games.

The guy tried to interrupt but I wasn't going to be fobbed off and asked him to let me finish, please.

I told him this club had showed no regard for the fact that many of their loyal and devoted fans were struggling financially to support them through thick and thin.

I also told him that my whole interpretation and definition of a football fan was somebody who paid to get in to watch a football match. With the exception of some employees and genuine helpers, the rest were not fans and if we were to calculate all those people who walked into our stadiums around the country every week without paying, it would amount to quite a lot of money. And when you consider how many of them walk into the posh lounges, even at cup finals, without paying one single penny, but just having the right contacts and moving in the right circles, you do wonder who is actually paying for football.

These people are, in effect, bunking in to watch football matches while the clubs not only turn a blind eye, but actually invite and encourage them.

"Can I stop you there?" he said.

"No, you can't." I was not going to be silenced. "As far back as I can remember, it has only ever been us fans who seemed to be paying to get into football matches. The rest are on freebies. Yet if we fans ever tried to get into a match for free, we'd be ejected and possibly even arrested. Tell me, how is that fair?"

This bloke at the FA must have wished he'd stayed in bed that morning as I gave it to him in chapter and verse.

"It's an absolute insult to us fans," I continued, "who *are* paying extortionate amounts of money, that our clubs are dishing out so many free tickets to people who can easily afford to pay anyway. I've never been able to understand this and find it so disrespectful to the loyal fans who they patronisingly keep calling the twelfth man…"

"But—" he managed to say, as I carried on in full flow.

"… and how annoying it is when decent, respectable fans, who have travelled thousands of miles in cold, wet, miserable weather to support their teams can't get a ticket for the cup final and yet certain privileged people are just handed tickets, often on a lovely warm, summer's day, even though they haven't attended any of the other games."

"But—"

His attempt to get more than one word in failed again; I wasn't going to shut up that easily.

"Having said that," I continued, "I do acknowledge that there are certain celebrities who are also great fans and these people have my utmost respect. But there are those, who believe they belong to some kind of exclusive club, rubbing shoulders with their cronies and taking tickets from the fans who truly deserve them. There's absolutely no excuse for this and everybody must realise how insulting it is, but nobody ever does anything about it."

I think he'd heard enough at this stage and was raising his voice as he interrupted by telling me, "But, Sir, I'm only the night porter and I don't even like or understand football. If you would just be patient for one moment, I'll go and get somebody for you—"

"Well, why didn't you tell me that in the first place?" I grumbled. "Making me go through all that for nothing…"

"But…"

This poor chap still couldn't get a word in and now he was getting told off.

Eventually I got through to the right department and had to go through all that spiel once again. This person at the FA told me they couldn't comment as these clubs had their own ticket arrangements.

"*These* clubs," I said and perhaps I was now being naïve, but I was quite disturbed to discover that this so-called arrangement applied to many other clubs as well.

I asked him if he'd heard of the Roman poet, Juvenal, who wrote about the politicians in Rome keeping the city's people under the thumb with bread and circuses.

"The thinking went," I told him, "give them food and entertainment and they won't rebel." A bit like us fans with our hot dogs.

Here was another bloke who must have wished he'd stayed in bed that morning, as I said to this guy, "When you say *these* clubs, don't you mean *our* clubs? Without us fans, there are *no* clubs."

I told him this wasn't on and if no one in authority could intervene, then I would have to do something about it myself, although I was fully aware that merely writing and complaining to our clubs wasn't going to change anything. I said goodbye and thanked him for his time.

I then telephoned a national newspaper (no not that one; they're finished) and spoke to a journalist who also found this so disrespectful and agreed with my frustrations, but informed me there wasn't much he could do, as this type of thing unfortunately did go on. He also told me he didn't work in the sports section, in fact he said he didn't particularly like football and with the greatest respect, he couldn't quite understand why fans like myself continued spending many thousands of pounds over the years, paying for swimming pools and mock Tudor houses as well as subsidising wags and mistresses. But he did offer me some interesting advice.

He said, "I totally understand how annoyed you must feel and if you really want to make people aware of your feelings, you'll be better off trying to generate some public interest."

"Like what?"

"I'm not sure; maybe a protest or something?"

"What... like a football strike, asking fans to stop going to the match?" I asked.

"Well it wouldn't have to be that extreme," he said, "and to be perfectly honest, I couldn't see many of your fellow fans supporting you, but maybe some kind of campaign that would at least capture the imagination. Basically, something that would make enough noise to publicly make people aware of the disrespectful way in which fans are being treated. Once you have that platform, you then have a story and once you have your story, people may listen, but until then, unfortunately, there's not much you can do."

I thanked him for his advice as well as his time and bade him farewell, but I couldn't stop thinking about what he said. He was right, I supposed. The only way people would take any notice would be to carry out some kind of protest, but it would have to be something really unusual and different. Like he said, something that would capture the imagination of the public. It was later that night when I had that light bulb moment.

The following morning, I telephoned our friend back at the FA and came out with a statement that was to alter the course of my whole life.

"From now on," I informed him, "I'm refusing to pay to get into any more football matches and this will be my personal protest. I have decided enough is enough and something seriously needs to be done. From now on, I want to see the fans come first. Maybe I have a lot to thank this man in a suit for," I added. "Apart from opening my eyes to what really goes on behind the scenes in football, he has also given me the courage to challenge a system that is grossly unfair and disrespectful to genuine, loyal fans everywhere."

I don't know whether this FA representative immediately understood what I meant, but as the straight talking politician, Tony Benn, often stated, 'say what you mean and mean what you say.' So I said it again.

"Are you saying that you still intend going to watch football matches, but are refusing to pay to get in?"

Got it in one. "That's exactly what I'm saying," I replied.

"Really? And how do you propose to do that, then?"

I told him I couldn't reveal that information. The reality was, I didn't have the slightest idea yet, but I couldn't let him know that. What I did make clear was that because of what I had witnessed, I was making this my protest on principle and I pledged that unless *everybody else* paid to watch football like we fans were forced to, I wasn't going to pay either.

I had never done anything quite like this before in my life and as I said, I hadn't the faintest idea how I was going to get away with it and at that time I suppose it was really more of a spontaneous reaction to the anger I was feeling, but I'd said it now and the more I thought about it, the more I convinced myself that maybe it wasn't as ridiculous as it sounded.

My wife and our Jeggsy weren't so sure, though, and thought I'd lost the plot.

"What if you get caught?" they asked me.

"I'll go public," I said, "and then that way, at least it will be out in the open that there's absolutely no respect for us football fans whatsoever."

I also wondered how these ticket touts

managed to get their hands on so many tickets and I needed some questions answering.

I kept reassuring myself that I wouldn't really be doing any more harm than those people who had no respect for us fans ... end of story. (No, not this one, there's still quite a way to go yet).

"And what happens if you don't get caught?" they asked.

I said, "Well, I'll just have to carry on until I do, but it's inevitable that I will be caught eventually." I told them both not to worry as everything would be alright and, in any case, somebody had to do something to highlight the many injustices we fans were now facing.

But deep down, I knew there would be problems ahead and this was going to be easier said than done. I had no idea how I was going to achieve it, but there was no going back now. I'd made my promise and this was to be my personal protest; I was still going to go and watch football – I just wasn't paying to get in any more.

Four
A Steward's Enquiry

With a new football season about to start, it was almost time to begin my protest. Now the enormity of what I was planning began to sink in. What was I actually thinking when I made this promise of refusing to pay into any more football stadiums? It wasn't too late to call it off, as the season hadn't actually started yet.

However, I knew that for far too long football fans had been and still were being treated like second class citizens and even though there were now many different fans groups opposing injustices, it still didn't seem to stop fans being ripped off every single season. In fact, if anything the situation was becoming a lot worse, with parents under extreme pressure to buy several new shirts every season and despite our clubs receiving a massive increase in revenue from TV companies and sponsors, we were still being charged a fortune to watch our teams play. Somebody had to do something about it and it was decided that I had to go through with this protest and I couldn't back out now. I just needed to sort out one or two minor details, one of them being... how the bloody hell was I actually going to do it?

With less than two weeks to the big kick off, I was also faced with another big problem. How, exactly, was I was going to make people aware of my protest? I mean, once I made it public, then all our clubs would find out that I was refusing to pay into their football grounds and they would all be looking out for me to make sure I didn't get through their turnstiles without paying. Talk about falling at the first hurdle. There was only one thing for it and I knew if I was going to get away with what I was planning, it would mean keeping quiet until I was ready to go public.

I confided in a very small group of family and one or two friends, but not before they were all sworn to secrecy. I told them if word ever got out, I would be exposed immediately and as soon as the football authorities knew what I was up to, then that would be the end of the campaign. So it was decided and agreed that nobody outside this trusted circle would know about it... well, for the time being, anyway.

My close confidants and I all agreed that some way was needed of recording details of my protest and we were thinking up quite a few different ways in which this could be done. There were a few suggestions such as recording the protest with a video camera, but this wasn't very practical and recording on mobile phones hadn't properly arrived yet. Another idea was to make an anonymous broadcast on a radio football show or even an anonymous announcement in the press, but as I said, that would just serve to inform everybody what I was doing and as soon as the clubs got wind of it they would pull down the shutters and be on their guard and maybe even bar me from their grounds.

After many more late-night discussions, our Jeggsy suggested that I should attend every Premiership club (without paying of course) and after each successful admission, I could mark and record the occasion with some kind of memento. The best memento I could think of was something which would benefit less fortunate people. So I decided to ask each club I'd managed to gain free entry into to send me a signed football, which could be raffled off for a charitable cause. We all thought it would be a good idea for the clubs that we had supported over the years to put something back. Of course, I couldn't tell them what I had done, otherwise they wouldn't send me a ball.

We agreed to nominate *Children in Need* as the chosen charity and once I had gained free entry into every Premier ground and I had the complete set of signed footballs, we could raffle them all off and end the protest.

Our Jeggsy said, "I can't wait to see Terry Wogan asking how you managed to collect every Premier league football."

If I'm being honest, I was absolutely terrified at the thought of going ahead with this protest, but now that a good cause like *Children In Need* was going to benefit, it kind of gave me the courage and the confidence to give it a go. I was determined to highlight how badly we fans were being treated and if we could raise a few quid for a good cause at the same time, then so much the better.

I wasn't trying to make fools of our clubs or make anybody look silly, but I wanted to publicise it properly and I knew this could only be done with a different and unusual kind of protest.

All I had to do was to keep a low profile until I was ready to go public.

One of my mates compared it to being like an international footballer, but instead of being awarded a cap each time I played for my country, I would receive a signed football from each club I managed to gain access in to, even if they weren't aware why they were sending the ball.

When I sat down and thought about it, I assumed the away games shouldn't pose too much of a problem as I'd be visiting many different grounds and they wouldn't know my face, but there could be problems at my own club, Everton. As my protest was to never pay into any more Premiership grounds, how was I meant to get into Everton's Goodison Park for every home game without paying? After a few weeks, people would recognise me and I'd probably end up being ejected and barred from the ground.

One of my mates who supported Liverpool suggested I should ask Everton if I could play for them as they were always on the lookout for shit players and if I played for them, I wouldn't have to pay to get in. After failing to understand the joke, a thought suddenly struck me.

"Hold on," I said, "that joke you just told, might not be as daft as it sounds."

"I wasn't joking," he replied.

"Listen, what if I did work at the club?"

"What do you mean?" he asked, still grinning.

But I was being serious now. "You've given me a great idea here," I said. "Me and our Jeggsy always used to say we should work at Everton as Stewards as it was costing us a fortune going to the game every week. That's what I'll do... I'll see if they're looking for any stewards."

So first thing on Monday morning I phoned Everton and asked if there were any positions available for match-day stewards. They told me there were and after sending in my CV, I was delighted to be invited for an interview. During my interview I explained that in my normal profession in the engineering industry, I was responsible and qualified to carry out many safety procedures, including first aid as well as health & safety. I couldn't believe it when I was given the very enviable job of stewarding the television gantry.

I checked with my trusted circle if getting a job at Everton qualified me to ask them for a signed ball. They agreed that it was and in fairness to the club I'd supported all my life, they were more than happy to support my charity event for *Children in Need.*

I can remember thinking how easy that was until somebody went and spoilt it by informing me I couldn't get a job at every other Premier club.

I knew it wasn't going to be easy obtaining free entry into every Premiership ground and as I was soon to discover, there were some real nerve-racking, scary adventures in store for me, but I was determined to complete the set by acquiring every premiership football, make my point, oh... and raise a few quid as well.

I naively thought getting a job at Everton was the perfect answer to the home games, but how very wrong I was. Needless to say, things didn't quite work out the way I had planned.

Five
The TV Gantry

I was absolutely amazed when I was taken to my post for the very first time, especially when I saw all the TV equipment, and it was so interesting to see how the football matches I had been watching all these years were actually televised. Just imagine being told your job is to simply sit down and watch the game from possibly one of the best vantage points in the ground... it doesn't get better than that. Although the wages only amounted to about £8 per game (I know, I should have got myself an agent), at least I didn't have to worry about finding the money to watch my team any more.

This seemed ideal for me and for a fan who was going to the match every week, spending extortionate amounts of money, it made a lot of sense. At least I knew I was sorted for the home games for now, so I only had to worry about the away games, as my protest of not paying to get into any football matches was now firmly etched in stone.

Supporting your team is one thing, but to go and work at the club you support must be a dream for most fans. Well, it certainly was for me.

How ironic it was for somebody embarking on a campaign of refusing to pay into any more Premiership grounds, to be employed as a steward on the TV gantry and whose role it was to prevent anybody bunking in and entering this area apart from the BBC, ITV and SKY commentators. I wasn't sure if it was because I was qualified in certain safety courses in my normal profession, but with my new job about to start, I certainly wasn't arguing.

During my time there, I can't remember one

single occasion when any fan ever tried to enter this area, apart from my mates that is, who used to take turns to play on my generosity. In fact I was quite surprised how many of my mates now wanted to support me in my protest once I'd landed this steward's job.

So there I was at every home game, sitting in one of the best seats in the house watching my team play, not just without paying but actually being paid for the privilege. I thought all my birthdays had come at once. One week I'd be sitting alongside the BBC's commentators, Barry Davies or John Motson when Everton were on *Match of the Day* and other weeks it would be Sky's Martin Tyler with Andy Gray and some other celebrity guests. ITV were also there regularly with the late Brian Moore, Clive Tyldesley and Elton Welsby.

Most of these people were very friendly and down to earth but there were one or two prima donnas who thought they were above speaking to the likes of me. That never bothered me though, and if they couldn't make the effort to speak to me, then I wouldn't speak to them. But I have to say I got on well with most of those I met.

One afternoon, Everton were playing Manchester City in a live Sunday game, which was being screened by ITV. The commentator was the late Brian Moore. I used to love his passion and his exciting commentaries and, as a child, I used to love his screaming on a Sunday afternoon when the likes of Pop Robson had scored for West Ham. I still enjoy watching his commentaries today on YouTube.

Brian Moore's co-commentator that day was the

first £1 million player and former Nottingham Forest striker, Trevor Francis, and one of his jobs was to select his man of the match.

Anyway, near the end of this particular match, the time had arrived when Brian Moore asked Trevor Francis to make his choice. I was sitting next to both of them and talked to them occasionally off-camera during the match.

When he was considering which player to choose, Trevor turned to me and whispered, "It has to be Kevin Sheedy, don't you think?" With Everton beating Man City 2-0 and Kevin Sheedy scoring a brilliant goal, I think everybody was agreed Kevin Sheedy was indeed man of the match. But it was very thoughtful of Brian Moore and Trevor Francis to include me, and the TV crews would quite often ask my opinion. They probably thought who better to ask than one of the fans?

Brian Moore and Trevor Francis on the TV Gantry with ITV

There was one occasion, though, when my opinion backfired on me big time. This was when the former Liverpool and Republic of Ireland striker Michael Robinson arrived on the TV gantry with Spanish television. He was a smashing bloke and very friendly with everybody and spoke fluent Spanish.

We had a nice chat before the game and he told me that although he now lived in Spain, he returned home to England of a weekend to cover a top English match.

"Just run that past me again, Mike," I said. "You live in sunny Spain during the week and come home at the weekend to watch a top English match? They're not looking for any TV gantry stewards are they, Mike?" We both had a laugh at that.

If you're reading this, Mike, I hope you can forgive me for this next bit. I take all the blame.

I was sitting next to Michael Robinson and as he was the co-commentator for this match which was going out live to Spain, naturally they were commentating in Spanish.

During my time on the TV gantry, I used to sit there and listen to other results coming in from around the country on my radio Walkman. This particular week, after about ten to fifteen minutes, I heard on my radio that Spurs were getting hammered at home to Chelsea, 4-1. Bearing in mind this was pre-Abramovich, when Chelsea were not expected to win, it really was a bit of an upset at that time.

Anyway, when Michael's Spanish colleague was commentating, I whispered to Mike that Spurs were getting thrashed by Chelsea, 4-1.

He looked at me and said, "You're kidding!"

No, Mike, I've just heard it on my radio."

Just at that moment, he was receiving the news himself in his ear phones.

"You're right," he agreed. "They're getting beaten 4-1."

As I heard more scores starting to come through and Michael Robinson was himself getting confirmation, I had by now gained his trust and he was passing these scores to his co-commentator.

Some other news started coming through on my rather unsophisticated Walkman, via local radio, that the former England captain, Terry Butcher, the Manager of Coventry City, had sensationally been sent off at Highfield Road.

"Are you joking? Mike asked when I told him. "Wow, that's amazing, being the manager as well" "That's what I thought, Mike."

We were both amazed at this news. With Terry Butcher being a former captain of England and very well known in Spain, it wasn't long before this news was being transmitted live to Spain. I remember sitting there, looking like Oliver Hardy and feeling pretty pleased with myself for my Spanish contribution and I couldn't wait to tell my mates after the game.

At the end of the match, Michael Robinson turned to me, shook my hand and thanked me for keeping him informed and joked that he'd have to get me a job with Spanish TV. We wished each other all the best and said Adios. He was a true gentleman and I had really enjoyed his company.

After the game I told my mates what happened and as we were driving out of the Mersey Tunnel, the day's football stories and reports were still coming through on the radio. Then somebody announced they were going over to Highfield Road, Coventry.

"Shush," I said to the lads. "Here's Terry Butcher… fancy getting sent off when you're the manager!"

I couldn't believe what I was hearing when the reporter began, "On a cold, wet and windy afternoon here at Highfield Road, Terry Butcher, who substituted himself in the 65th minute of the game…"

We all looked at each other.

"I thought you said he got sent off, Peter," somebody said. "I could have sworn that reporter just said he was substituted."

"He did get sent off; well, that's what it said on my radio, I'm sure of it."

We continued listening to the story as the reporter confirmed once again that Terry Butcher had indeed been substituted. Yours Truly had obviously made a huge gaffe and panic began to set in very quickly as I realised the implications of what I had done.

One of the lads said, "What about Michael Robinson?"

"Never mind Michael Robinson," somebody else quipped. "Worrabout the whole of fuck'n Spain? They all think Terry Butcher got sent off!"

By now I was really panicking and we all started laughing, although my laughter was fraught with nerves. They were now calling me El Pedro. What a cock-up I made that day. Sorry, Mike. I take all the blame; it was my fault completely. The next time Spanish TV came to Everton, I phoned in sick.

One of my other jobs was to ascertain whether there were any medically trained fans, such as doctors or nurses – sitting near the TV gantry. In the unlikely event of an accident or anybody feeling unwell, you really wouldn't want to be on your own. I got to know most of the fans sitting in this area and I always enjoyed talking to them anyway, as they were my people. They would often ask me what the commentators or players were like to work with and some would hand over notebooks for autographs. We'd have a bit of a laugh when I asked why nobody ever wanted mine.

I found it very interesting to discover the many different professions of people sitting in the Upper Bullens Road stand, situated just behind me on the TV gantry. I would often look around and think here were such a wide variety of people from so many walks of life, but for just one day at the match, they were all the same, just fans. I know it's had its fair share of bad publicity over the years, but one of the most beautiful things I've found with football is the way it can bring people together. You may not even know the name of the person sitting next to you but you can enjoy a mutually understandable conversation, or even give them a big hug... something that would never happen outside the stadium. We may indeed all lead separate lives, but once inside that stadium, if you'll pardon the pun, it's a totally different ball game.

One particular week, there was a bit of a commotion near one of the refreshment bars. When I arrived there, I found an elderly man who had collapsed and didn't appear to be breathing. I knew where a doctor usually sat and quickly went to fetch him. We both started CPR and within a few seconds were joined by a nurse who asked if we needed any help. If you've ever been in this situation, you will understand that people who know what they are doing are always most welcome.

You may have seen the former footballer turned

actor, Vinnie Jones, demonstrating on the TV ads how to carry out chest compressions to the tune of *Stayin' Alive* by the Bee Gees, to get the rhythm right. A lot of medical students have been taught this technique and although it may sound a bit ridiculous, it has actually proved to be very effective. Another tune that can be used is *Nelly the Elephant* and I suppose as long as nobody can hear you singing, it doesn't really matter as long as you are managing about a hundred beats per minute.

First Aid really can keep people alive until expert help arrives and I've always believed it should even be part of the national curriculum for our older kids in school; you simply never know when you're going to need it.

To go back to the elderly man, we were then joined by the St John's Ambulance Brigade, who in my opinion are the real heroes at football matches everywhere. These people are not sufficiently recognised for their great work, week in, week out and I for one feel very reassured by their presence at football matches. I would recommend that any young person join the St John's Ambulance Brigade as I believe this gives them a good grounding, with the added bonus of learning first aid properly (as well as getting into a football match for nowt.)

We managed to resuscitate the ailing gentleman who was then taken to hospital by a waiting ambulance. Unfortunately, I discovered later that the poor man had passed away.

A couple of weeks later, a young bloke came up to the TV gantry and introduced himself as the man's son and asked if I was the person that helped his father. I told him I was amongst quite a few people who tried to save his dad, but I only had basic first aid training and that my contribution wasn't as effective as the other people there. He shook my hand and thanked me anyway for my help in trying to save his dad. I told him I was very sorry to learn he had died.

"Sorry?" he said. "Please don't be sorry. We were delighted he died here at Goodison Park." He told me his dad had been coming here for more than sixty years and all his family found it very comforting to know he died at the place he loved. We then gave each other a hug as he said goodbye. I knew exactly where he was coming from and understood how fitting it could be for people to leave this life in such a way, which in this gentleman's case brought some comfort to his grieving family.

Although it's obviously very sad, it does tend to happen more often at football grounds for some strange reason. I don't know for sure, but perhaps it's the excitement of the game.

The Everton legend, Dixie Dean, died of a heart attack after watching Everton play their closest rivals, Liverpool, in 1980 and exactly five years later, former Everton manager, Harry Catterick, also died of a heart attack shortly after watching Everton draw against Ipswich Town. The former Scotland manager Jock Stein collapsed and died after Scotland qualified for the World Cup at the end of their game against Wales in Cardiff, also in 1985.

Another part of my job was to collect the team sheets from the players' tunnel and bring them up to the TV gantry. This was a chance to stretch my legs and also a great opportunity to meet some of the players before the game and it gave me a small insight to the other side of the fence.

I'll never forget the time when Tottenham Hotspur came to Everton. Gary Lineker was playing for Spurs and it was his first time back at Goodison Park since leaving Everton for Barcelona.

Coincidentally, my wife and I got married on the same day as Gary Lineker and his first wife, Michelle, and we both went on to have boys around the same age. So the night before this game, I asked my wife if she had a new garment for their son, George, as a 'welcome back to Everton' present. She found something, still unwrapped and suitable for a boy, which I took with me to the game.

Anyway, before the game, I was near the changing room waiting for the team sheets when Gary Lineker popped over to say hello to some of the Everton staff. He really is as pleasant as he appears on TV, and it was then that I gave him the present and congratulated him on the birth of his son and welcomed him back to Everton.

He put his arm around me, said a big thank you and told me Michelle would be delighted with the present. I mentioned we were married on the same day and he wished my wife and me all the best.

He then led me into the Spurs changing room and showed his team mates the present, telling them he 'knew something like this would happen.' He was really touched with the present and although I knew he obviously wasn't in need of it, he really appreciated the thought. It was nice to see Gary Lineker back at Everton and I'm sure he was delighted with his warm welcome back to Merseyside.

Some of the Spurs players were jokingly shouting "Get out! No scousers in here!" I shouted back at them that they were in for a beating today and it was all good banter.

I spoke with Gary for a few more minutes, but just before I left, I asked him if he could do me a small favour.

"What is it?" he asked.

I told him I worked on the TV gantry, directly opposite to where the teams came out.

"I know where it is," he replied. "I used to play here, remember?"

I asked if he'd come over and give me a wave when the teams came out onto the pitch.

"Is that all?" he said. "No problem."

I couldn't wait to get back up onto the gantry and as John Motson was there that day with the BBC, I told him what I'd arranged with Gary Lineker.

He doubted whether Gary would remember and told me not to build my hopes too high as he would probably be fully focused on the game.

"He will, John," I said. "He promised me."

John Motson didn't share my optimism, but I was convinced he would and I asked one of the camera men to film it for me.

Well, about twenty minutes before kick-off, the Everton and Tottenham teams came out onto the pitch in track suit tops to warm up and, noticing Lineker heading towards the gantry, I told the camera man to get ready. But Gary then turned away without looking up and started warming up in the other direction. A minute or so later, he came close again. Convinced he would wave this time, I alerted the BBC camera man once again.

But, as before, he turned the other way, without waving. John Motson reminded me that although Gary

Lineker is a genuinely nice bloke, professional footballers were at this stage, prior to the match, too psyched up and focused on the game to possibly remember. The two teams then began leaving the pitch after their warm up and went back down the tunnel to discard their track suits and prepare to come back out for the kick-off.

I was a bit disappointed, but I understood what Motty said; he probably was focused solely on the game and besides, it wasn't all bad, as Gary had been kind enough to take me into the Spurs changing room to meet the rest of his team.

At five to three, Everton and Tottenham Hotspur emerged from the tunnel to a deafening reception and what happened next will stay with me for the rest of my life. Gary Lineker and the whole Tottenham team came over to the TV gantry, looked up and gave me a wave.

I was absolutely gobsmacked. He must have arranged it with his team mates after I left the changing room. Boy was I surprised. I turned around to John Motson who was just standing there, laughing and shaking his head.

"I told you he wouldn't let me down," I said to Motty. "Didn't I tell you?"

Gary Lineker... a true gentleman, thank you very much.

One week, I even got a cheer from the Goodison crowd myself. Every now and again, the ball would be kicked up into the stands and you would often see the fans throw the ball back onto the pitch. As the TV gantry is right at the front of the stands, the ball quite often ended up beside where I was sitting.

This particular week, the ball headed up towards

the gantry and I'm not sure whether it was just instinct or seizing the chance to achieve a lifetime ambition, but as it came towards me, I stood up, positioned myself, and instead of catching the ball as most do, I headed it back onto the pitch. It was a header Andy Gray would have been proud of. I still don't know why, but I then raised both arms high in the air as if I'd just scored the winning goal.

The crowd cheered like mad and I could see all the fans sitting around me, laughing. For most of my childhood, I'd dreamed of heading the ball at Goodison Park and although it may not quite have been playing for Everton, it was good enough for me and I still managed to get a cheer from the Everton fans.

I can still see the Everton full back, Andy Hinchcliffe, and some of the other players looking up and laughing. After the game, some of my fellow stewards were laughing and patting me on the back, as if I'd scored the winning goal. Andy Warhol once said everybody would have fifteen minutes of fame; mine was more like fifteen seconds, but well worth it.

I also watched many exciting games during my time working on the TV gantry, including the Everton v Liverpool FA cup replay which finished 4-4. The match was an absolute classic and for sheer passion and excitement, this game had it all. With Liverpool in front four times and Everton refusing to give up and coming back, it really was a thriller.

This was also Kenny Dalglish's last match as manager, (in his first spell in charge) as he resigned the following morning after it was suggested the pressure of the job was taking its toll.

Sky TV and the BBC were televising the game

that night, which was rather unusual as you didn't normally see more than one TV company, but with this being such a massive game, most channels were screening it. That night I was sitting alongside Martin Tyler, Andy Gray and the rest of the Sky sports crew.

What struck me more than anything else was the way the commentators and some very big people in the world of football were reacting privately to the events unfolding on the pitch, which was why I chose to sit alongside the Sky Sports crew that night, (think about it) and remembering they were only human beings, affected in the same way as we fans. I'll always remember Andy Gray, standing up and literally squeezing and hugging me each time Everton scored and then sitting down again and trying to compose himself whilst commentating with Martin Tyler.

The atmosphere that night was absolutely electric. It was probably one of the most exciting I've ever experienced at a football match and you could see how divided the TV crews were as they demonstrated their loyalties off-camera, although they had to somehow remain impartial when they were onscreen. It gave me a great insight to how these football pundits watch the match on our TV screens and you really do see that they are just like the rest of us with a passion for football.

On the TV Gantry with Andy Gray

Andy Gray told me it was much worse on the nerves to be watching rather than playing. He said being involved in the game carried you along but when you're only watching you're helpless to do anything about it.

Everton and Liverpool had to replay a week later, with our family and the rest of Merseyside divided once again. Dave Watson scored the winning goal for Everton which eventually settled this epic cup tie. Just as well... I don't think the nerves could have taken much more, but as I was about to discover, this was nothing to what was waiting for me in my protest.

Six
It's Nice to be Important, but More Important to be Nice

Working on the TV gantry was a brilliant job but although I was getting into the home matches for free, this did not entitle me to get into away games. I soon found out from a few of the more experienced stewards, though, that if you brought your badge with you, there were certain stewards at away grounds who would turn a blind eye and let you in for nowt. It was like some kind of tacit agreement between stewards at different clubs and likewise some of the stewards at Everton would return the compliment when they came to Goodison.

Having said that, it was by no means guaranteed and there were gate men and stewards at other clubs who wouldn't (pardon the pun) play ball. You would often come across the odd individuals who, once they donned their yellow stewards' coats, became Little Hitlers.

It was at one of these clubs when a member of the Third Reich was patrolling the gate and refusing to let any of us stewards use our passes. I won't name the club, but they play near the River Trent and Brian Clough used to be their manager.

On this particular day, my mate, Dennis and I avoided Adolf patrolling the gate and made our way to another turnstile, where I pulled out my steward's pass. This gateman promptly radioed for assistance and told us that somebody important was on his way down to see us. Somebody important, I thought, that's just what we need, getting kicked out before we've even managed to get in. One of the head security men arrived, who I will call Bill. He looked at our passes and told me in a quite authoritative manner that these were not tickets.

"No, of course not," I replied. "They're our stewards' passes, we work as stewards for Everton Football Club and we're here to assist you and ensure the Everton fans behave themselves." It was the only thing I could think of.

He said he had never heard of other teams bringing their stewards to away grounds before and that they had their own stewards, so why would Everton be sending theirs?

I didn't need to remind myself that I was conducting a protest of no longer paying to get into football matches and I also had my heart set on obtaining an autographed Nottingham Forest ball for the collection. I knew I only had one chance to convince Bill and I had to come up with something really good.

So I took a deep breath. "We do this everywhere," I insisted. "When the two teams come out onto the pitch, we stewards start clapping the opposing team and our fans follow our lead and join in. In addition to this, if we see any potential troublemakers, we go over and speak to them, defuse the situation and remind them they are representing their club as ambassadors and are responsible for Everton's good name. We're also trained in first aid, oh and one more thing, we do all this for nowt, by giving up our Saturdays voluntarily."

That's absolutely marvellous, he said. "What a great idea... we should start doing that here at Notts Forest." He thought for a moment. "In fact, I'm going to contact Everton and thank them for sending these volunteers and tell them what a great bunch of stewards they have."

Dennis immediately gave me a worried look and I stepped in quickly and told Bill he didn't have to do that and it would only embarrass us, as we were quite modest people. Of course, if he had contacted Everton, we would all have been sacked.

Anyway, after this totally ridiculous and fabricated explanation was accepted, Bill allowed us into the ground, free of charge. I remember thinking, wow, that's how I'll get into every ground from now on, but, as I was to soon discover not every ground had a lovely bloke like Bill.

When the Notts Forest team came out first, a lot of the Everton fans began booing them.

I said, "Dennis, you're meant to be clapping their team!" and we both started laughing.

Everything seemed to be going great when after about fifteen minutes into the game, Bill came over to us, looking very serious.

"Peter, I need to speak with you now if you don't mind, please?"

I said to Dennis, "Shit, it looks like he's phoned Everton; we may as well get ourselves ready to leave mate." I knew it was too good to be true.

"What's the matter, Bill?" I asked.

"Peter, I could really do with your assistance for a few minutes, please?".

"Of course," I said. "What is it, Bill?"

He said there was an Everton steward outside the turnstile who wanted to come in and help out as well. Dennis and I were struggling to keep straight faces and I whispered that I thought our story was original, but they all must be using the same one.

Apparently this person claiming to be an

Everton steward said he'd mislaid his pass and Bill said if he was a steward I would know him and would I mind just confirming that he was indeed a steward. I didn't like the sound of this, but I got the impression from Bill that I didn't have much of a choice. I thought if it keeps him happy, I'm going to have to play along with it.

So Bill, Dennis and I made our way to the gate and as we were walking towards this stranger who I'd never seen before in my life, he was looking at me with a 'please don't let me down' expression. I'm not sure who was more nervous, this bloke outside the gate, me or Dennis.

I thought to myself, what the hell am I supposed to do here? I can't not help one of my fellow Evertonians, but in another way I didn't want to take Bill for a ride, especially as he'd been so kind to let us in. By this stage, I had taken a bit of a liking to Bill, who came across as somebody's lovely grandad and I really didn't want to be disrespectful to him. But when I looked at this bloke with those big sad eyes looking up at me, I thought, how can I let him down, especially after travelling all that way? We couldn't just leave him outside, on his own as well.

I knew that whatever words came out of my mouth in the next few seconds would determine this poor bloke's fate and if we were in a position to help him out, I thought we should do. It's only one more person, I thought, and surely a big club like Notts Forest can afford to let one more person in free of charge? I also hadn't forgotten about the way our clubs gave loads of tickets away to privileged people, so without any further ado, I heard myself shouting, "Jimmy! How are you, mate? You're a bit late, aren't you?"

The guy I was calling Jimmy and trying my best to convince Bill that I knew him, was looking behind him to see who I was shouting at. Obviously his name wasn't Jimmy. So I shouted to him again, only this time I began winking at him.

"Jimmy! How come you're late, mate? The game kicked off a quarter of an hour ago.

The penny dropped. "Oh yeah, I'm great, er... I was held up in traffic."

Bill said, "You do know him then, Peter? He is a steward?"

"Of course he is," I replied. "Jimmy's one of our senior stewards, aren't you, Jim?"

"Yeah, that's me," he said. "Jimmy, one of the senior stewards."

I looked at Dennis, who was shaking with suppressed laughter.

So Bill let in this bloke who I didn't know from Adam, thanked us both and asked if he could bother us again if needed.

"No problem, Bill," I said. But I must admit, I did feel a bit bad about Bill, but there was no way I could have left one of my fellow Evertonians stuck outside.

"I don't know who you are, mate," the Jimmy bloke said to me, "but thanks a lot, I owe you one. There was no need to make me a senior steward, though; that was a bit over the top." He then gave me a searching look.

"By the way, why is it they have Everton stewards at an away match... and how come you're working?"

"We're not, mate."

"What? You mean…?"

"We've done the same as you just did."

"You mean I was depending on you two to let me in and you'd just bunked in yourselves?"

As he walked away, shaking his head and laughing, we heard him mutter, "Cheeky bastards."

We were back watching the game, and booing Notts Forest every time they kicked the ball when Bill arrived once more and asked if I would mind helping him out once again.

Dennis thought it was dead funny and laughed at me.

"You're going to get this all through the game," he said.

"I know," I said. Bill was making absolutely sure I worked for my free entry. "What's up this time?" I asked him.

He said there was an Everton fan outside saying his mate was inside the ground with his ticket, that they'd somehow split up and the fan had no money on him. Bill wondered if I may know his friend and maybe try and assist in getting his ticket for him.

So now I found myself standing next to Bill and questioning another one of my fellow fans who was attempting to get into the game along the same lines as this Jimmy bloke, Dennis and I.

"What happened to your mate?" I asked him. "Have you any idea where he might be?"

After a long drawn out explanation by this bloke, I asked Bill if I could make a suggestion… could we let this man in to find his friend and bring back his ticket?

"But Peter, how do we know he'll come back?"

Bill asked.

"Look," I said to the bloke, "if we were to let you in to find your friend, do you promise to come straight back with your ticket?"

"Course I will and I won't be long at all," he answered. "As soon as I find him, I'll be straight back."

Bill agreed to let him in and thanked me for my help.

I couldn't believe it when Dennis spoke to this fan in a raised voice. "You've got fifteen minutes, mate," he said, "or we're coming looking for you!"

I looked at Dennis and asked him if he could remember how we got in, reminding him that we shouldn't even be in here ourselves. I think the sense of authority went to Dennis's head, but it was absolutely hilarious. When Bill wasn't looking, this bloke quietly asked me if he really had to come back. I whispered back that I didn't care if I never saw him again and shook his hand.

I never got the chance to tell the fan that we were just like him… but if you are reading this and happen to recognise yourself, Dennis was looking everywhere for you.

At the end of the match, Bill came over to thank us both for our help and as it turned out, the fans were quite well behaved that day and everything just turned out sweet. Then, just before we were leaving, Bill had the last word.

"Don't worry, lads," he said with a little wink. "I wasn't going to contact Everton."

The good thing about Bill was that although he probably knew all along that it was just one big blag, he was experienced enough to see the benefits of letting us in, unlike his colleague, Adolf, who had no understanding of a little common sense. Bill was obviously aware of the saying, 'it's nice to be important, but it's much more important to be nice.'

Thanks for a great day at the City ground, Bill, a true gentleman and a genuine thank you to all the lovely people at Nottingham Forest who kindly sent me my second ball for a very worthy cause. Notts Forest, take a bow.

Seven
The Prawn Sandwich Brigade

When Sunderland were playing Liverpool in the 1992 FA cup final at Wembley, my old mate, Ray, who I worked with and was a big Liverpool fan, asked me if I fancied going down to London to watch the final with him on Saturday.

I thought that was nice of him. "I didn't know you had tickets," I said.

"I haven't," he replied.

"How can we go down there, then?"

"Why? What's the problem?" Ray asked.

"Well, there's the small matter of us not having any tickets," I reminded him.

"Worrabout the protest, then?" He said if I was really serious about fans not getting tickets for big games like the big cup finals, then I'd have to take my protest to other clubs apart from my own team, Everton, and even to FA cup finals, no matter who was playing.

He did have a point, but I couldn't help noticing how keen he was to support my protest, especially with his team, Liverpool, now in the final... oh, and that small matter that he didn't have a ticket.

He said, "I'd like to support you in your protest and this being an FA cup final, it's the perfect venue to protest to the Football Association. Oh, and we'll have a great laugh as well."

I had to admit that whenever we did get together, we always had a good laugh and we'd both been working long hours together in Shotton Paper Mill, so I thought, why not? There was just one stipulation, though. If we were to stand any chance of getting into a stadium like Wembley and with it also being the FA Cup final, the biggest game in the football calendar, it would have to be done properly. There could be no half measures, as we simply wouldn't get in otherwise.

"No problem," he said. "What exactly do you have in mind?"

I told Ray that we'd have to dress up really smart and look the part. If we were going to pull it off, we'd have to pretend we worked at Wembley and simply walk into the stadium with the rest of the staff.

"Wha... isn't there another way?" he asked.

"Yes. We could always turn up at Wembley at about two-thirty, half an hour before the final was due to kick off and pay three hundred quid each to a ticket tout."

"Do I need to wear a tie?" Ray asked.

It is said you never get a second chance to make a first impression and this is very true, so on the Saturday morning, dressed up in our smart suits not shell suits; and without our black curly wigs, we drove down to dat der London.

We arrived at Wembley quite early, looking the part, and I made sure my steward's pass was safely tucked away in my pocket. It was about ten o'clock in the morning and as the fans hadn't arrived yet, we stood a much better chance of getting in. Also, if you worked at Wembley, that would be about the right time to report for work.

My Everton pass reared its ugly head once again when we arrived at the gate and although Everton weren't even playing, it looked really official. I told security we were reporting for work.

Glancing at my pass, they wanted to know

where we were stewarding.

"The TV gantry for Sky Television," I answered without hesitation.

Ray shot me a worried look as security asked if we knew our way up there.

"Of course," I said with an outward show of confidence that masked my fear of being found out.

I couldn't believe it when they opened the gate and we were allowed to enter. To be perfectly honest, I wasn't anticipating a result like this straight away and had been half expecting to have to try some of the other gates in the hope that one of them would let us in. So to get in the TV gate at the first attempt was like hitting the jackpot.

I don't think I'd ever known Ray to be so quiet as we walked into an empty Wembley stadium. It was still quite nerve racking though, especially as I could see out of the corner of my eye that the security guards were casting glances at us and whispering between themselves. They must have had one or two doubts about us and, if that wasn't bad enough, I wasn't sure whether to turn left or right or continue straight ahead and I realised we were by no means home and dry. Suddenly I noticed some steps leading up to a staircase and remembered one of the guards asking if I knew my way up there, which suggested to me this must be the correct route to take. If it's not, I thought, we've had it.

With security still in view, we began to make our way up the stairs, desperately trying to appear as if we knew where we were going. When we eventually reached the top of the stands, nothing could have prepared me for the spectacle I was about to see. This unbelievable view was almost impossible to comprehend as we both looked down at the truly magnificent arena and its beautiful pristine green turf. But in another way, it was also quite an eerie feeling.

To my dying day, I swear, I'll never forget being overcome with emotion, gazing down at this iconic stadium... the home of football, which had for many years produced so many fantastic memories for me and for millions of other people all over the world. For a few awe-filled moments, I just stood there and gaped at the spot where the Queen presented the World Cup to Bobby Moore in 1966 and I could see a toothless Nobby Styles dancing around the pitch. I could also see the bench from which the Sunderland manager, Bob Stokoe, had leapt up at the final whistle to run over and hug his goalkeeper, Jim Montgomery, after beating the mighty Leeds United in the1973 final.

Tears rolled down my face as I saw the Everton and Liverpool fans sitting alongside each other, singing 'Merseyside, Merseyside,' in the Milk Cup final in 1984, the final that became known as the friendly final, because of our very close bond.

I could also hear Kenneth Wolstenholme's immortal words "They think it's all over, it is now."

But for me the most emotional memories by far that day were the wonderful finals that took place in our house as I was growing up. Every one of those brilliant events may well have taken place here on this Wembley turf, but for me personally, the memories will forever belong in our front room with the curtains closed.

I found it impossible to hold back the tears as this famous pitch below me was actually responsible for most of the happiest moments of my childhood. The vision and the whole experience of the world-famous, empty stadium that day will stay with me forever. I'm not ashamed to admit I was crying my eyes out as I could hear my mum ask who would like another cup of tea and my late, treasured dad asking me, as Everton hadn't made it that year, who was I supporting that day. I could have stayed there all day as I had so many wonderful memories of this incredible arena, until...

"Ay, are you okay la?" Ray was shaking my shoulder. "Why aren't you listening to me? Those security people look like they're still looking at us, you know."

"Dey do dough, don't dey, dough?" I said, drying my eyes and composing myself.

"What's wrong? Why are you all upset and looking down at the pitch like some kind of knob-head in a trance?"

"I was just reminiscing, mate... just reminiscing."

"Worrabout?"

"I'll tell you again, mate."

I'd never experienced anything quite like the feeling I had that day. I'm not exaggerating when I say it was one of the most moving experiences I've ever had in my life and I just wanted to keep it to myself a little bit longer. It had a huge effect on me, but in a very positive way. It was almost as if those loved ones who had shared such happy childhood memories with me and who were sadly no longer here, were actually back with me again just for today, saying, 'Don't worry about a thing here at Wembley, Peter; everything is going to work out great.'

Ray continued to give me strange looks.

"From now on, mate, everything is going to be fine," I told him.

Although still feeling a bit nervous, we made

our way towards the massive television gantry where reporters and commentators from the BBC, ITV, SKY and other TV crews from all over the world would shortly be doing their stuff. I was also aware of the security guys still looking up at us from this vast, empty stadium just waiting for us to make one mistake.

I noticed Wembley wasn't like other league football grounds, as there were so many different private security and stewarding companies and we were trying to work out who were the best people to approach. It only needed one mistake from either of us for one of these companies to report us on their radios and that would have been the end of this final for us.

"We've got to look like we know what we're doing," I said to Ray "and hope for the best. Okay?"

Ray now had determination etched all over his face. Protest or not, his team, Liverpool, was playing in the FA cup final and there was no way he was missing that. He wasn't going to allow a minor issue like not having an FA Cup Final ticket get in his way, so we pressed on.

I quietly showed one or two companies my steward's pass and explained that our company had over-booked with their stewards and we were available if they needed our help. Unfortunately most of these companies were already fully manned and it wasn't looking good. I sensed we were rapidly running out of options and I knew that once all the fans had entered the stadium, there wouldn't be a single seat left in the house and we would end up looking out of place and being ejected from the ground.

Just as another company declined our offer of help, a lady in charge of one of the stewarding firms approached me and asked if we were looking to help out,

"Two of my people haven't turned up and we could do with a couple of stewards to stop anybody coming into the hospitality section without a pass," she explained.

Ray and I exchanged hopeful glances. I couldn't believe it... had she been sent by an angel, or somebody who was looking out for me this day and knew we needed some help?

"I'm afraid, as you're not registered with us, though, we can't pay you, but we can give you two top class seats in return for your help."

Bingo!

This was one of those offers in life which didn't need any further consideration and we accepted her offer immediately. I couldn't believe our luck.

"You know what that means," Ray whispered to me. "It means we've got to stop anybody bunking in." We both started laughing, as two people in charge of stopping anybody bunking in had just bunked in themselves.

Ray and I couldn't stop laughing with each other about it, especially when I asked him, with my voice of authority, where his pass was. It was about to get even better when this lady came back over and apologised to us and said we didn't have to work now as the two people had turned up, but we could still keep our seats if we wanted to.

"Oh, okay," I said, nonchalantly. "Yeah, we may as well then, thanks." Just as well, I thought to myself, because we didn't have any other seats.

Incredibly, we'd landed on our feet yet again. At quarter to three we sat down to watch the 1992 FA cup final between Liverpool and Sunderland in two of the best seats in the house as another beautiful memory of this iconic stadium was about to unfold.

About fifteen minutes after the match started, I went to the toilet and although I didn't know it at the time, our day out at Wembley was about to take another incredible turn. As I left the toilet area, I struck up a conversation with a couple of blokes, not something I make a habit of doing in men's toilets, but one of them asked me which company I was with. They looked pretty posh and then it dawned on me, we were in the corporate hospitality area and they must have been part of the prawn sandwich brigade. They were all with different companies there... which company could I say I was with?

I couldn't tell him I'd just walked in with my Everton steward's pass, which carried as much weight as a cigarette coupon and Everton weren't even playing here today. But then I thought the chances were that this guy wasn't a real football fan anyway and probably wouldn't even know that Everton weren't playing.

"I'm working with Sky Television," I told him.

Suddenly, he was really interested. "Oh, I see...who's commentating today?"

Without thinking, I just said Martin Tyler, as he more than likely was, anyway.

"Ah. Which one is he?" he asked.

My suspicions were confirmed immediately; he didn't have a clue about football. If he was a football fan, he'd know who Martin Tyler was. My first thoughts were, how many real football fans couldn't get hold of a ticket for today's game, and how many people like this bloke were in here and shouldn't be? (Yes, I know what you're thinking, but Ray and myself had a vastly different agenda.)

Then he said, "Why don't you pop into our executive lounge at half time for a drink?"

I felt a bit mean then and thought, what a really nice man and a very kind gesture, until he spoilt it by suggesting I brought Martin Tyler in with me. I realised of course that his only reason for inviting me was to get Sky TV's Martin Tyler into his lounge to impress his cronies. I knew that for sure when I overheard his colleague, who thought I'd gone, ask why he'd invited me into their lounge at half time. This other bloke wasn't as friendly and thought he was far too important to speak to the likes of me. They were obviously unaware that there were still some people outside the toilets preventing us from moving on and as I was static for a few moments, I could still hear what was being said in the toilets. They'd naturally assumed I'd left the area, but I could hear the one who invited me in telling his posh mate that he wasn't really inviting me, but just using me to get Martin Tyler from Sky TV into their lounge. His toff mate thought this was a stroke of genius and found it very amusing. As I listened to the two of them laughing behind my back, I shook my head and thought to myself, that's what's wrong with the world today. Nobody seems to care about anybody any more and it's all about 'what's in it for me?'

I must admit though, I was now laughing as well, because I wasn't with Martin Tyler, the Sky Sports commentator, or Sky TV for that matter... just my old mate, Ray, a carpet fitter. I couldn't wait to get back to tell Ray about our invitation into one of the executive boxes at half time. A very wise man once said, 'He who laughs last, laughs loudest.'

Ray's jaw dropped open and he started laughing

when I told him.

"You kiddin' me, mate?"

I explained about bringing Martin Tyler with us.

"Well, how are we going to do that when we're not even with Martin Tyler?"

I just looked at Ray and grinned. "This bloke knows nothing about football and doesn't even know what Martin Tyler looks like…"

Ray's laughter was short-lived. "Absolutely no chance!" he said. "You can get that thought out of your head right now. I'm not doing it. I'm not pretending to be Martin Tyler. I've only come here to watch the match and you've already got me dressed like some knob-head in a suit, had me working as corporate hospitality steward, and now you want me to be a commentator for Sky Television."

The two of us were laughing our heads off by now and I told Ray I was only kidding. "Don't worry, mate; I think I've already worked out this little problem."

At half time and with my throat very sore from all that cheering and shouting for Sunderland, Ray and I made our way into our friend's hospitality lounge and once inside, we were immediately handed two glasses of champagne by two delightful young waitresses.

John, who had invited me, came over and asked straight away if Martin Tyler was coming down. It was a bit like meeting a girl you really liked but she was only interested in where your mate was. I must admit I was a bit disappointed at being used in this way but the excellent champagne and mouth-watering cuisine I could see on display quickly won me over.

"I'm afraid Martin won't be able to make it until after the game as he's getting ready for the second half,"

I told John. "This is my friend, Ray."

"Do you work for Sky Sports as well—?"

"Yes," Ray replied, almost before the question was out, "and I also work with Martin Tyler as well!"

I had no idea Ray was going to say this. It was totally over the top and sounded far too corny and well-rehearsed but at the same time, dreadfully funny.

"What was all that about?" I whispered to Ray.

"I'll tell you worrit's about, mate. You know you and I aren't really welcome in here; in fact if we'd knocked on that door asking for a drink of water, they would have contacted security and had us beaten up, ejected and then arrested." He laughed. "No, we're not welcome here, but Martin Tyler is. That's why I said it."

"Make sure you bring Martin in after the game, won't you?" John insisted.

For the next fifteen minutes, Ray and I enjoyed prawn sandwiches and sampled some top class bubbly and fine beers and wines from all over the world. Talk about the haves and have nots; this was definitely the haves and have yachts. As we made small talk with John and his business colleagues, we noticed how some of them liked to click their fingers at the waitresses for more champagne, which we thought was very rude. The waitresses were two lovely, polite young girls from Dublin and I felt a bit sorry for them. These so-called business executives didn't even make eye contact with the girls as they held out their empty glasses for a top up. They obviously didn't think waitresses were worth acknowledging.

I made a point of apologising to the waitresses and telling them how disrespectful this was and that Ray and I were embarrassed by their ignorance. They told us not to worry as they were used to that kind of behaviour and besides, later on, when they were drunk, they would only be getting cheap plonk, anyway.

We confided to the waitresses about Martin Tyler and they both went into hysterics. After that, each time someone clicked their fingers, the waitresses shot us knowing looks, trying not to start laughing again. It was plain to see how false these people were and the more they had to drink, the more objectionable they seemed to be, to each other as well as the waitresses.

As Ray and I were talking, one of John's cronies confronted us, demanding to know who we were and what were we doing in his lounge. When our friend John saw what was happening, he quickly came over and thinking that we couldn't see what he was doing, began winking as he explained to his rude colleague (although he couldn't remember our names) that we were bringing in Sky Television's commentator, Martin Tyler, after the game.

Of course, his associate's rude face was suddenly transformed. Excited by this news, his eyes glinted greedily and his mouth stretched into a sly smile. I was almost expecting a predatory lick of the lips. After apologising to me and Ray, his response was to click his fingers to the waitresses for two more drinks. The waitresses came over, trying not to laugh as they poured our drinks. Ray and I just about managed to keep straight faces as we thanked the girls.

Ray said to me, "Just look at this idiot who's suddenly all over us like a rash and knows nothing about football either, asking us what does Martin Tyler look like, but is nevertheless now delighted that a Sky TV commentator is coming into his lounge to impress his business associates."

I had to remind Ray that Martin Tyler was *not*

coming, as we both started laughing again. Even more amusing was that we could see them casting secretive looks at us and wondering what the joke was.

I still couldn't help thinking of all the fans outside who had followed their team all season and were now unable to get a ticket and yet we had these ill-mannered creeps who were not the slightest bit interested in football, enjoying a team bonding exercise and most probably writing the expenses off against their tax bills.

The bell rang in the executive box and it was time to return to our places for the second half.

"For fuck's sake," Ray said, "it's like being in the fucking theatre."

"Come on," I said, "Martin's waiting for us!"

We both creased over again with laughter, having forty-five minutes in which to work out how to explain to John and his phonies why Martin Tyler wouldn't be visiting their executive suite after the game.

"Maybe it's best if we don't go back?" Ray said.

"I thought that, but it's gonna be murder trying to get out of here in this crowd," I replied.

"Yeah, that's a point… and after all, we have been invited," Ray said.

After the match we made our way back into the lounge, where our new business associates were now very much the worse for wear. I explained that Martin was tying up a few loose ends and would be down once he concluded his post-match report.

"Did you like that, Ray?" I asked. "… concluded his post-match report? I learnt that from the TV gantry at Everton."

Ray grinned. "Yeah, good. You even had me believing it."

We cringed at some of their antics and they became even more pathetic as they kept asking Ray and me who had scored and what was the name of this or that player, etc. We were disgusted that these individuals didn't have a clue about football, but were only there to take advantage of whatever was offered in order to serve their own interests.

One of the posh brigade asked what the final conclusion was.

Ray whispered to me, "What was the final conclusion? Does he mean what was the fucking score?"

"Who knows?" I answered. "The only conclusion I can arrive at is that a significant number of Liverpool and Sunderland fans have been unfairly deprived of tickets today."

After more finger-snapping to keep the bubbly flowing, the prawn sandwich brigade had by now begun singing rugby songs and playing stupid games. These idiots thought they were being amusing and that people nearby found them funny. In fact they looked absurd and it was even more sickening to watch the junior members of this company having to pretend they were funny.

It was all so very false, but what I did find amusing was that every time the door opened, John, his rude friend and all their ridiculous cronies jerked their heads round in unison, no doubt expecting to see Martin Tyler walk in.

"Here's Martin," Ray remarked, each time the door opened. I never imagined that simply opening a door could make me laugh so much. It was absolutely hilarious. Even the waitresses were coming up to us in fits of laughter with comments like, "Ooh, this'll be

Martin Tyler, then!" We also had it confirmed by the waitresses that the finger-clicking hooligans were now officially consuming cheap plonk, although it looked good in the ice buckets.

I remember one of John's colleagues suggesting they come back next season as they were having such a great time.

"They don't even know who's bloody playing next season," I remarked to Ray, "and they're making plans to return next year. No wonder we fans can't get any fucking tickets!"

Yes, I was angry, and this was only one corporate concern; there must have been dozens of them there that day and each executive box hosted about twenty people. How the hell were these private companies, who knew nothing and cared even less about football, getting their hands on so many tickets at the expense of the real fans?

It's quite okay to criticise ticket touts and rightly so, but why do we not object to these prawn sandwich merchants, as well as certain celebrities whom we might respect and admire but whose famous bottoms are actually occupying our seats? We look up in awe at the famous stars and the many privileged people who suddenly like football's big games and are handed free tickets at cup finals and then we wonder why there are none left for us. But when it's all over and another season begins, we are welcomed back with open arms and called the twelfth man again. We buy our season tickets for another campaign and a long, cold winter looming with matches nobody else wants to go to and we're flavour of the month once again. It's a recurring cycle that has existed for as long as I can remember and when the cup finals and big matches come round again, we moan amongst ourselves, engage in a few post-match radio phone- ins, write the occasional letter to our local paper and don't hear any more about it until the following season, when it happens all over again. How have the football authorities been allowed to do this to us and... come on, fellow fans... why are we allowing them to do it?

"I'm going to contact the FA first thing Monday morning and ask what's going on," I said.

"And are you going to tell them how *you* got in as well?" queried Ray with a grin.

John came over to me and Ray and asked us, not for the first time, when Martin was coming.

"For fuck's sake," Ray said, "I'll go and see what's keeping him."

I gave Ray a quizzical look. How was he going to do that?

After about five minutes I went outside to see what was happening and there was Ray, near the toilet, smoking a cigarette.

"I take it you didn't find Martin, then?" I asked him.

Just then, as another rugby song started up inside, Ray and I called the two waitresses over, gave them their first and only tip of the day, said goodbye and thanked them for a lovely day. They thanked us too, for a great laugh, and said it was the funniest and most enjoyable day they'd ever had working at Wembley and although they were not into football, they would always remember the 1992 FA Cup Final and never forget Sky TV's Martin Tyler.

Just as we were leaving, John's friend from the toilet, who I'd caught laughing at me behind my back earlier, was walking past and I couldn't resist asking him what the score was today.

"I don't know," he said. "I'm not really into football that much."

"The score," I told him, "was: The Fans, One; The Prawn Sandwich Brigade, Nil," and left him to think about it as we made our way out of Wembley.

Eight
End of the Road

Manchester United's Old Trafford was next on my list and to be perfectly honest, I was beginning to think I was invincible and that my steward's pass was a licence to get me in anywhere. With the benefit of hindsight, I now realise that complacency was also setting in, which in a way was giving me a false sense of security.

Whilst visiting Old Trafford, some of us Everton stewards were preparing to use our passes to get into the stadium and I saw it as an easy opportunity to acquire the third Premiership signed ball for my collection. Once outside the Theatre of Dreams, we were trying to find one of their stewards or gatekeepers who didn't mind turning a blind eye, but we weren't having much luck and although I couldn't put my finger on it, there was something not quite right... you know, when you get that sixth sense feeling that something is wrong?

It's no big secret that the Mancs and the Scousers aren't the greatest of friends and I don't know whether or not this played a part, but no matter which gate we tried, we were told in no uncertain terms we weren't on. But just as we were about to call it a day and accept defeat, my mate and I managed to find a decent gateman who was more than happy to oblige and kindly allowed us in free of charge. Happy days, we thought, as we made our way into the ground; it was very satisfying to walk into this wonderful stadium, the home of one of the biggest clubs in the whole world... after Everton, of course.

However, once inside, we noticed there was something wrong. We couldn't see the rest of our fellow Evertonians. The reason for that soon dawned on us; we'd only entered the United section of the ground for some obscure reason. My mate was convinced the gateman didn't like scousers either and must have found it highly amusing to deliberately send us into the lion's den. I wasn't so cynical as to believe he would do such a thing as he was an elderly bloke and I thought he was genuinely trying to be of help. However, you didn't need a degree in linguistics to notice we were not speaking with the same accent as our rivals, nor even wearing the same colours, as more and more people around us were beginning to realise.

For a brief moment, I was reminded of that cigar advert, with the music, when everything seems to go wrong and you think... ah, what the heck. Fortunately for us, it wasn't a bad part of the ground, but more like a family section and my mate and I knew then that the gateman was genuinely being helpful.

Although I wouldn't say we felt threatened, we certainly stood out like the proverbial sore thumb and with quite a lot of attention now focused upon us, it wasn't long before one of their senior stewards came over to us.

"What are scousers doing in the Man United section of the ground?" he asked. "The rest of the scousers are over the other side." He jerked his head towards the Everton supporters.

I couldn't help but notice his repeated use of the scouser word and, without sounding paranoid, it didn't seem to be in a friendly manner, either. I mean, we could have been Man United fans who just happened to be scousers and although I know that's as likely as Wayne Rooney singing *You'll Never Walk Alone*, it was still a possibility and a bit presumptuous of him to think we were Evertonians who had just bunked into the United end of the ground. Okay, so he guessed correctly, but that was hardly the point.

He demanded to see our tickets, which we obviously didn't have and again he wanted to know why the scousers were in here. There it was again, that word *scousers*, and at this point it was quite fair to assume we had a bit of a problem on our hands.

I told him we didn't have tickets as we were Everton stewards and I began reciting the same spiel that I had given Bill at Nottingham Forest a couple of weeks earlier, about clapping the United team when they came out, blah, blah, blah. Of course I was wasting my breath, as the whole world and his dog knew only too well there was absolutely no possibility whatsoever of any scousers, be they Everton or Liverpool supporters, clapping Manchester United coming out onto the pitch. Okay, there may have been a very remote possibility of a lonely individual up in the stands clapping Nottingham Forest, but this senior steward and I both knew we'd never be clapping Man United in a million years. The other unfortunate thing for me and my mate on this day was that this guy wasn't Bill from Nottingham Forest, either. Oh no, this this was the head of the Gestapo, Mussolini, the Anti-Christ, and Gary Neville all rolled into one.

He then asked us which gate we came through and was hell bent on finding out which of his gatemen had breached security by allowing us in without a ticket. There was no way we were going to tell this official which gate we came through; we were in trouble and we knew we'd been rumbled, but there was no point in getting the poor gatekeeper into trouble as well.

He was now shouting and bawling and

demanding to know who let the scousers in here (that word again) and when he found out who that was, they would be sacked on the spot. At that precise moment, my mate and I both knew that the identity of that person would never be revealed in our lifetimes, especially when he mentioned another S-word... the sack. We insisted that nothing would make us divulge this information and he eventually realised he was going about it all the wrong way. Changing his approach slightly, he then said if we told him which turnstile we came through, he would consider the matter closed and the gateman wouldn't get into trouble. Did he really think we were daft enough to believe that for one second?

"If you're really prepared to close the matter," I said, "why do you need to know which turnstile we came through?"

We knew this tyrant was after blood and there was not the slightest possibility we were going to cause this gateman to lose his job, even if he did happen to be a Man United fan. He had been kind enough to do us a favour and there was no way we were letting him down.

When the steward realised he was wasting his time and we were definitely not going to tell him, he changed his spots again and became even more enraged, now screaming and threatening to call the police unless we told him which gate we came through. It was quite hard at this point to restrain ourselves from laughing and the more he shouted, the funnier the situation became. But even if we had been separated and tortured painfully and slowly, I was one hundred percent certain my mate wouldn't talk. So there was nothing they could do to this bloke.

The incident reminded me of owning up in

school at the age of about seven when a teacher wanted to know who kicked the ball through a window. This official must have thought he was berating a couple of kids. He was turning purple with rage and was without question one of those intolerant people who would bring back the birch and capital punishment as well as invading not just Poland, but Switzerland tomorrow. The way he was behaving, you could be forgiven for thinking we'd just bunked into the cup final at Wembley.

My mate said, "Do you know he's doing this for charity, or do you think *scousers* aren't capable of doing nice things?"

"Eh! Eh! Calm down! Calm down! For goodness' sake, pal," I said, "we're not a couple of football hooligans. We've only come to watch the match and there are enough seats available for us to sit on." Sure, I know this senior steward had his job to do, but I just think he went completely over the top with us and I still didn't see why he couldn't make us welcome, like Bill at Nottingham Forest did.

Anyway, we were unceremoniously ejected from Old Trafford and I suppose it was inevitable; my luck had to run out eventually, even though it was quite early into my protest. On the way out, I sarcastically thanked the official for making us so very welcome and asked him what was the difference between us well behaved stewards and some of those other privileged people who merely turned up to the big games when it suited them, when the weather was nice.

"The difference is," he roared, "that they have been invited, but you scou... erm... people, have not."

"You were going to say scousers then, weren't you?" I jibed. "Well then, we're going to have to change all that, aren't we? In future, perhaps these privileged people will have to pay for their tickets just like all the rest of us."

The sarcasm in his parting smile as he slammed the door on us, spoke volumes. I had obviously touched a nerve.

As we walked out of Old Trafford, I asked my mate if this entitled me to a Man United ball for the collection.

"I did gain free entry into the ground, didn't I?"

"Yeah, I suppose you did," he replied, "but I wouldn't ask for it just yet."

A week later, when I went to Everton to work on the gantry at one of our home games, I was called into the office. They'd received a letter of complaint about *Scousers* bunking into Old Trafford from a very irate senior steward who was now demanding to know from my bosses at Everton which gate I went through. I felt a real sense of foreboding as my superiors wanted a description of the man who had let me and my mate in. I couldn't believe this despot from Manchester was still determined to find out which one of his gatemen had let us in and I knew then for absolute certain that the nice old guy who had kindly let us in would be sacked once they found out his identity. For all I knew, this could have been the gateman's only source of income and there was no way on this earth I was going to be responsible for getting him the sack.

My mate wasn't a steward, so I knew that as long as I didn't reveal who the gateman was, there was no way of them finding out.

"I can't even remember which gate I entered through," I said.

"If you don't tell us which gate as well as a

description of this man, you are going to be sacked," I was told very directly.

I remember standing there thinking that if I was just about to lose my job here, I needed to tell them something.

"All I did last week," I began, "was go to watch a game of football, without causing any trouble, just like I have been doing all my life. I merely entered a football ground free of charge and now you want to sack me because some over-zealous jobsworth at Man United wants to make an example of one of his gatemen for kindly letting me in."

This met with no response so I continued. "What about all those people who bunk in every week, like all those privileged people who aren't real football fans, but friends of people in the know ... and which they've been doing for years? Why don't we ever ask who allowed these people in... and incidentally, why don't any of these people ever pay to get in? These same people who have never put their hands in their pockets or made any financial contribution to football whatsoever?"

For years I had been wanting to say that to somebody in authority and even though I knew they now wanted to make an example of me, I felt heaps better for getting it off my chest.

Now there was a reaction.

"You have one of the best jobs in this stadium, working on the TV gantry; you don't have to pay a penny to watch any games and you get paid as well. Why do you want to lose that?"

He was right, it was a brilliant job and after a few moments of thinking about it, I told him I thought it was Gate Z and the gateman was a spotty, ginger-haired midget with a Manchester accent. Of course, they knew straight away I was lying because there was nobody at Old Trafford, with a Manchester accent.

My inquisitor then told me that if I didn't want to mention who this gateman was, he would provide a sheet of paper and an envelope and leave the room for a few moments. When he returned, unless the gate and the person's genuine description was inside the envelope, I would be sacked with immediate effect.

For the next few moments I stood there as all those beautiful memories of my job on the TV gantry flashed through my mind: Gary Lineker and his Tottenham team mates waving to me, my cock-up in giving the wrong information to Michael Robinson with Spanish TV, the time I headed the ball back onto the pitch. Andy Gray hugging me when Everton scored against Liverpool and all those other brilliant games, sitting in one of the best seats in the ground. There really were some great memories.

When the official came back into the room, he looked inside the envelope and just stood there, shaking his head. I was then asked for my steward's pass and was immediately relieved of my duties as a steward.

Losing my steward's pass was like losing an arm or a leg and I knew I had met my Waterloo. I also knew getting into football grounds from now on was going to be a lot more difficult without my pass. My campaign would continue though, but this time I'd make sure I didn't get caught. In fact, I was now more determined than ever to complete the set of footballs and enter every Premiership ground as part of my protest, free of charge. As somebody once said, you'll never be good at anything, unless you're bad at it first and I knew I could only get better. But if I was to continue the protest of getting in for free, I knew I had to up my game.

I realised that it was going to be much more difficult from now on, but it would not mean the end. I just accepted that getting into grounds in future was going to present some new and exciting challenges.

Nine
A Stranger is a Friend You've Never Met

So, with no Steward's pass to help me now, how was I supposed to continue with this protest and get into football matches for free? I had already decided I wouldn't be paying to get into any more grounds until I'd managed to collect twenty-two signed Premiership balls and I'd also committed myself further by telling people that I would raffle them off for *Children in Need*. So I knew I couldn't really back out.

I suppose there are all kinds of ways of getting into football matches without paying, but the difficult bit is finding out what they are and actually carrying them out. If you aren't too bothered about whether you can get away with it every week, then you must accept that it's not always going to work. If, however, you are conducting a personal protest and refusing to pay entry into any more football grounds, then you don't have much of a choice. Well, I didn't... it *had* to work.

I still couldn't quite believe what I had taken on and I'd lost count of the amount of times I nearly backed out, only to keep reminding myself that if I dropped the protest now, I was just allowing us fans to continue being disrespected. Each time that word, disrespect, entered my head, it spurred me on even more and if it meant continuing to gain entry into grounds without paying, then that's what I would do. I kept telling myself that it was hardly the crime of the century and if it served to highlight how decent and loyal fans were being ripped off, then it was definitely worth doing. And what could anybody say or do about it if the proceeds from my protest were going to a brilliant cause like *Children in Need*, which for me and my conscience was a great leveller? No, I kept telling myself, there was no going back. I was not going to pay to get into any more football grounds until I had collected twenty-two footballs, which I knew I couldn't receive until I had entered all Premier league clubs free of charge.

I also knew I had to strike while I was still quite wound up. If I had waited any longer, I don't think I would have gone ahead with it. Attending the away games only involved visiting that particular ground once during a season, but going to my own ground, Everton, would mean a fortnightly visit. I knew I had to find an easy way to get in, as I was refusing to pay into *all* football matches until I had completed my protest. My old stewards' office was at the other side of the ground, so as long as I stayed away from there, I should be okay. I'd also picked up a few tips during my time as a steward and thought I could use this to my advantage. I felt a bit like gamekeeper turned poacher and if any stewards I knew spotted me, I could pretend I was now one of the prawn sandwich brigade by walking in through reception. With no turnstile and no police presence operating at this entrance, as long as I dressed smartly enough, I could walk in without looking out of place.

If I was lucky to get away with it, I knew I'd have the same problem at the next home game in a fortnight's time and if I was going to continue walking in through reception, I needed to get my face known, and as quickly as possible. Instead of hiding and keeping my head down, I needed security to get used to seeing my face and accept me as a welcome guest and not an intruder. Well, that was how I used to look at people when I had my steward's hat on.

At twenty to three I was swept along by a very busy crowd as I made my way to the reception entrance. Once outside and dressed in my posh navy suit, I was almost ready to go ahead with my new plan. I was observing everything and everybody such as guests, staff and security. I'm really not sure what I was looking for as a lot of people had now descended around reception, with kick off drawing near. I figured this was an opportunity not to be missed, but I knew I would have to make my move very soon before I lost the protection of this huge crowd.

Walking through the open glass doors, the area resembled a smaller version of a hotel lobby and I could see two or three smart looking members of security who were checking passes and tickets. I slowed down, even allowing people to pass me, as I was still unclear of how I was going to get through. Looking beyond security, I could see into the reception area, where there were many people shaking hands and greeting one another. My problem was, I had neither pass nor ticket, nor even anybody to shake hands with. I knew then that just wearing my suit wasn't enough for me to blend in with everybody else. I could now feel my heart pounding and I was becoming very nervous indeed. Panic can be a strange feeling, as I was now seriously contemplating abandoning my plan and just making a run for it. Why was I putting myself through all of this?

I needed convincing that what I was about to do was the right thing and it had to be pretty quick. My only thoughts now were that I was carrying out a protest of refusing to pay into any more football matches until football fans were shown some proper respect. Get a grip of yourself, I told myself; have the courage of your convictions and stay focused on the plan.

At that point, there was a group of people behind me in the queue and one of them asked me if this was the correct way into one the corporate suites. In my most positive and confident voice, I heard myself saying, "Yes, it is and I'll even show you where to go."

To my good fortune, a couple of them gave me their passes to check, which I then displayed to security who confirmed that we were indeed headed in the right direction. Wow, was I really in? I couldn't believe it. Instead of disappearing amongst the crowd, I knew this was my opportunity to get myself known to each member of security. After thanking them for their help, I introduced myself and made absolutely sure I got their names. I even made a note of them, as from now on I wanted to remain on first name terms and I was hoping these men would be here in two weeks' time, at our next home match.

After the match, I was delighted that each one of them remembered my name and even said, "Take care Peter," and "Look forward to seeing you soon."

What a result and I wasn't talking about the match.

That first time walking through reception was easier than I expected and my posh navy suit obviously looked the part, as I was allowed to walk straight through. It seemed too good to be true and I was expecting to be greeted by the same faces every week.

However, things started to go horribly wrong at the next game, as my luck appeared to dramatically change. I turned up at reception, just like I had a fortnight earlier and dressed to the nines. But standing at the door today was one of my old steward bosses,

Frank, and I realised I had a huge problem on my hands, as he knew all about me being sacked.

Before I'd even seen Frank, the butterflies were already fluttering twenty to the dozen in my stomach, but in the next instant he was coming over and asking me how I was doing, which just made everything a thousand times worse.

"Fine, thanks," I answered nervously.

"You're looking very smart, Peter," he said, smiling at me very sarcastically.

"Thanks very much. I didn't know you worked over on this side of the ground Frank," thinking to myself, just my frigg'n luck.

"No, I don't usually, but they were a bit short over here today," he said, maintaining his sardonic expression.

Yeah, they fuck'n would be, I thought to myself again, managing to keep my own rictus grin steady.

I then walked past him, towards one of the reception guys taking the tickets and passes. I glanced round and Frank was still looking over, smiling, probably wondering what I was doing there and who was I with.

I actually remember asking myself at that precise moment, what the hell *was* I doing there? I don't have a ticket to get in, I thought, and this Frank fella hasn't taken his eyes off me. It's not too late to just turn around and pretend I've left my ticket in the car, while I still can.

But it w*as* too late, as the guy on reception was now asking me where my ticket was. There was quite a long queue behind me and I told him I had it on me somewhere, as I searched through my pockets.

"Can you get a move on, please?" he said.

"You're holding everybody up."

"Sorry about this," I said, now becoming even more nervous. "I'm sorry, but I don't seem to be able to find it." As I turned, I could see Frank walking towards me and he was now grinning happily and obviously thinking to himself, 'Peter's trying to bunk in here without a ticket and he's been rumbled.'

I was trying my best to keep cool, but I couldn't as my plan was going horribly wrong.

Frank, still grinning, then asked the guy on reception if everything was okay. I was just about to explain that I'd left my ticket in the car... and then drive home, when seemingly from nowhere, a man suddenly appeared.

Holding a ticket in front of my face, he said, "Is this your ticket here? It must have dropped on the floor." As he spoke, he winked at me.

The reception guy rolled his eyes. "No wonder you couldn't find it. Okay, hurry up and come through, please," he said, "you're holding everyone up."

I looked at my old steward boss Frank and smiled... no actually, I didn't smile; I grinned at him from ear to ear, but Frank no longer had that grin, or even a smile on his face, just a puzzled frown as we both knew I'd come within a whisker of being caught.

I walked through behind this fellow who had slipped me the ticket and followed him into the lounge.

"Thanks very much," I said, "you just saved me from getting kicked out."

"You're very welcome," he replied.

I asked him how come he had a spare ticket. He looked to be in his late sixties, was well dressed, but more casual than business looking and although he looked smart, he didn't appear to be part of the prawn sandwich brigade. There was something very different about this man that I couldn't put my finger on, but I could remember seeing his face around the lounges and outside reception.

He seemed to ignore my question and said to me, "I've seen you around here quite a lot recently."

I then asked him if he knew some of the players as I noticed him in here last week, which was also one of the best lounges. He just shook his head and laughed. I was looking around to see what the joke was but he just smiled at me.

"Tell me, why do you come in here when you don't have a ticket?"

I told him I must have lost it somewhere on the way to the game.

"Why don't you tell me the truth?" he asked.

Oh, what the hell, I thought, and began telling him about my protest and explained that we fans had been treated like second class citizens for too long. I told him the story of the man in a suit collecting twenty complimentary tickets, when the fans were expected to pay top prices and I was carrying out a protest and refusing to pay into any more football grounds because of this.

He started laughing. "Do you know who you remind me of?" he asked.

"Who?"

"You remind me of myself about twenty years ago."

Of course, I was intrigued by his remark. "What do you mean?"

He told me that what I'd just done looked so obvious and it was only a matter of time before I was caught. Then he revealed that he hadn't paid to get into a football match himself for the past twenty years.

"How come?" I asked, "Are you protesting as well?"

His jolly laugh bubbled up again. "Yes, you could say that."

There was something very compelling about this man. He introduced himself as Michael; he said, it's not Mike or Mick, but Michael. I quickly replied that my name was Peter, not Pete, nor P, but Peter and we both started laughing.

"Yes, definitely me twenty years ago."

I couldn't explain it, but I just knew at that precise moment that I was going to get on very well with Michael. If there's one thing I love doing in this life, it's meeting people. I am always talking to people, in airports, on trains – anywhere, in fact – and I was very interested in what he had to say. Michael was certainly one of those people, 'once met, never forget.'

He told me he admired my courage and that it took guts to walk into football grounds without paying.

"Do you feel nervous about what you're doing, Peter?" he asked.

My answer was that because I felt so strongly about my protest, it kind of helped me, but I'd be lying if I said I wasn't nervous, walking into grounds up and down the country every week. I also told him that I'd pledged not to pay into any more football matches until I had collected twenty-two Premiership balls. I would then go public and expose the many injustices of being a football fan.

"Seriously, Peter, if you continue walking through reception like this, it's only a matter of time before you do get caught and that will be the end of your protest."

I knew that perfectly well but I just didn't want to dwell on it. I wondered how he happened to have a spare ticket and I asked him. He replied by asking me a further question.

"If I were to show you an easier way to get into football matches without having to worry about security, would you be interested?"

"Of course I would," I said.

He asked me to meet him outside reception, five minutes before kick-off at our next home game and he would show me how it was done.

"Five to three's a bit late, isn't it?"

"Don't be late," he replied as he shook my hand and said goodbye.

The next home game in two weeks' time couldn't come quickly enough.

Sure enough, at five minutes to three, a fortnight later, Michael was outside reception and I walked over to shake his hand. He told me the key to success was having a new face and I was to be that new face. It then dawned on me why he'd slipped me the ticket two weeks ago and that he must have been as delighted to see me as I was to see him. However, he was showing me how to get in without paying, so I kept quiet.

"Right, Peter, this is what you do!" He pointed to a ticket collection window and asked me if I knew what it was.

I told him I didn't.

"That is where the players leave complimentary tickets in envelopes for their family and friends to collect." He explained that was quite normal at every football ground up and down the country, every single week of the season.

He continued. "You walk up to the ticket window and give in your name. The ticket lady will then look for your name and hand you your envelope."

"But how will my name be there when nobody has left any tickets for me?" I asked him.

"This is the clever bit." He briefly touched his nose with his fingertip. "You give in a name which you and I know she won't be able to find. But as she's looking through the pile, you will see other names on the envelopes and you must memorise one of them, so long as it's not one of the player's names, okay?"

I nodded, slightly bemused.

"She will then tell you she can't find your name and you'll have to say, well it must be in your partner's name and then give her that name you have memorised. She will look through the pile again and bingo… this time, she will find your name."

"How could that ever be my envelope, though?"

"You see, Peter, at five minutes to three, these people won't be coming to the match today and they are, in effect, spare tickets."

"Wow! I see what you mean, but I'll never get away with that," I said.

"I know you will," he replied, "because I've seen you walk through reception without having a ticket, so this should be a stroll in the park for you!"

"If it's that easy, why isn't every other fan doing it?" I asked him.

He said it was for the same reason that every other fan wasn't walking through reception; because hardly anybody would ever think of doing something like that and the ticket staff, just like security at reception, wouldn't expect anybody to do it, either.

"Oh my God, that's absolutely amazing," I told him.

He did have a point, because I had walked through a few receptions at other football clubs across the country without anybody batting an eyelid.

"Does it always work?" I wondered.

"Always. That's why the tickets are left there, to be collected by members of the public and you, my friend, are a fully paid up member of the public."

"Okay," I said, "I'll give it a go." So I took a deep breath and strolled up to the ticket window as nonchalantly as possible. There was a small queue; as Michael said, most people were now inside the stadium with only a couple of minutes until kick-off. When it was my turn, I hoped I looked confident enough to pull it off.

"Hello, love, I'm picking up some tickets."

"What's the name?"

"Jackson." I don't know why I said Jackson; it was the first name that came into my head. Although I may have appeared unflappable, the ducks feet were paddling like mad beneath the surface, but I really wanted to prove to Michael I could do it and I didn't want to let him down.

The ticket lady then turned around and began looking through a pile of envelopes for Jackson. However, and wouldn't you just believe it… there was a problem. She had turned her back on me to look through the envelopes and therefore I couldn't see the rest of them to look for a name. Just my rotten luck, I thought. With it being a small window, there was no room for me to see over her shoulder. What was I going to do now? I thought, this Michael bloke has been doing this for twenty years, I haven't even done two minutes and already I've cocked it up.

I turned round to look at Michael, hoping he could help, as I could feel a sense of panic setting in, but he wasn't even looking my way.

She then turned to me and said, "Sorry, love, there's no tickets here in the name of Jackson."

I said, "Are you sure? Could you check once again, please?"

Fortunately, this time, she turned around to face me. "You can see for yourself," she said and began looking through the pile once more, so that I could see all the envelopes. I spotted one with the name O'Brien written on it and thought to myself, that's the one I'll remember.

When she got through them all again, she apologised. "Sorry, love, but you can see there are no tickets here for Jackson."

"Er, sorry about this," I said, "but could you check in case they are in my partner's name, please?"

"What's your partner's name?"

"O'Brien." My heart had begun pounding by now.

She began riffling through the pile once again, when, lo and behold, she pulled out the envelope bearing the name O'Brien.

"Oh yes, here it is. There you go."

Thanking her for her trouble, I walked away with the envelope. When I reached Michael, he was smiling.

"See, there was nothing to it, was there?"

"No, Michael. Piece of cake," I replied, still shaking.

"Come on, then, open the envelope."

Inside were four tickets to one of the top

lounges.

"Michael, that's unbelievable, and it worked," I marvelled.

"I told you," he said. "It always works; it's even easier than two in the click. It's kid's stuff really, but nobody would ever dream of doing it."

Two in the click, incidentally, is when two people walk through the turnstile at once and as each click registers somebody entering the stadium; two people are actually walking in for the price of one, hence the term two in the click. In other parts of the country, I think it's called a squeeze.

I remember feeling we were kindred spirits and I was amazed at how laid back he was. It then dawned on me how he had a spare ticket for me at reception on the day I met him. There were obviously tickets left over in his envelope. I couldn't believe all this… and not just obtaining free tickets, but top of the range tickets to boot.

The following home game I went up to the window and gave in the name O'Brien again. This time it was bingo straight away and for the next few weeks. Whoever Mr O'Brien was, he hadn't bothered coming to the game and, as Michael explained, these were indeed spare tickets.

One week, Everton were playing a big match against Manchester United and Michael had warned me that he thought Mr O'Brien may be here this week and it might be a good idea to memorise another name in case I needed plan B. Michael was spot on once again; the ticket lady told me I was too late, as Mr O'Brien had already collected the tickets. It was a good job Michael had warned me as I was well prepared and able to pretend I was with Mr O'Brien. As I had seen another envelope with the name Davies on it, I told the ticket lady he was with us and she gave me that envelope. At five to three, it was fair to assume that Mr Davies wasn't coming either and the tickets once again would only be going to waste.

I still couldn't believe the simplicity of this new system of getting into football grounds without paying and by this stage Michael and I had become good friends. We would often spend our afternoons together at the match and although he was a bit of a rogue, you couldn't help but like him. Most of the staff knew him and would call out, "What can I get you to drink, Michael?" I often wondered if they knew how he got in, and would he still be treated like that, which made me laugh. He always gave them a tip after the game and apart from being very generous; he was also quite funny and a very polite gentleman. I was impressed with the respect he had for people and it really was a pleasure to be in his company. We would often sit in the lounge talking about our experiences at football matches and I found it remarkably uncanny how similar we both were. Like me, he abhorred hooligans and greedy clubs trying to extract every last penny out of their fans and he just loved having the craic.

He told me his wife had died a couple of years ago and he'd needed some stimulus in his life or he would have given up and I kind of understood what he meant. It was then that he told me the first of his many interesting sayings.

"Peter," he said, "live every day as if you will not see tomorrow, because one day you won't." He wasn't showing off or anything like that; he was being himself. I was more than happy to listen to him as I always left his company feeling uplifted; that was the effect he had on me.

I started taking my son to the games and occasionally my daughter would come in with her friend. I remember one week, a father and his two children had travelled from Ireland and asked Michael and me where they could buy tickets for the game.

Michael pulled out three tickets and said, "Why don't you have these? Our friends can't make it today. They are actually for the players' lounge."

Our guest from Ireland couldn't believe it. "Are you serious?" he asked. "Look what it says on the tickets, kids… The Players' Lounge. This is the first time I've brought my kids to Goodison Park," he said, laughing and hugging me and Michael. "Thank you so much."

After the game, we bumped into our Irish friend in the lounge. He thanked us once again.

"My kids have had the day of their lives," he added.

I also noticed Michael's face and how happy he was and I knew that making people happy made his day.

Michael then came out with another of his famous sayings when he said to him, "Can I ask you one favour?"

"Yes, anything," said the Irish man. "Just name it."

Michael asked him if he would also pass on this kindness to a stranger one day and then quoted a phrase that I was hearing for the very first time. "Please remember," Michael said, "a stranger is a friend you've never met."

I've never forgotten that phrase; it's stayed with me ever since that day. A lot of things Michael said have stuck in my mind and he had a calm way of making everything sound so simple, as if nothing was a problem. Although he appeared to enjoy life, I sensed that he was still missing his wife very much, but instead of sitting in the house and moping alone, he enjoyed going out and meeting people. Sometimes we would drop Michael off and although he lived in a modest terraced house, he gave the impression he never wanted for anything. He would always dress smartly and present this image of having money and enjoying life but, deep down, I sensed he was lonely and I couldn't help feeling sorry for him.

I spent the next couple of years sitting in many different parts of the ground with Michael, listening to his repertoire of brilliant and funny sayings. Sometimes we had top of the range tickets, other times just ordinary stand tickets. On some occasions, we had two tickets and at other times, we had as many as ten. The really funny thing was, you never knew from one week to the next, what was going to be inside the envelope.

One week, I was waiting for Michael outside. It was past three o'clock and the match had already started. I told my son I thought he must already be inside the ground. When I got my envelope and went in, there was no sign of Michael anywhere. Maybe he hadn't fancied going that day as he had missed a couple of games in the past when not feeling too well.

I said to my son, "After the game, we'll drop off the match programme for Michael and see how he is." When we got there, though, there was no answer to our knock at his door. A neighbour then came out and I told him I was looking for Michael and that I was a friend of his.

By the look on his neighbours face, I knew

instantly something was wrong. "You obviously don't know, do you?" said the neighbour. He then told me that Michael had died two days ago. I couldn't believe it. I knew he hadn't been feeling at his best for the last few weeks, but I had no idea he was that ill as he never complained about anything.

"He hadn't been looking too well for quite some time," the neighbour said. "Nobody seems to know what it was."

I think I knew, though.

I remembered his old saying about living everyday as if it was your last and I was convinced then that he knew he was dying and he was enjoying what time he had left with a bit of excitement in his life. I was so pleased to share those times with him.

At the following home game, after I'd collected my envelope, it just didn't feel the same. It felt a bit like somebody saying, 'you can have as much to drink in this pub as you choose, free of charge, but you must be on your own.' There didn't seem much point to it any more. It just wasn't the same without Michael.

My son and I walked up to where some people were queuing to buy tickets and I noticed a man about to buy a ticket. With tears stabbing at my eyes, I told him my friend wasn't coming to the match today and if he wanted his ticket, he was welcome to it as my friend would prefer somebody to use it, rather than it going to waste.

The man was naturally delighted and thanked me as I gave him Michael's ticket. Once inside the lounge, he came over to where I was sitting with my son and thanked me once again.

I said to him, "If I were to show you how to come in here every week, free of charge, would you be interested?"

"What, in these lounges? Free of charge? Are you kidding? Of course I would. But you don't even know me," he said. "Why would you do that?"

I shook his hand. "Because, as I once heard a beautiful, warm and very special person say, a stranger is a friend you've never met."

Ten
The Craic

Like a lot of people living on Merseyside, I come from an Irish family and in 1994 I had the pleasure of travelling to the United States to watch Ireland in the World Cup. As you've no doubt seen on TV on many occasions, there is always a carnival atmosphere when the Irish are playing and you never see any trouble from their fans, they just enjoy having the craic, win, lose or draw.

Incidentally, I know most people are familiar with the phrase, 'the craic' but I wonder how many people actually know where the word originates from. It has no direct translation in English, but is often associated with partying, enjoying the company of others and having one hell of a time. But perhaps what you don't know is that it's actually an acronym, as follows:

Ceol, meaning music in Irish
Rince - Dance
Amhrain - Songs
Inis Scealta - Story telling
Cainte - Gossip

Ireland were playing their opening match in the Giant Stadium, New Jersey, against Italy and I travelled to New York with my mate, Brendan – also of Irish descent, to watch the match.

This was quite possibly the biggest football match in Ireland's history. Even though we didn't have any tickets, we still decided to travel anyway. I had protested to the FA by refusing to pay into any football grounds in England; I also made my protest at an FA cup final at Wembley and I now wanted to take my protest to the very top, to FIFA and the World Cup finals.

Me and Brendan with American Airline flight crew en route to our first World Cup

As you can imagine, there was a huge demand for tickets and it was well-nigh impossible to get hold of any at all. But it was great, just soaking up the atmosphere of the World Cup and meeting up and making friends with so many Irish people, as well as enjoying a lovely week in the Big Apple.

During the day we would visit the usual attractions of New York, such as the Statue of Liberty, Broadway, Times Square and Central Park, as well as going up the World Trade Centre, which will sadly be remembered for the 9/11 attack. Coming from Merseyside, we also had to visit the Dakota building where John Lennon was murdered outside his own apartment by Mark Chapman in 1980.

As international venues went, this had to be one of the greatest places ever to stage a World Cup tournament and I think everybody lucky enough to be there knew that this was a one-off. At night we would meet up in a bar with the Irish fans, including two smashing lads, Richard and Fred that we met from Liverpool who had won the prize of a lifetime by entering a competition in the *Liverpool Echo* newspaper. This bar became our local and unfolding before our eyes and being televised live on almost every channel throughout the United States, was OJ Simpson being chased by police on the freeway. I've already mentioned how we always remember where we were when certain historical events took place… and now, whenever I see OJ Simpson on the television or in the newspapers, I always think of the 1994 World Cup USA. See what I mean? You just can't get away from football.

Former Liverpool player and now TV commentator, Jim Beglin, would occasionally come into this bar and he was a soft-spoken, friendly bloke who enjoyed talking to the Irish fans. He remembered me working on the TV gantry at Everton when he was co-commentating for ITV. Brendan and I spent a bit of time in his company and while we were out sightseeing during the day, he would be reporting for the media, from the Irish team camp.

Like everybody else, he knew how difficult it was to get hold of tickets for this match. New York was teeming with Irish and Italians and I knew we had an almost impossible task of getting in to see this match. Even if I did want to buy a ticket, there weren't any available to buy. He told us it was also very difficult for the players' families to get tickets, which only confirmed how difficult it was going to be, as I think the whole of Ireland wanted to be at this match.

On the eve of the match, Jim came in to our bar and, because of my previous experience of working on the TV gantry, suggested he would try and ask if I could help out the TV crew. He couldn't guarantee it and did emphasise he couldn't ask for the two of us.

It was very kind of him, although it meant leaving my mate who had travelled with me and been at my side from the start.

I told Jim we had travelled to the Big Apple together and although I appreciated his offer of help, I couldn't leave my mate. I also explained that this wasn't the first time we'd been stuck for tickets and something would turn up; it always did.

But deep down in my own mind I knew the chances of getting in to see this match were very slim, in fact almost impossible, and it was going to be a lot harder than any English league ground or even the cup final at Wembley. This was America and I knew the security for this match would be much tighter; I remember saying to Brendan that we'd need all the luck of the Irish and every one of our ancestors to pull this one off.

On the day of the match we woke up to a glorious sunny morning, one of those beautiful days where you're so glad to be alive. It reminded me of the FA cup finals years ago, growing up in our house when I couldn't wait to wake up; but instead of coming down the stairs to a bowl of Weetabix, I was now in a café in sunny downtown Manhattan having an 'all you can eat' American breakfast. Sitting near the window was amazing, literally watching thousands of people walking through Times Square, going about their business and I couldn't help asking myself where all these people were going today. I began wondering what kind of a day was in store for Brendan and me. I couldn't think of anything else now, apart from the excitement of sitting inside the Giant Stadium and watching my very first World Cup match of Ireland against one of the favourites to win the world cup, Italy.

We met up with Pat, Brian, Kevin, Phil and the rest of the Irish fans with whom we'd been partying all week and some of them didn't have any tickets, either. (Pat went on to marry Bernie, the mother of Swansea's Lee Trundle and we became good friends).

We all started making our way to Bruce Springsteen's neck of the woods, New Jersey, and to the hotel where the Irish team was staying. There were a lot of fans outside the hotel, most of them in the same position as Brendan and me.

One or two of them were lucky enough to pick up some tickets, but most of them had resigned themselves to staying in the hotel and watching the game on TV. A lot of people thought if they couldn't get a ticket for the match, the players' hotel was probably the next best place to watch the game and it became something of a focal point for the Irish fans. However, Brendan and I hadn't travelled four thousand miles to watch a game on the telly and we certainly weren't giving up just yet. There were hordes of press and media people from all over the world at the hotel and with the big Irish and Italian presence in the States, this was definitely no ordinary football match.

The temperature was absolutely soaring that day. Honestly, I've never known heat like it before, or since. When the Irish team emerged from the hotel to rapturous applause and cheers from the fans, you'd have thought it was the World Cup final. The atmosphere was brilliant. I noticed Brendan talking to some ticket touts who were asking over a hundred dollars a ticket, which at the time was quite a lot over the odds.

"This is a one-off match," Brendan told me. "We'll probably never get the chance to see a World Cup match again. Er, I was considering buying one."

I didn't have to remind Brendan of my opinion of ticket touts.

Knowing my situation, he suggested a compromise. "I'll pay and you can owe me the money," he suggested.

"Thanks, mate," I replied, "but how's that not paying?"

"For fuck's sake, I'll pay and you don't have to give me any money back at all. That way, you haven't paid for your ticket. Worrabout that then, Peter?"

"No. Sorry," I said. "I know you mean well, but I'm not letting you buy my ticket from a tout."

Not long after I stepped off my soap box, a hotel official walked over and announced that the press coach was about to leave for the stadium and would the remaining members of the press kindly make their way to the coach now.

"I've worked as a steward on a TV gantry," I told Brendan. "I wonder if that qualifies me as a member of the press? Look, you go and buy your ticket and I'll take my chance on the press coach."

"Forget it, Peter. You'll never get away with it," he said. "They're all wearing identification badges and there's tight security everywhere!"

I remember thinking to myself they could only say no, and I wasn't buying a ticket, nor was I watching the game on TV in the hotel.

I said to myself, One day, when I'm writing my book, I can't write in Chapter Ten '... watched match in hotel on TV...' I've already committed myself to this personal protest of refusing to pay into any more football matches, so I have to go through with it.

I knew this was my one and only chance.

I told Brendan to go and buy his ticket and that I would be fine. I gave him a big hug, told him not to forget the luck of the Irish and I would hopefully see him inside the ground. Then I strode towards the coach which was just about to leave.

I tried to look as confident as I could, smiling, possibly too much, at everybody as I boarded the coach. I headed straight to the back, sat down and caught sight of Brendan through the window, just looking at me and shaking his head. I still wasn't sure if this was going to work but it was too late now; there was no going back.

An American official boarded the coach with a policeman and I thought, 'Oh my God, I've been caught and the coach hasn't even bloody left. I'm going to have to say, oh, sorry, my mistake, I thought you said all those going to the Giant Stadium, get on the coach, or something like that.'

Fortunately, they were just making sure everybody was on the coach and I think this police officer turned out to be our motorcycle escort. The official then asked all the press to check one last time that they all had the correct identification with them, as we wouldn't be able to come back for anything, and added that security was also very tight at the stadium. Just what I needed to hear. As if I wasn't already nervous, he'd just made absolutely certain I was even more so now.

The coach pulled away slowly, too slowly for my liking. I could see Brendan below, still shaking his head, as we smiled rather nervously at each other. I felt like that bloke in the movie *Midnight Express*, or Richard Attenborough getting on the coach in *The Great Escape* and my heart was pounding with the buzz of adrenalin. The coach proceeded to the stadium, carrying journalists, photographers, media representatives... and me. They were all talking to each other on the coach and it was a bit lonely sitting there, as nobody spoke to me.

On arrival, I was surprised to see how quiet it was, but kick-off was still some hours away, just like it had been at Wembley with my other mate, Ray. The fans would not be allowed in for another couple of hours, at least. This was to give the press, and everybody else who worked at the stadium, time to set up and prepare for their work. Although being on my own was a bit scary, in another way it was probably for the best as I stood a better chance on my own, if you know what I mean.

We drove down a tunnel and into an empty stadium. Everybody stood up and began to move towards the exit. I could see most of the press, who hadn't seen each other for a while, shaking hands and greeting each other, but nobody knew me, of course, which was a bit of a problem. What was I getting myself into here?

However, I thought, when in Rome... or in this case, New Jersey, and began mingling and saying hello to anybody who walked past me, even though none of them had the faintest idea who I was. I made sure the Americans heard my English accent in the hope they would think I was an English journalist and, so far, nobody seemed suspicious.

I was now beginning to feel a little bit more relaxed and then it dawned on me that I was actually fulfilling a lifetime ambition. As a schoolboy, I had always wanted to be a football journalist. My head teacher, not the greatest source of inspiration, once told me what sounded like, as long as I had an orifice in my posterior, I would never make it. Okay, he was right, I never made it, but how I wished he could have seen me, getting off the coach that had 'PRESS' emblazoned on its front window. I remember laughing to myself and thinking I'd have given anything to see his face today.

There was still quite a long time to wait before the fans were allowed in and I just kept walking round this vast, empty stadium, hoping to kill some time and trying to look as if I belonged there.

Trying to look inconspicuous in an empty stadium isn't easy.

I thought I was home and dry until a policeman suddenly appeared and I realised he was walking towards me.

"Excuse me, sir," he began, "I need to have a word with you." My heart missed a beat when he said he'd been watching me walking round for quite a while.

"Would you mind telling me who you are, please, sir and why you are not wearing an ID badge?"

I then noticed all the press were wearing their badges, displaying their photographs, except me. I hadn't realised, when walking round, that I must have drawn a lot of unnecessary attention to myself. Instead of keeping my head down or having a sleep in the toilet until the fans arrived, I was walking round like some kind of eejit. I mean, I'd done the hard bit by getting in and now it looked like I had been found out. Buying those tickets from the touts outside the hotel now didn't seem such a bad idea.

I could hardly tell this cop I wasn't wearing it because I was really a welder and not a journalist and my head teacher was right all along. I also couldn't tell him I was refusing to pay into any more football matches, or that I was too stubborn to buy a ticket from a tout. So I came out with the first and only thing that came into my head. I told him I was an English journalist, I had just gone to the toilet and my badge was clipped to my jacket downstairs. As it was an absolutely sweltering hot day, it seemed quite a plausible explanation and with my Merseyside accent, he may realise I wasn't an Irish or Italian fan bunking in and he might just believe me.

There was another move I quickly needed to make which, if it worked, may just be better than my first. There's an old saying that the Irish answer a question with a question, so I decided to give it a go. Immediately after explaining about my jacket downstairs I asked him this question:

"Is it okay for members of the public to have a photograph taken with a police officer whilst on duty? Only I wanted one to show my children when I get home to England. They'd love to see their dad with a real American police officer."

Now if there's one thing the Americans love doing, it's showing true American hospitality and, fortunately for me, this police officer was what you would call a real American.

"Sure, Buddy," he replied, unconsciously pulling himself up to his full height. I was hoping that by now he'd forgotten why he came over to see me. I have to say, though, he was a true gentleman, as were most Americans we met that week. I knew this police officer had to do his job and I think I convinced him that I wasn't a threat to security. He very kindly stood beside me while a passing worker obliged by taking our photo, after which he shook my hand, told me to have a nice day and to 'make sure you wear your badge, Buddy,' as he continued his rounds. Phew! The luck of the Irish again, I said to myself.

Inside an empty stadium with an American police officer, feeling a bit uncomfortable.

But it was a very close shave and I learned my lesson. I knew there could be no more mistakes and if I was to remain with the press, I had to start thinking like the press. So I immediately bought a Match day programme and pulled out a pen and paper and now looked a little bit more like a journalist. Not wanting to push my luck though, I found the nearest toilet, entered a cubicle, sat down and began to read. I thought if anybody came in and asked why a member of the press was residing in a shit-house, I could always tell them I worked for the Sun Newspaper.

After an hour or so, I was awoken by some noise and was very relieved to hear they had now started allowing the fans in to the stadium.

It was a lovely sight, watching the Giant Stadium begin to fill up and I knew I was home and dry. I soon met up with Pat, Brian, Phil and Kevin as well as most of the other Irish lads we'd been with all week. I kept walking round looking for my mate Brendan and anybody who was at this match will recall you were able to walk 360 degrees around this stadium. It was lovely to see the Italian and Irish fans shaking hands with each other and taking pictures, unlike the many English grounds I was used to where the fans were segregated to prevent them from killing each other.

I also met the famous Davey Keogh for the first time at this match. Fans in Ireland will need no introduction to Davey, who has to be Ireland's most famous fan. Everybody... and I mean *everybody*, knows Davey, including the players and staff.

Incidentally, Keogh in England is pronounced Key-oh, but in Ireland it's pronounced Kuewo. The reason I'm explaining this is because he always carries a massive banner to every (yes, *every*) Ireland match, which reads, 'Davey Keogh says hello' and yes, it does rhyme.

I'm not sure how true this is, but I've heard countless stories that sponsors have asked Davey if they can print their logos on his banner as he's that well known and his banner is almost always screened on TV. Whenever I watch Ireland on TV I always look out for his banner and say to my wife, "Davey Keogh says hello."

Me and Davey Keogh, minus his shirt in the Giant Stadium

The Giant Stadium was now enjoying a carnival atmosphere. Liza Minnelli was on the pitch, adding her own brand of entertainment to the event. I heard another, unconfirmed, story that when the fans were doing the Mexican wave, she thought it was for her benefit. She was reported to have remarked on TV that she thought the fans were brilliant, especially when they did that waving in harmony thing for her!

Liza Minnelli greets the Press... and me

When the teams came out, the noise and atmosphere was something I had never witnessed at any other match before in my life and I knew then how lucky I was to be present at this very special occasion. I will never forget sitting alongside two Americans in perfect seats just behind the goal. They told me they had woken up that morning wondering what to do with their Saturday.

One of them had said Ireland were playing Italy in a World Cup soccer match in New Jersey and that his company had two tickets for the occasion, if they fancied going. Apparently, his friend told him he wasn't doing anything else that day, so why not?

I asked my two American friends who they were supporting and they said they were cheering for Ireland as they were of Irish ancestry. I wasn't sure whether or not to believe that, as they were both Afro-Caribbean, but you can take it from me, they were definitely Irish that day.

All through the match I was explaining to the boys what was going on. Offside, though, was a bit tricky and I've always found it difficult to explain anyway, especially to two people who had never seen a game of soccer… I mean football, before.

These two guys were great fun and very nice people. What did it for me though was when the Irish fans were singing, 'Ooh, ah, Paul McGrath" (which is pronounced Mcgrah); my two companions were singing, 'Ooh, ah, doody dah; ooh, ah, doody dah,' which, to me, was hilarious.

When I told them what the real words were, one of them said in his laid back American drawl, "Whatever it is, man, it's a fuckin' great song."

Sheer quality, and apart from Ray Houghton's

winning goal, these two guys provided the highlight of the match for me. It still brings a smile to my face every time I think of them.

As I said, it was a very special moment when the players walked out onto the pitch and were welcomed by the Irish and Italian fans. Given the number of Italians living in New York, it was expected they would have the majority of the support, but I couldn't believe my eyes when I looked up to see three quarters of the stadium bathed in green. It was an incredible sight that I will remember for the rest of my life and I'm still convinced to this day, that's what won Ireland the match.

When the ref blew his whistle for full time, the Irish fans were absolutely ecstatic. What a result, Ireland beating the mighty Italy. I can still picture John Aldridge and Jason McAteer passing me as they walked off the pitch and looking round and smiling as they heard another scouse accent saying well done to each of them. As the singing and cheering fans were leaving the ground, I now began to wonder how was I going to get back to Manhattan, which was about an hour away.

As I was still with the press, I thought it would be best to let the large crowd disperse. I noticed some of the outside broadcast TV crews were preparing small barbecues, something I had never witnessed at a football match before, or since, for that matter. An American TV crew asked me who I was with. I just said the BBC, trying to remain anonymous.

"Welcome to our BBQ, Buddy, it's always a pleasure to share a few drinks with the BBC!" a voice said.

I looked around to check it was really me they were talking to. Of course, I didn't want to appear rude to our American hosts and I also wanted to remain in the ground a little longer until the huge crowd had dispersed. And it would be much easier getting a bus back to Manhattan when it was a bit quieter.

The American TV crew were having a whip-round for their barbecue, of five dollars each. I put my five dollars in and as they were cooking burgers, I nominated myself as barman and began pouring the drinks, nicely cooled in ice buckets.

After serving a few drinks, I noticed the BBC Match of the Day commentator, Barry Davies, walking over in my direction. He had recognised me from the TV gantry at Everton.

"Hello," he said, "what are you doing here?"

I thought, oh my God, I've just told all the Americans I work for the BBC and now one of their top commentators is asking me what I'm doing here.

"Hello, Barry... oh, I'm working with local radio."

"Really? I didn't know any of the radio stations were here."

Neither did I, mate, I thought to myself, but what else could I say, caught on the hop like that? Anyway, I had to act quickly, as all the Americans were watching.

"Boys," I said, "please allow me to introduce Barry Davies, the best commentator in England." (Sorry Motty... oh, and Martin.)

After shaking Barry's hand, I gave him a cool drink as we sweltered. I then noticed former Arsenal and Ireland internationals, Liam Brady and David O'Leary, who were with Barry. David O'Leary introduced me to his wife, Joy. I handed them all a drink as we discussed the great game that had just taken place.

Barry asked me where was I staying and how was I getting back. He told me they were staying in Manhattan, and quite close to my hotel. I told him I was getting the bus back.

Barry, always the gentleman, said, "Our driver's waiting outside for us. Why don't you jump in with us?"

"Thank you very much," I replied, with some relief, and handed him another drink.

I wondered if I was dreaming as I left the Giant Stadium, New Jersey in a luxury, air conditioned SUV, accompanied by David O'Leary, his wife Joy, Barry Davies, Liam Brady and their friend, Simon. Once again, the luck of the Irish had reared its beautiful head. When was this fabulous day going to end?

Driven in by the Press, watched a great game and now being delivered home by the BBC. Could it get any better? As we passed the many Irish and Italian fans walking along, I was looking out for Brendan, hoping to give him a lift, but didn't see him. We had a good craic in the car on the way back to Manhattan. David O'Leary told me he was from Glasnevin and Liam Brady said he was from Whitehall, both situated on the north side of Dublin's River Liffey. I told them my dad was from Crumlin, on the south side of the river.

'One of the nicest people in football' Barry Davies,
from our time on the TV Gantry.

When we arrived at the Sheridan Hotel, I
thanked Barry, said goodbye to them all and began my
short walk around the corner to my rather modest hotel
and, in true fairy-tale style, like Mr Ben, returned to my
normal life. Oh well, never mind...

I was surprised how very quiet it was back at
the hotel, then realised the fans hadn't returned from
the match yet; a bit like it had been in the stadium a few
hours earlier. After a shower, I went down to the bar
and sat there on my own with a cool beer, reflecting on
the unbelievable day I'd just enjoyed. I was still
pinching myself and wondering if I had really been
driven into the stadium with the press, watched one of
the greatest matches of my life from a perfect seat, free
of charge, had a barbecue after the game and then been
dropped off at my hotel by David O'Leary, Liam Brady
and Barry Davies.

"Do they sell lottery tickets around here?" I

asked the barman.

Some of the fans began arriving back in jubilant mood. After a couple of hours, many more had arrived back. I began to worry, as there was still no sign of Brendan. I knew he had his ticket, though, and assumed he must be celebrating somewhere.

Eventually, after about three hours, Brendan walked through the door. He looked very sunburnt, tired and a bit dishevelled.

"Over here, Brendan, mate!" I shouted.

Actually, he was completely knackered and looked like he'd been dragged through a hedge backwards and then again for good measure.

"You okay?" I asked.

"It was horrible getting back," he explained. "We had to walk miles from the stadium. Then we got a bus and it broke down so we had to get off and walk a couple more miles to get another bus. It was murder. I couldn't even get a bottle of water in this unbelievable heat." He gave me a searching look. "How long have you been back? You look like you've had a shower."

I bought him a cold beer, bursting to tell him what had happened, but after listening to his ordeal, I thought it may not be the right time, as he didn't look too great.

"Did you manage to get into the match?" he asked.

"Never mind about me, what about you?" I said. "Wasn't it a great result and what a brilliant goal..." trying every possible diversion to avoid telling him about my experience, as he wasn't in the best of moods.

"So did you get in?" he asked again.

"Brendan, you take my stool and let me get you

another drink." I was now seriously considering telling him I'd been kicked off the press coach, walked ten miles into the next town, got arrested for jaywalking, beaten up by the bad cop in the police office, put in a cell with a few butch guys and just released on $10,000 bail, without being allowed to make one phone call to the DA.

Fortunately, a song broke out and after a couple of drinks, everybody was singing and celebrating and Brendan felt sufficiently refreshed to begin telling me how much of a brilliant match it was. I knew then it was okay to tell him what really happened.

"Wow," he said, "that's brilliant. You know worrit is, don't you, Peter?"

"Yeah," I replied, as we both raised our glasses in a toast and said, in unison, and not for the first time that week, "It's the luck of the Irish!"

Eleven
Boys on the Black Stuff

Although I took my protest to the World Cup by refusing to pay my admission fee there, I wasn't looking to get an Irish football for my collection. What I did get was to meet some great Irish supporters who to this day are still great personal friends of mine. That has to be one of the most beautiful things about football; meeting such a varied mix of people who support many different teams, yet at the end of the day are really like the rest of us who just love football.

The World Cup is one of the greatest occasions for any football fan, it's that special. Even people who aren't particularly interested in football suddenly become captivated by it all. The World Cup is also responsible for so many other strange and incredible situations. For instance, how strange it is to see Everton and Liverpool fans baying for the blood of Wayne Rooney whenever they play Manchester United and also the Man United fans hurling obscenities at Steven Gerrard. But once the World Cup starts, the insults stop and all those Liverpool and Man United fans are cheering on every move that Wayne Rooney and Steven Gerrard make. Suddenly, we all love them. It's crazy isn't it? Could that be the reason why we're known as fickle fans?

Another thing I've noticed, once the World Cup starts, is that even if your country isn't involved, you still want to feel a part of it. Although England didn't qualify for USA finals in 1994, I know of quite a few English fans that actually travelled to Dublin to support Ireland and enjoy the carnival atmosphere. They obviously thought if they couldn't make it to the United

States the next best place to be was Ireland. I can remember being a Scottish fan in 1978 when Argentina hosted the World Cup. In Spain at the 1982 tournament, I was shouting for Northern Ireland and I've lost count of the amount of times I've been a Brazil fan.

I still love going back to Ireland and everybody still talks about those brilliant World Cup memories when Jack Charlton was the manager. Jack Charlton's reign as Ireland manager will be remembered by the Irish people for generations to come. He is one of the most successful managers in the history of Irish football and whenever Big Jack travels around the Emerald Isle, he's treated like royalty.

I love listening to all the old football stories over a lovely pint of the black stuff and having the craic. I was told one story about Big Jack and whether it's true or not, or just exaggerated, I'm not quite sure.

I was told that whenever Big Jack visited pubs and restaurants, the landlords never used to bank his cheques as they had his signature on them. Instead of paying his cheques into the bank, these proprietors would immortalise them behind glass and display them on the wall as a souvenir and proof that the big man had been in their establishment. Goodness me, if I were Big Jack, I'd be visiting every pub and restaurant in Ireland and I'd even probably move there permanently.

After the world cup, I kept in touch with Pat, Brian, Kevin and Phil to name but a few and I watched Ireland with them on so many wonderful occasions. I travelled to matches at Lansdowne Road as well as travelling further afield to places like Latvia and Portugal and if you've never been away to watch an

Ireland match, irrespective of where you're from or who you support, I would definitely recommend it.

What I particularly noticed when watching Ireland was the very informal and laid back relationship their national team seemed to have with their fans. From my personal experiences, they really do seem to have a very close bond and I've often wondered if it may have something to do with the friendly and respectable way their fans behave. I'm not sure why it is, but there doesn't seem to be the chasm that exists with the England team who are guarded away from their fans and to my way of thinking, live in a completely different world.

When I travelled to Latvia, I was chuffed to bits that John Aldridge and Jason McAteer both remembered seeing me when they walked off the pitch in New Jersey. I actually gave John Aldridge a Russian hat as he and the rest of the players who were in the next hotel to ours, were travelling back early and wouldn't have had a chance to buy one. There was also another occasion in Portugal when Jason McAteer kindly gave me his shirt.

On the flight to Riga, (Latvia) Pat and Brian introduced me to the Irish comedian, Brendan O'Carroll, who is now taking the world by storm as Mrs Brown. He was wearing his hat with the initials BOC (Brendan O'Carroll) on tour. Despite his fame, he was just one of the fans and you couldn't help but notice his respect for other people. He was a true gentleman, who certainly went out of his way to make me very welcome. As you might imagine, we also had a brilliant laugh on that flight... another experience I'll never forget.

I also bumped into Ireland's number one fan, Davey Keogh, once again, with his big banner. After the match, we all celebrated long into the night, without any trouble whatsoever.

As I said, meeting so many Irish fans in New York resulted in a lot of new and valued friendships. Pat, Brian, Kevin and Phil would often visit Liverpool and I would often visit Dublin. After watching one match at Lansdowne Road, the Irish lads took me to Rumours night club in the heart of Dublin where the players used to go. Getting into the VIP section was no problem with my Merseyside accent and once in there I was drinking and talking with most of the players.

Roy Keane has a reputation for being hard and aggressive, but I have to say that when I met him I found him to be very softly spoken and polite. I told him I used to live and work in Cork, his home city, and for the next few minutes we spoke about his beautiful city on the River Lee.

This was another illustration of the very close bond between the Irish players and their fans. I still can't quite figure it out but this rapport is something I've never seen or heard about with the England team.

A few months after the world cup in the USA, Pat and Brian brought their local Irish amateur team over to England to play in a football match we organised. I put together a team from Merseyside and we decided to stage our own version of England versus Ireland, in aid of a local charity, the *New Born Baby Appeal* in Liverpool. The team was Rivermount FC, a local team from Finglas in Dublin where Brendan O'Carroll is from.

I wouldn't profess to be a football promoter or anything like that, but having organised one or two charity events, I was quite looking forward to this one. For the months building up to this game, I was telling

Pat and Brian by what margin they were going to get beaten and just for the craic, we decided to have a bet, but this was no ordinary bet. As we were arguing and bragging who was going to win, we decided whoever lost would have to pay a forfeit. There was even a few quid put down, for charity of course. I didn't mind so much losing a few quid, as it was going to a good cause anyway, but I really didn't fancy losing a forfeit, especially to Pat and Brian, as you never knew what they had in mind. For this reason I had to go all out to win this match and to make absolutely sure of this, without telling Pat and Brian, of course. I managed to get hold of the former professional Liverpool players, Joey Jones, David Johnston, Alan Kennedy and my wife's cousin, Kenny McKenna, who played for Tranmere Rovers, to play for my team. It promised to be a great day and I was also delighted to secure the services of Sky TV's Rob Palmer and Rob McCaffrey, who could both play a bit as well.

Left Lee Trundle, Dave Johnson, Rob Palmer, Rob Mcaffery, Joey Jones, Me (centre) turning into that man in the suit, Jan Walton, kicking off the match with Rivermount FC

To say I was confident was a bit of an understatement and I couldn't wait for the day of the match, to see Pat's and Brian's faces when they saw my team. When my side walked out with former Liverpool and England international players, I couldn't stop laughing. I also had one hell of a forfeit for them if… I mean when, they lost.

However, my smiles quickly faded when Rivermount walked out and I saw that Pat had brought his stepson and their surprise player, Swansea's City's Lee Trundle.

I confronted Pat and Brian immediately and complained that this wasn't fair, as Lee was still a professional footballer. Okay, maybe I had been a little dishonest for bringing in the former Liverpool players, but at least my players had retired, unlike Lee who was still playing professionally and was a lot younger than any in my team. My plan had definitely backfired and Pat and Brian now had the laugh on me.

Jan Walton, world-renowned mother of the Merseyside sextuplets (yes, six daughters), was invited as representative of the *New Born Baby Appeal*, blowing the starting whistle to what was quite a competitive match.

It turned out to be one hell of a match, which finished in a 3 - 3 draw. As is so often the case though and much to the delight of Pat and Brian, England lost once again on penalties. Pat and Brian gave me plenty of stick and although I lost the bet and now had to honour my forfeit, it wasn't all bad, as the match was a sell-out and we raised quite a lot of money for the *New Born Baby Appeal*.

I had booked one of the function rooms in the Holiday Inn Hotel in Liverpool and we laid on a really big party for our Irish guests afterwards. It was here that I was to learn of my forfeit. Pat and Brian said I had to go on the stage and sing a song.

Phew, I thought and as Yosser Hughes used to say, "I can do that."

The two of them started laughing and said, "You haven't heard what you have to sing yet." They continued laughing and exchanging knowing looks and it would be an understatement to say that a little panic was beginning to set in. I had this strange feeling the song they wanted me to sing was not something I would be comfortable with. I was quietly praying to myself that it wasn't the song I had in my mind.

But unfortunately for me, it was and they were still laughing and said, "Peter, we know you're a very big Evertonian and as it's for charity—"

"No fucking chance," I said, before they could finish their sentence. "I'm not singing *You'll Never Walk Alone*, no way. It ain't happening."

They were laughing like mad as I pleaded with them to let me sing anything else, other than my dearest rivals' anthem. For years, if that song ever came on the radio or TV, I would get up and leave the room and now these two were asking... no, actually, they were telling me I had to sing it. I offered to make a very generous donation to charity and even begged them to pick another forfeit.

"I would never ask you to do something like this," I protested, but before I could say another word, Brian was up on the stage and announcing that an Evertonian was just about to sing YNWA for charity. Everybody was cheering by now and my two Irish friends were not letting me talk my way out of this.

There was only one thing for it; I had to bite my

lip and keep reminding myself it was going to a good cause. It was the only time I've ever received a standing ovation for singing and I hadn't even started yet. Then I heard myself beginning to sing those words; 'When you walk... through a storm...' Apart from it feeling very weird, it also felt horrible. How was I ever going to live this one down?

When it was eventually over, Pat and Brian were the first to come over and congratulate me as they led me to the bar to buy me a large drink.

"By the way," Pat said, "what was the forfeit you had in mind for us if we'd lost the bet?"

"Oh, you two were both singing *God Save Our Queen,*" I replied.

I told Pat and Brian they'd better have some good singers with them because there was another bet riding on the singing. Once again I had resorted to some underhand tactics and without telling Pat and Brian, I hired a professional Elvis impersonator, pretending he was one of my mates from school. I just hoped his Lancashire accent wouldn't give it away. This was my big chance to even the score.

When 'Elvis' came on he was brilliant and brought the house down.

It was now my turn to laugh. "Beat that if you can," I said, over the moon that my tactics had triumphed.

Once again, though, my joy was short-lived and I really ought to have known better, especially with Ireland's track record in the *Eurovision Song Contest.*

Unbeknown to me (and very unfairly once again), they had brought with them Ireland's popular professional singer, Tommy Carey. This was bang out of order as Tommy sang not one, nor two, but a host of songs that were actually part of his repertoire.

Tommy was an outstanding performer. If you closed your eyes when he was performing, you could have been listening to Gene Pitney, Elvis Presley, Roy Orbison, Tom Jones, Jim Reeves, Charlie Landsborough and so many more artists. You name it, he could sing it.

I looked over at Pat and Brian, who were now creased over. I'd been stung once again.

"He's a pro," I complained. "That's not fair."

"Right, and what about Elvis?" they asked.

"He's my mate."

"Really? Your mate, is he? And how come he has a Yorkshire accent?"

"It's actually Lancashire," I said.

They asked me what his real name was and I told them we'd always just known him as Elvis.

"You've never met him before in your life. We know what you're up to."

Okay, so I'd been rumbled once again, but we really did have a fantastic day, full of fun… and in all fairness, I would have to concede that Tommy Carey was a bit better than my Elvis, anyway.

The former Liverpool players who played in our match had tried to organise one of the current players to present a cheque to the *New Born Baby Appeal* at the party, but there was a problem at the last minute and unfortunately, there was no longer a Liverpool player available. Now this was a bit of a problem, because I had actually advertised in the local press and on the radio, that a Liverpool footballer would be making the presentation. I even had tickets printed indicating that a surprise, current Liverpool player would be present. Now I really was in big trouble.

I wasn't sure what I was going to do. A real promoter would have had this boxed off by now. But I wasn't a promoter, just an ordinary fan, a little bit out of his league for taking on something so big.

As I was standing by the stage, Brian came rushing over to me.

"You're not going to believe this," he said, "but I've just seen the Liverpool and Irish footballer, Mark Kennedy, in reception!"

"Brian, are you sure it's him? Is he still there?"

"Well of course I'm sure; it's definitely him."

We both dashed off to reception and there, large as life, as Brian had said, was Mark Kennedy talking to some friends.

I couldn't believe it; he must have been sent by an angel to help us in our hour of need and to cap it all off, he was Irish as well. In fact he was perfect. If Liverpool had asked us which of their players we wanted for our charity event, we would probably have asked for Mark Kennedy. Talk about the luck of the Irish.

"What are we going to do?" Brian asked.

"Brian, mate, we've got no choice but to ask for his help. There's a room full of people in there expecting to see a Liverpool player presenting our cheque in about fifteen minutes, so we can't let him out of our sight."

After shadowing Mark Kennedy all round the foyer, I eventually plucked up the courage to approach him just as he was about to leave the hotel.

"Excuse me, Mark, sorry to trouble you… I know you're just about to leave, but…" I hastily explained we had Rivermount FC from Dublin in the other room and how they had helped us to raise quite a lot of money for charity, doing themselves and Ireland very proud.

"I've told everybody in the local newspapers and on the radio that there would be a Liverpool player presenting the cheque and we've been let down at the last minute. "I just, er... well I wondered if you'd mind presenting the cheque, please? It would only take a couple of minutes—"

"Okay," he said, smiling.

"... and as you are also from Dublin, I thought you might be able to help us out..."

"Okay," he repeated.

"It's just that we were expecting to get another player, but—"

"Peter, shut up," Brian interrupted. "He has said yes twice, he's going to do it."

"You mean you will present our cheque?"

Mark said he would be honoured to do it.

"That's great, thanks," was all I could say. Phew, I couldn't believe how close we came to looking like idiots.

Up on the stage, Brian and I thanked Rivermount FC and the former Liverpool players who had played that day, as well as Rob Palmer and Rob McCaffrey from Sky Sports, our famous Merseyside mum, Jan Walton, Lee Trundle, Kenny McKenna and last but not least, Elvis and Tommy Carey. But the loudest cheer of the night was undoubtedly when I announced, "We promised you a Liverpool footballer was coming here tonight and now could you please put your hands together for Liverpool and Republic of Ireland superstar, Mark Kennedy."

Mark was given a standing ovation as he came up on the stage to present the cheque and I caught a glance from my wife who looked at me, smiled and shook her head, knowing how close we had been to looking very stupid and nearly having to apologise to everybody.

As he left the stage to another standing ovation, the music started and the dancing began. Pat, Brian and I thanked God for sending Mark Kennedy to our rescue; to us it was a miracle how we managed to get out of that one.

Mark Kennedy was baffled by it all.

"You know when you just announced that you'd promised a Liverpool player," he began, "What if I hadn't been in this hotel tonight? What would you have done then?"

I grinned at him. "I would have had to tell everyone that the Liverpool player was also doing an Elvis impersonation for us as well."

As we all laughed, Mark said he was delighted to help and if we were planning anything like that again, he would be glad to help us out... with a bit more notice, if possible.

Thanks for saving the day, Mark Kennedy, another top man.

Twelve
Having a Ball

The protest was now in full flow as I was looking to obtain the rest of the premiership balls, by refusing to pay into their grounds.

I kept wishing my good friend Michael was still alive. Apart from missing him deeply, I had also felt absolutely bullet proof when he was around. He gave me so much confidence; I believed I could walk into No.10 Downing Street when I was with him. Have you ever felt like that about certain people in this life? You know, those who can make you feel really great about yourself when you're in their company? Well, he was certainly one of those people. But sadly, he wasn't here any longer and with no steward's pass, either, I knew that my chances of completing this protest were now a lot slimmer. From now on it was going to become even more difficult.

A handful of people knew about me collecting a signed football from each club I'd gained free entry into and they were constantly asking how many balls I'd managed to collect so far. With only a couple of Premiership balls sitting on top of our kitchen cupboard, it was fair to assume I hadn't got very far.

But Michael had left a legacy; a legacy of inspiration, which I hoped would be enough to drive me on to continue… that, plus the fact that I was still annoyed with the way fans were being treated. *Children In Need* also gave me the determination to carry on with my protest. I knew I couldn't give up and I also kept reminding myself about another one of Michael's numerous sayings: 'You only ever fail when you stop trying.'

I kept telling myself the only way to fill the top of the kitchen cupboard with all twenty-two signed Premier League footballs, meant gaining free entry into twenty-two Premier League clubs. There was no other way.

I would nearly always travel to these games without the faintest idea of how I would be getting in and I'd be lying if I said I wasn't nervous, but in another strange kind of way, trying to get into the match without paying and the unpredictability of it all, made it so much more exciting, not to mention absolutely nerve racking.

I used to think back to when we were younger and the word worry didn't belong in our vocabulary. It was like riding on the big dipper at Blackpool all day long without any fear whatsoever. I know for a fact I'd never be able to do anything like that today.

I also thought of the days when some of my mates who supported Liverpool, used to pay about 30p to go into the boys' pen at Anfield, which gave young kids a cheap option of watching the match (something you don't see much of in today's 'money rules all' game). Once they were inside the boys' pen, those brave enough to dare would climb over the frightening giant of a mesh fence to get into the Kop, which would have cost about £1.50 then. Instead of standing alongside their soprano-voiced peers, they could now join in singing with the adults in the famous Kop.

We couldn't do this at Everton though, as we had a mesh roof in our boys' pen, which resembled a cage, preventing anybody from climbing out into the Gwyladys Street End, but young kids wanting to make their limited finances go that little bit further would use their ingenuity in so many different ways in those days and that was half the fun. The Liverpool playwright and big Liverpool fan, Dave Kirby, perfectly sums up these memories of the boys' pen in one of his many brilliant poems, aptly named The Boys' Pen which I still enjoy watching on YouTube.

When I travelled to Sheffield United one week with our Jeggsy, I actually decided to tell a gateman that I was carrying out a personal protest of refusing to pay to go into any more football matches as we fans were being treated like dirt. He suddenly shouted over to one of the stewards to come over quickly, as he needed his help.

Here we go, I thought, I'm in big trouble here. I couldn't believe it, though, when he then requested the steward to open up the side gate and allow me and our kid to enter.

"I absolutely agree with you," he said. "Football fans are being treated like second class citizens and it's about time somebody did do something about it. Good luck with your protest, mate."

I must admit I hadn't been expecting anything like that and I can remember thinking that was so much easier than I thought. From now on, I thought, that's what I'll do, I'll just be truthful and explain to people how badly we fans are being treated and they'll just let me in for nowt.

Wrong. When I tried this same honest approach at Tottenham Hotspur the following week, their gateman called the Police and I was about to be arrested, until I told him I was only joking. Just as well not all the cockneys were like him, though, and a blessing that my son, Tom, was only small, as two in the click reared its ugly head for the first time in about thirty years. And instead of there being 26,303 fans inside White Hart Lane that day, if fans had been treated with a little bit more respect there would have been 26,304.

As each signed ball arrived at the house, so my confidence grew and I was now entering clubs through their reception areas as well as with the envelope trick and any other opportunity that may present itself on the day. It was another option where I would dress smart, blend in and simply walk past security. Our clubs would never suspect any fans of attempting this sort of thing. Although it proved to be another very effective way of gaining free entry, the objective was the same, but just another way of going about it.

But after doing this with great success, I began to notice something else happening... it wasn't really feeling like a protest any more. I felt like I needed to walk through with a giant placard, or something to explain what I was doing, otherwise who the hell would know there was any protest going on at all? The other thing I noticed, which gave me a bit more cause for concern was that, just like an alcoholic who craved a stronger drink, I was now looking for more daring and adventurous ways to enter these grounds.

It was no longer enough just to walk in through reception. What was the point of that? So what if I got in without paying? Big deal; hundreds of privileged people did it every week anyway and nobody batted an eyelid, or gave a damn. I knew if this protest was to have any appeal or mean anything at all, I really needed to up the ante. It was time to be more adventurous and vary the ways in which I entered these grounds.

I've heard pop stars and other performers say that once they lose that stage fright feeling, it's time to stop performing and I was beginning to understand what they meant.

I travelled to our next away game at Chelsea's Stamford Bridge with my mates, Kevin, Darren and Dennis with a more daring plan in mind. I remembered once seeing a young lad jumping over a turnstile and everybody was looking. At the time, I thought he was absolutely crazy. Although, I considered it quite extreme, another part of me also wondered how he had the nerve to do such a thing. I mean it was so risky and not something you could talk your way out of in the way I did each time I walked through a reception area. There was no explaining or apologising that you've made a mistake and entered the wrong gate after blatantly jumping over it. I'm not sure why and it might sound completely nuts, but his action had a strange sense of excitement about it and I couldn't help wondering what must have been going through his head at the time. It wasn't until we were outside Stamford Bridge that I was about to find out how he felt. This was to be my method today.

My mates couldn't believe that I was seriously considering jumping over the turnstile and they all looked rather shocked.

"Aren't you a bit old to be doing something like that?"

"You sure you can jump that high, mate?"

But I was determined to do it. "See you inside," I said.

They each shook my hand and wished me well as I made my way up to the turnstile.

Once there, I said to the gateman, "Look, I'm really sorry about this. I know you have a job to do and I mean this with the greatest of respect to you and to Chelsea Football Club, but I'm carrying out a protest of no longer paying to get into any football matches due to the total disrespect shown towards us football fans…"

He just looked at me as if I was some kind of nutcase and without further ado, I put my hands on the turnstile and swung my legs over it, clearing the hurdle with a jump that Red Rum would have been proud of.

The rush of adrenalin was something I had never before experienced in my whole life. It was unbelievable. Honestly, it was absolutely amazing, but I wouldn't recommend doing this every week just to get in for nowt, as it was just too nerve racking.

I've heard people describe something happening too quickly to even think about it. Other people have described, say, an accident as happening in slow motion. Well, that was how it felt to me and it was like an out-of-body experience, because for a very short time, I didn't feel that I was really there.

But because this was a protest and in my mind quite a justifiable protest, it was a different kind of nervousness, if you know what I mean. Whenever I've watched TV news bulletins about people around the world holding protests, I've always wondered how they had the courage to do such a thing. Now I was beginning to understand. Although I was scared stiff, I was able to do it because I believed in my protest.

Once inside Stamford Bridge, I stood hiding behind a crowd of people from where I could see the gateman describing me to the stewards and the police.

"He's a small bloke, wearing a blue shirt," I heard him say.

Once the police and the stewards heard 'wearing a blue shirt' I saw them laugh and turn around, no longer interested. As Everton and Chelsea both played in blue, they knew they had a better chance of finding a scouser in the Kop. (Sorry, I couldn't resist that one).

I was amazed by what I had just done. I would never have dreamt of doing anything like that had it not been for this protest and I was beginning to see a side of me I didn't know existed. I won't deny that I was very excited by it all, but I was also a bit worried about what was happening to me.

My mates came over, laughing their heads off and still couldn't believe what I had done.

"You okay, mate?"

I told them I was absolutely fine, in fact I felt fantastic and I couldn't wait for our next away game.

When I started this protest, I was very disenchanted with football and Saturdays for me had lost their sparkle. As you know, I was particularly cheesed off with the way a lot of privileged people were taking tickets from the real fans, but there were also a few other issues in football I wasn't very happy about. Somehow this protest had revived a passion that had been missing for quite some time and Saturdays or any match days couldn't come round quickly enough now. I would almost describe it as an addiction; the challenge of each game was now becoming more and more exciting and some of the methods of getting into the grounds were about to become even more daring. Some people were now asking me how I was going to get in to the next game and could they come and watch me do it. The truth was, I hadn't the faintest idea how I was going to do it until the day of the match, but I could understand their interest, as even I used to wonder what the next game would bring.

I travelled to Queens Park Rangers hoping to

pull off one of the most daring attempts of the protest so far and I knew if this one was going to work, there could be no room for error. It would have to be done properly as I would only get one chance. I was waiting outside the reception area with quite a lot of supporters from both teams, which is a regular thing for fans hoping to get a glimpse of their heroes and maybe even an autograph. As soon as the Everton team coach arrived, I knew I had to make my move and get it right and as Del Boy used to say, fortune favours the brave.

Dressed in my Everton tracksuit and looking no different to the Everton team members, I walked over towards them and, looking as if I'd just got off the coach, calmly walked into Queens Park Rangers football club with the official Everton party. Some of the players and the rest of the party were glancing at me and I noticed a few of them talking amongst themselves and looking round at me. I hoped they wouldn't say anything to the QPR officials, who so far wouldn't have known that I wasn't a member of the Everton party.

I kept thinking, I've supported you lot since I was a child, please don't say anything now. And fortunately for me, nobody did. They definitely knew what I was up to, but must have realised I didn't look like trouble or any kind of threat and a few of the players were even looking at me and laughing. I can't be sure of it, but I would like to think that our players were looking after me that day, as I always knew our boys wouldn't let me down.

Once inside the ground I made my way up the tunnel and being dressed in my track suit, I didn't look out of place walking onto the pitch. But I didn't want to push my luck too much. I knew I had another Premier League ball and I'd made my point. It was time to make myself scarce and take a seat in the crowd.

I would normally have been full of nerves doing something like this, but I remember having no fear that day. It may have been because I thought I was becoming invincible, but my confidence was definitely running so high that I was ready to try anything. Merely walking through reception didn't do it for me any more; I'd done that and as they say, got the T-shirt; that was far too easy now. I knew I needed a harder challenge and I couldn't wait for the next one.

Around this time, I was working on a welding contract in Leeds. We used to work nights and commute every night up the M62. I struck up a friendship with one of the workers in the factory and we got on really well together. As we were always talking about football, I confided in him about my protest. As it happened, Everton were due to play at Elland Road, the Leeds ground, that coming Saturday and I was planning to attend. Naturally, I would be trying to gain free entry into the ground and I was delighted when my friend from Leeds told me he had a mate who worked on the door of the press lounge at Elland Road and that he would phone him and see if he could fix it for me to get in.

His friend agreed, making it an easy ride for a change, but it was a new and different way of getting in, as well as adding the Leeds ball to my ever-growing collection of signed Premier League footballs.

He contacted his mate, then told me it was all sorted and gave me his description... 'a big ginger-haired bloke.' He told me to give him a little wink when I got there and not to worry as he would be expecting me. I suggested that just to make it look good, I would bring one of my old Everton steward's passes so that anybody looking would think it was a press pass.

"Yeah, that's a good idea," he said, "I'll tell him that."

On the Saturday, I travelled with Terry to Elland Road. Terry happens to be a big Leeds fan although he lives near me on Merseyside. Once outside the ground, we made our way towards the press lounge and standing at the door was a big, ginger-headed bloke who was looking over in our direction. I knew this must be our man, so I immediately gave him a wink. There were a few people in front of us, though, and I was trying desperately to get his attention. I never took my eyes off him for one second.

When I caught his eye, I gave him another wink and I didn't know if it was because there were other people about, or maybe he just didn't see me, but he didn't acknowledge me at all. I realised he couldn't make it too obvious as there were other security and staff members around as well, but to be honest I was expecting some kind of acknowledgement from him even if it was just a nod. Of course, I didn't want to get him into trouble so I didn't say anything in case anybody else was watching. Meanwhile, I had made sure I stuck to the plan by bringing an old Everton steward's card, pretending it was some kind of press pass.

As Terry and I moved closer, our big gingered-haired friend looked over towards us once again and not for the first time that day I winked back and this time, even smiled at him. There was still no response and I was now pretty certain he was remaining aloof on purpose in case anybody noticed and put two and two together. All I hoped at that moment was that he hadn't bottled it and changed his mind. He was now asking all the members of the press… oh, and me and Terry, to have our passes ready as we made our way towards him.

"Passes, please," he asked, as Terry and I walked right up to him. I continued winking and smiling at him and then showed him my Everton steward's pass that was well out of date.

"Okay, everybody move along now, please," he said, as I shuffled my feet and winked and smiled at him some more. I was beginning to feel a bit awkward to say the least; winking and smiling is not something I normally make a habit of doing to strange men, or any men, for that matter.

It had to be said that Ginger was very cool and never uttered one single word as Terry and I both walked past him and into the press lounge. I was relieved we were in, but I was a bit disappointed he didn't acknowledge us, or even give us a smile. I just felt he could have made it a bit easier for us and he was rather too cool for my liking. Anyway, the main thing was, he did let us in; we were in Elland Road and I knew the kitchen cupboard would be displaying another football during the week.

After the game we went back into the press lounge, again without any acknowledgement from our ginger-haired friend, and we even attended the post-match press conference afterwards. The Leeds manager at the time, Howard Wilkinson, was in attendance and refreshments were included. I wanted to walk over and thank Ginger, but I thought he must be worried about other people or some of his colleagues watching, so I decided it was best to say nothing.

My friend had done me a great favour, though, and I couldn't wait to go in to work on the Monday and thank him personally.

When he walked in, I never got the chance to say thank you as he was anxious to speak first.

"Peter, I'm sorry about Saturday, mate," he blurted out.

"Oh, never mind. I fully understood that your mate couldn't speak to us. At least he let us in," I replied.

"What do you mean?"

"Well, I understood why he couldn't talk to us or anything, but at least he was good enough to let us in."

"I haven't got the faintest idea what you're talking about, Peter, but I'm just apologising because my mate couldn't go to the match on Saturday. Sorry to let you down—"

"What do you mean, he couldn't go?" I was totally confused. "But he let us in. I showed him that ridiculous looking old steward's card... and I even winked and smiled every time he looked my way."

"I don't know who it was you winked and smiled at, Peter, but it most certainly wasn't my mate. His wife was taken ill and he never went."

"You're winding me up," I said.

"No, Peter, I'm not, honestly. He phoned me yesterday to apologise for not being able to make it the day before, but he said if you wanted to return next season, he would make sure he would be there this time and let you in."

"Oh my God," I said. "I don't know who that big bloke was on the door at the press lounge then, but he had gingerish hair and I walked straight past him, flashing an out of date Everton steward's pass. God... I was winking and smiling at him for a good five minutes. No wonder he wouldn't speak to me!"

People arriving for work were stopping to listen; they were all laughing their heads off. I had a good laugh myself afterwards but for the moment I couldn't take in what had happened.

Isn't confidence an amazing thing? Have you ever had that feeling of certainty, that blind faith in something, only to discover you never really were that certain after all?

I was just thinking about a very similar situation, something that happened to me in Holland, on a job. I was climbing about a hundred feet up a wind turbine with the reassurance of being securely strapped to a safety harness, only to discover when I eventually reached the top that my harness wasn't in fact attached after all. I almost froze with fright as I looked at the loose harness that should have been attached and a familiar rush of panic immediately enveloped me. Honestly, I felt sick to the stomach, which was a bit similar to how I felt on being told that news from my mate in Leeds. After the initial shock, I was fine and we continued to laugh about it all through the shift – and do you know something? Yes, it does appear to be true that ridiculous things always seem to happen to me.

Whilst travelling to Ewood Park, Blackburn with my son, Tom, I was in one of those honest to God, no messing about type of moods and bluntly told a couple of gatemen I was carrying out a protest and that I was refusing to pay to get in. One of them started laughing and I asked what was so funny.

"They're on to you, mate," he said.

"What do you mean?" I asked.

He told me the gatemen and stewards had received information about a football fan carrying out a protest of refusing to pay into any football matches and had been briefed and told to be on their guard. They politely apologised and told me they couldn't let me in.

So they were on to me, eh? Word was certainly getting around. Never mind, I thought, when one door closes, another one opens… yet another one of my old friend Michael's sayings. So off we went in pursuit of the Blackburn ball to add to the collection in our kitchen.

We tried nearly every other gate as well as the envelope ruse that Michael had taught me, but there were none left and it wasn't looking too good. I was looking up to the sky now, asking Michael if he could help us out of this one when suddenly, out of nowhere, a bus pulled up right beside us with one of the youth teams on board. A large group of lively youngsters began scrambling off the coach. As it was very near to kick off, a Blackburn steward had to open one of the exit gates to let them through… and before you could say Sir Jack Walker, the Blackburn ball was on top of our kitchen dresser.

I enjoyed so many different ways of getting into football grounds during my protest, but one of my all-time favourite occasions had to be at Manchester City's old Maine Road stadium. I was explaining to a steward about my protest, when one of his colleagues heard what I was saying and made his way over.

"Hey," he said, "I know who you are, mate. I've heard all about you. You're that bloke who's refusing to pay to go into footie matches aren't you?"

I thought to myself, here we go again, here's trouble, this sounds like another Blackburn job, and I remember thinking that all the clubs must now be on to it. However, the only thing worse than being talked about, was not being talked about and if it was good enough for my mate, Michael and Oscar Wilde, it was certainly good enough for me.

"We've heard all about you," he continued. "How's the protest coming along, anyway?"

"Very well, thanks," I said, a little unsure about him. I told him I was collecting a signed football from each club I managed to get into and that once I had the full set of twenty-two, I would be raffling them off for *Children In Need* and I had nearly all of them.

With that, he opened the gate, patted me on the back and said, "Nice one, mate," and wished me all the best as he let me in. Once again, I couldn't believe my luck. It was also extremely heart-warming and very nice to know that there were now people out there who not only agreed with what I was doing, but in their own little ways were also supporting me and it was something I will never forget.

I had also been told by some players and former players, how badly they thought fans were treated and what I was doing was quite understandable.

The top of the kitchen cupboard, I'm pleased to say, was now looking beautifully adorned with almost every Premiership football as they were coming in thick and fast.

Our Jeggsy used to laugh when they arrived. "I wonder what they'd say if they knew how you got them?"

I would just remind him that the balls were going to a very good cause and as long as everybody was happy, I didn't believe I was doing any harm. With just two balls to go, I was almost there and a visit to Highbury, the home of Arsenal, was next on my list, which would prove to be the second hardest ground to get into.

Thirteen
It's Not What You Know...

When my nephew, James, was younger he spent a lot of time in hospital and although I never heard him complain once, I still wanted to cheer him up and as he loved Liverpool I wrote to them and phoned, asking if he could be considered as a mascot for one of their games. However, my requests appeared to be falling on deaf ears and I seemed to be getting nowhere.

I fully understood Liverpool must have been inundated with similar requests and with a fan base pretty well covering the globe, I knew it wasn't going to be easy.

It was around this time that my wife and I went to watch the brilliant band, the Electric Light Orchestra who were performing at the Royal Philharmonic Hall in Liverpool. After watching a magnificent concert we were making our way to the exit when I noticed the then Liverpool FC Chairman, David Moores, walking out alongside us with his wife. We were walking quite slowly and I asked them if they enjoyed the concert and they said it was fantastic, as ELO had in fact brought the house down.

I asked my wife if she thought I should tell David Moores about me writing to Liverpool regarding my nephew, James.

"Why are you asking me?" she replied. "You know you are about to, anyway."

Whatever did she mean by that? Anyway, I thought it was worth a try and I knew I would never get another chance like this in a million years. It really did seem like a once in a lifetime opportunity and I can remember thinking, well he can only say no.

When we had left the theatre, I introduced myself, "Excuse me, Mr Moores, my name is Peter Farrell. I really don't make a habit of doing this, but would you mind giving me a couple of minutes of your time, please?"

He gave me a guarded look, obviously wondering what on earth I was going to say to him, and cautiously said okay. I knew that what I was about to say in the next couple of minutes was going to have to be one of the best pitches of my life.

I told him my young nephew had been in and out of hospital since he was a child and that I had telephoned and written to Liverpool on a few occasions enquiring about the possibility of him becoming a mascot at one their games. I explained to David Moores that I was getting nowhere and didn't know what else to do.

I also said that I knew Liverpool, in common with a lot more clubs, were constantly helping sick children, but I was just hitting a brick wall and wondered if he would be able to help me out.

He stood there patiently and listened to every word I said without interrupting or trying to make an excuse for leaving. He then looked at me for a few moments, I think to make sure I had finished saying my piece, before saying it's always nice to talk to Liverpool fans. I shot a worried glance at my wife who suddenly turned the other way and must have been wondering how the hell I was going to get out of this one. I don't know why he assumed we were reds and how would he react once he discovered we were not and actually supported his greatest rivals, Everton? I still laugh today whenever I think of it.

Do you go to Anfield often, he asked?

Oh my god. I can hardly tell him that I can barely bring myself to go into that place just once a year when my team Everton play there.

So, with a nervous laugh I said. "Er, ha ha… no, I'm afraid we're not actually real big Liverpool fans."

"Do you just go to Liverpool occasionally then?"

I'm not sure how, but I was now convinced that he knew only too well that we were blue noses.

"Well…no, not exactly. We don't go at all." I stuttered.

I then told him our family was kind of split down the middle, with loads of Liverpool fans in, oh yeah, really loads, ha ha, and a few Evertonians, as well.

Here I was, asking the Chairman of Liverpool football club for a favour and he was about to find out that we were Evertonians.

"Really? And which side of the middle would you happen be on?" he wanted to know.

Suddenly, it was no longer funny, the situation had become really difficult and he didn't appear to be smiling anymore.

I nervously laughed again "Actually, we're both Everton fans, ha ha. Fancy that, eh? Evertonians."

I swear, I will take the look on his face to my grave, as he stood staring at me sharply for a few seconds.

"So you're not Liverpool fans, but actually Evertonians? I thought as much," he said.

My wife and I looked at each other, now really worried.

Erm, I see. Now that could be a problem," he replied.

Frowning, he shook his head. "You shouldn't have told me that," he said. "Sorry, I can't help you..." but then his frown slowly turned into a broad, sardonic grin. People who know David Moores will no doubt understand and relate to what I'm saying here, as he really did have a very dry sense of humour.

It was great Everton/Liverpool banter which I loved, and I must have caught him at an opportune moment. He had obviously enjoyed the concert as well and appeared to be in a very good mood.

Just as well ELO were brilliant tonight, I thought to myself.

He was very sympathetic and good-natured and although he said he couldn't promise or guarantee anything, he gave me his PA's telephone number and told me to call her on Monday morning and mention our conversation. He said he would certainly look into it for me and be in touch.

He then asked me how our James was and we also spoke about ELO and the wonderful theatres we have in Liverpool for a few more minutes before we parted.

I shook his hand, thanked him for his time and wished him all the best. "Oh, except when you're playing Everton, of course!"

On the way home, I was still absolutely amazed and very puzzled how he could have known we were Evertonians. I've heard stories of some people claiming they can tell the difference just by looking at people, as I gave him no clues, yet he definitely knew and I was now curious to know how?

My wife then told me she thought she knew how he sussed we were blue noses.

"You introduced yourself, remember, and told him your name.

Just then the penny dropped. I was named after the former Everton captain in the fifties, Peter Farrell. David Moores must have had a good old laugh to himself, thinking I'll wind these blue noses up.

Talk about being in the right place at the right time; the Chairman of Liverpool Football Club certainly did look into it for me. I'm delighted to tell you that my nephew, James, walked out at Anfield as mascot for Liverpool against Arsenal, just three weeks later, holding hands with the Liverpool captain, Stevie Gerrard and the Arsenal skipper, Thierry Henry, when the two teams met in the FA cup. And just to round off a beautiful day I'm even more delighted to tell you that Arsenal won 3-1. Sorry, James and sorry, David Moores, but it's that Everton/Liverpool banter once again.

James with Steven Gerrard and Thierry Henry

It's funny how things happen in life though and whenever I hear an ELO track now on the radio, I always think of our James, Stevie Gerrard, Thierry Henry and of course David Moores. But the one thing I can never get out of my mind is how serendipitous it was that we met the Chairman of Liverpool that night. I certainly don't want to undermine David Moores' concern and warm kindness for my nephew in any way, as he was genuinely interested in helping James, but the fact remains that if we hadn't gone to watch ELO that night, then quite simply, young James would not have been mascot. This, I suppose, bears out the old cliché that it's not what you know, but who you know and although I'll always be extremely grateful to David Moores and Liverpool Football Club (who were both fantastic), I'm also very mindful that not everyone would have had that chance.

After he was mascot, James said to me, "Thanks very much, Uncle Peter."

"Don't thank me, mate," I told him, "thank David Moores, another top man... oh and the Electric Light Orchestra, for putting on a great show."

It's strange how serendipity has played quite a part in my life. I can recall another time when I was filling up my car at a petrol station one afternoon in Liverpool. I was kind of daydreaming and wondering what to get my eldest daughter for her twelfth birthday, when who should pull up alongside me but the former Liverpool and England captain, Phil Thompson. As he began filling his tank I nodded and said hello and he did likewise.

Liverpool were playing Newcastle United later that evening and I mentioned to Phil Thompson that Liverpool would have their work cut out as the

Geordies were playing quite well.

"No problem," he laughed. "You must be an Evertonian?"

"I am," I said, "but my daughter supports you lot."

"Sounds like she has a bit of sense," he joked.

That Everton/Liverpool banter again. It was funny really, but as we were both filling up our cars, mine being slightly more modest than his, of course, and exchanging small talk, he was looking at the petrol pump, probably thinking, 'I wish this thing would hurry up and there was I, looking from him to the pump, thinking I'd just had a brainwave what to get my daughter for her birthday.

Now my kids are probably fed up of me telling them there are two types of people in this life. There are those who have things happen to them and then there are those who make things happen and I've always tried to instil in them to never be afraid of making things happen. But the right opportunity doesn't always present itself; situations and opportunities come and go every day of our lives and can pass us by without us actually even realising they were there to begin with. I wasn't going to let this chance escape easily.

"Hey, Phil," I said, "it's her birthday next week. Would you mind making her day by letting me bring her down to Melwood, (Liverpool's training ground) to see the players train as a birthday treat, please? Tell you what; if you do I'll keep everything crossed for you tonight against Newcastle." (Just as if...)

He must have thought, cheeky blue nose so-and-so, but I don't think he had much time to knock me back and get into a conversation, as he had a very big game to prepare for and anyway, by now there were other cars queuing up behind us for petrol.

"Okay, why not?" he said. "She is one of us, I suppose."

Again, just as with David Moores, I happened to catch the right person at the right time. I mean if I'd written to the club, or even Phil Thompson himself, maybe on another day the answer would have been no.

He gave me the phone number of the training ground and told me who to ask for. The following week, I took my daughter and nieces to meet their Liverpool villains... I mean heroes, and they all had a great day.

Once again though, as grateful as I was to Phil Thompson, just like I was with David Moores for their warmth and kindness, I couldn't help thinking I wouldn't have been so fortunate if I hadn't had the good luck to meet them. Why me? I then started thinking that, although I only met them very briefly, what if I'd known them personally? Could I have just contacted them and asked for their help? I mean, are these the perks and privileges of being in the know, that would never normally be available to the likes of myself or the ordinary fan in the street?

I hope that doesn't make me sound really ungrateful; believe me, that is far from the truth because, as I said, Liverpool FC were superb in making James's day and David Moores and Phil Thompson both proved to be genuinely helpful people as well and I am more than aware that there are those who would have flatly refused my requests, but it still makes me realise the meaning in the saying, 'it's not what you know, but who you know.'

Fourteen
Good Old Arsenal

With just two more grounds to go, Highbury, the former home of Arsenal was only a few days away. This one was keeping me awake at night as it was proving to be one of the hardest grounds to get into. Having tried unsuccessfully to get into Highbury for the past couple of seasons, it seemed to be one of those places where just about everything was going against me. Each time I tried to walk in through their reception area, there was always an obstacle in the shape of an eagle-eyed, uniformed commissioner who, by the look of him, would have none of it. In addition, there were never any tickets left over in the envelopes at the players' ticket collection window and the turnstiles were nearly always policed. The few people working at the non-policed turnstiles appeared to have been forewarned about my actions and were now on full alert, looking out for me. It may sound paranoid, but I think most if not all of the clubs were by then fully aware of my protest, which probably explained why it was becoming more difficult towards the end.

There was also another small problem with Arsenal that niggled me. You see, I had already received the signed Arsenal ball, even though I hadn't actually managed to gain free entry into their ground yet.

Let me explain... when I started the protest, my original plan was to contact each club in alphabetical order. I contacted Arsenal first and told them I was collecting a signed ball from every Premier League club for charity. In fairness to them, they were extremely helpful and kind enough to send me an autographed ball. My plan was to then get into these stadiums, without paying, whenever Everton were due to play them.

This sounded like a good idea, until somebody posed the question: what if I didn't manage to get into that particular ground, yet still obtained their ball? That seemed to me to be a fair enough point. So I then decided to only ask for a signed ball once I had gained free admission into their ground.

As I mentioned, Arsenal and the rest of the clubs were all superb and not a single club declined my request for a signed ball.

My protest was never solely directed at our clubs, or any individuals at our clubs for that matter. My beef was more with the people responsible for running football and the whole unfair system that went with it. There were many disrespectful issues that needed addressing and it had to be acknowledged that certain individuals did have over-inflated egos, some of whom seemed to believe they were more important than the game itself and obviously way above us adoring fans. Some of them were in highly privileged positions which they exploited to the full. I also felt that our clubs, possibly without realising the full implications, were being mistakenly drawn into these cosy, but rather disrespectful relationships.

I wasn't looking to cause trouble, either, but I knew if I was to have any realistic chance of getting people to sit up and take note of my protest, then it had to be unusual. I also knew how difficult it was going to be, especially near the end, but I'd come this far and I couldn't give up now.

When my son and I travelled to London on the Saturday morning, I realized this would be the final roll of the dice. I suspected their security would be looking out for me and apart from anything else, this protest of travelling around the country was costing me an arm and a leg.

Once outside Highbury, it wasn't long before my suspicions were confirmed, as I heard one of their stewards on the radio, informing his colleagues to be on the look-out for an Everton fan who was carrying out some kind of protest and would be trying to get in without paying. He went on to say they had received information that he would be here today and attempting to jump over one of the turnstiles. Somebody at Chelsea had obviously informed Arsenal about my Red Rum moment and if I was to get into Arsenal today, you could safely assume it wouldn't be through, or even over, one of their turnstiles.

I stood beside one of the stewards, listening to his radio.

"What's the trouble with this Everton fan then, mate?" I asked him, casually.

"Oh, just one of you Scousers trying to jump over one of the turnstiles," he replied.

"Why would he do a thing like that?"

"Oh, it's some kind of ridiculous protest, I think, but if you ask me, I think he's just showing off and looking for attention."

Now I know some people may have considered my protest ridiculous and to others, it may have seemed a complete waste of time. Of course, they were entitled to their opinion, even if I didn't agree with them, but showing off wasn't a comment I was prepared to accept and there was no way I was going to let this steward get away with saying something like that. I'd been through far too much for that and even though I was getting into grounds for nothing, there were some grounds, like

Arsenal, where I had to return to a few times due to my failure to get in. On top of which, travelling expenses were going through the roof.

People who know me will confirm that it would be an impossibility for me to stand there and keep quiet. So I said to him, "Is that what you really think?"

He didn't answer but I think he was a bit surprised by my reaction, as he turned round and gave me a searching look.

I continued. "Do you know about Rosa Parks, who was ordered to give up her seat to a white passenger, on a bus in Alabama, USA, when black people were being treated like second class citizens? She refused. Do you think it was because she may have been protesting about something she strongly believed in? Or do you think she just wanted to show off?"

"Rosa who?" he asked.

Now I wasn't suggesting for one second that my protest was of anything like the magnitude of the black civil rights marches, but I was deeply offended that anybody could think of somebody trying for the last few years to gain some respect for football supporters as being a show-off. Looking for attention, I could accept, because I definitely was looking to publicise and highlight the plight of us fans. But I definitely wasn't showing off and he really touched a raw nerve.

He shook his head. "I don't get you…"

"Then allow me to explain," I said. "I think the person carrying out this protest has had enough of seeing genuine football fans supporting their team all season in all kinds of weather and then finding themselves unable to get a ticket for the final. I think he's also incensed with the fact that young families are struggling to make ends meet when our clubs are bringing out three or four different kits every season… not to mention changing the names of our grounds."

The steward opened his mouth to reply but I hadn't quite finished.

"And I believe he's also pretty pissed off about the constant increase of ticket prices, preventing young fans from having the chance of going to watch their team play, like you and I did when we were young."

"Not me, mate," he answered. "I don't like football."

I knew at that point I was wasting my time but I asked him to have a good look around here today as well as inside the stadium and to just ask himself why there were hardly any kids here.

"I've never really noticed," he said, "but now that you mention it, there doesn't seem to be that many."

"Well, I think that's why he's carrying out his protest—"

Suddenly a voice interrupted on his radio, enquiring if there was any description of this protester.

He turned to me and asked if I had any idea what the protester looked like.

"Oh yes, I've seen him a few times. He's a big blond-haired ugly looking bloke with glasses, a quiet sort of bloke and he always works alone." I described someone more or less the direct opposite of me.

"Well, If you see him today, you can tell him it's the end of his protest, because he's going to get caught and arrested if he tries anything today," he replied.

I felt like saying, why don't you tell him yourself? But on this occasion, I decided it was best to keep schtum.

He then relayed my fabricated description on his radio; "Er, yeah. Big, blond-haired, ugly geezer with glasses, travelling alone."

I knew it wouldn't be long before it dawned on this steward that if I respected this protester so much, I would hardly be giving his description away and taking the risk of him being arrested. It was time to disappear quickly, before the penny dropped.

If it was hard to get into Arsenal for the last couple of seasons, it was definitely much harder on that day as I knew they were looking out for me. I was still very nervous, but just to spur me on, I kept saying to myself that this was not a ridiculous protest and I knew that our kids, the next generation of fans, really were being excluded from our stadiums. Honestly, this was what provided me with all the courage and inspiration I needed for one more attempt at Arsenal and this time they weren't going to stop me. I was determined to succeed.

Tom and I made our way towards the reception area and for the third year running, I stood outside watching the players, staff, VIPs, celebrities and hordes of privileged people make their way inside. A few cars pulled up and certain people began getting out and walking in. One of them was the former Labour MP and Minister for Sport, Kate Hoey. As her official car drew up right outside the entrance, I instinctively felt this just might be the opportunity I was looking for and I knew I had to act quickly.

I thought, I've always voted for Labour and supported Kate Hoey and her Party. In fact, I've actually helped Kate Hoey and the Labour party on numerous occasions over the years and I only need her help for just a few minutes today.

I also thought if she knew what I was protesting about, she might even support my campaign. I figured she wouldn't really mind helping me and being a sports minister, as well as a Labour politician, she may just understand me exercising my democratic right to protest. After all, mine was a peaceful protest, with the benefits going to *Children In Need*. Well, that's how I tried to justify grabbing hold of Tom's arm and preparing to deploy my weapons of mass distraction.

Just as she was about to enter the reception area, I said, "Hello Kate, this is my son, Tom. We're both Everton fans, visiting Highbury for the very first time today." *(With me failing to make it into Highbury on previous occasions, I wasn't lying).*

She smiled. "Hello Tom, I hope you have a very nice day," she said.

"Thanks very much, Kate," I replied. "I hope we do as well, especially on the pitch against your team," and with that she laughed.

Now then, was it our fault the commissioner on the door assumed Tom and I were with Kate Hoey, the Minister for Sport? Honestly, the timing was perfect and I wasn't about to disillusion him as Tom and I walked through reception right behind her. You couldn't buy a bottle of this type of adrenalin anywhere; it was absolutely nerve shattering, but so incredibly exciting… the buzz was unbelievable.

Once safely inside Highbury, I didn't push my luck by saying anything else to her; I was so overjoyed that I had finally made it into Arsenal's ground. However, we still weren't out of the woods, as we now had to make our way up the players' tunnel and get past the numerous stewards and club officials, then out onto the pitch heading for where the Everton fans were sitting. I couldn't have picked a harder way of getting a seat in the Everton end. There were Arsenal officials and staff everywhere and unfortunately for us, we no longer had Kate Hoey to protect us. I knew we were bullet proof whilst walking with her, but now that we were back on our own, we were very vulnerable once again. This was now a much different bottle of adrenalin and a very worrying one.

I told Tom to keep quiet; if we opened our mouths, they would know straight away that we were Evertonians and shouldn't be anywhere near this part of the ground. As we continued walking through this minefield, I told him to keep his head up and to keep smiling. When we reached the top of the players' tunnel, I knew we no longer had the safety of pretending to be staff either. We'd be members of the public once again and as soon as we left the tunnel, we were in even more danger.

As we came out onto the pitch we began making our way slowly and as calmly as possible over to where the Everton fans were. This was really dangerous territory and had it been a normal walk, the Everton fans didn't look to be that far away. But this was no normal walk and involved walking around the pitch which at that moment seemed like a good mile. If anybody approached us now, wanting to know why we were walking around the side of the pitch, I knew we were in big trouble, especially as we had no tickets on us. In fact, when you think about it, even if we did have tickets, what the hell were we doing walking around the side of the pitch anyway?

I may well have managed to get inside Arsenal's stadium, but if we were stopped by anybody, we were out again; it was as simple as that. I was desperate to get to the Everton supporters' section as quickly as possible, but running would only draw unnecessary attention to ourselves, so we had to force ourselves to walk slowly. It felt like one of the longest journeys of my life, no kidding.

As we got closer to the Everton section, it was looking good, until out of the crowd as if by magic and walking rather quickly towards us, was a policeman. Oh my God, I thought, this is where we get kicked out. This policeman wasn't looking too happy, either, and I could hear him shouting over to the stewards, wanting to know why there were two people at the side of the pitch. It was pointless trying to run, that would have been suicidal.

I suddenly noticed Gunnersaurus, the Arsenal mascot. This big fluffy creature was waving at the crowd. Immediately, I grabbed Tom's arm and asked somebody to take our photo with Gunnersaurus and could they hurry up, please? This policeman was now pretty close and the shouting was a bit louder as he asked in a very authoritative manner what we were doing on the pitch. I had to ignore him so that this person could take our photo, which made him even more angry.

Rescued at Arsenal by Gunnersaurus

"What do you think you're doing out of your seats and on the side of the pitch?" he demanded to know.

My first thought was to say, "What do you think we're doing? I'm conducting a fan's campaign by refusing to pay into any premier league clubs and we've just walked in behind Kate Hoey as we don't have any tickets." But once again, it was best if I said nothing, as I really couldn't go another season without getting into Arsenal.

"Sorry," I said, "I just wanted a quick photograph with Gunnersaurus for my son here. I hope you don't mind."

"Well I do as a matter of fact," he replied. "By your accent, you're Everton fans, right?"

"Yes."

"Right, you're going straight back to where you came from! And how the bloody hell did you manage to walk onto the side of the pitch without being stopped?"

He wasn't happy at all, but as he began walking us towards the Everton section, I had to laugh to myself... once again, just like when we were with Kate Hoey, we had that protective armour. This time I felt a bit safer, as we now had the long arm of the law escorting us to our seats. Correction; we didn't even have seats, but this police officer who was still shouting and swearing made sure we did. I knew we were now as safe as houses and getting a personal escort from the Metropolitan Police Force made it even more difficult for me to keep a straight face. I remember thinking; I hope Kate Hoey isn't looking down from the directors' box at all this, or that steward who asked me for the description.

When we arrived at the away section he pointed a finger and said, "Now get back in there and do not enter the pitch again."

"Okay," I said. "We won't."

He then shouted and instructed the stewards to make sure nobody else came onto the pitch. I couldn't believe what had just happened; we found ourselves a couple of great seats and we could now finally relax and enjoy the game. From a personal point of view, I was very pleased that I had finally managed to get into Highbury and I couldn't have done it without the help of Kate Hoey and the Metropolitan Police Force.

I now had twenty-one signed Premier League footballs spread out on top of the kitchen dresser, with just one to go... which proved to be the hardest one of all, as this was no ordinary ball.

Fifteen
The Full Monty

With just one more club to go, I was almost there, which of course meant just one more signed football to take its place on top of the kitchen cupboard to complete my target of all twenty-two Premiership balls. However, the pressure was really mounting and taking its toll. I was feeling absolutely exhausted, having probably bitten off more than I could chew with this protest. I always suspected the last ball would present the biggest challenge of all and just to add to the pressure, this wasn't just another Premiership ball. Of all the twenty-two grounds I was refusing to pay my admission fee into, the very last club just happened to be our nearest and dearest rivals, Liverpool.

I think most people know about the two major football clubs in the city of Liverpool and the great rivalry that exists between them. I just happened to belong to the blue side and being a die-hard Evertonian meant the boys in red were our arch-rivals and certainly not a club I would want to ask anything of. But, because of my protest, all that changed and I could never have imagined in my wildest dreams ever wanting a signed football so much from the team that had caused me the most heartbreak throughout my childhood and well beyond. The plain fact was, I desperately needed to get my hands on the Liverpool ball.

Getting anything from Liverpool on the football field over the years had always been a struggle and gaining entry to the Anfield ground free of charge was going to be equally challenging. I hadn't planned on this being the last ground, but due to a couple of previous failures there, it was unfortunate that it ended up that way. I knew that every club was now probably aware of my campaign and security at Anfield would be well briefed and on the lookout for me.

During the previous season, every turnstile had been heavily policed and there was an extra policeman stationed at the other side for good measure. I even tried their ticket window with the envelopes trick that my old friend Michael taught me, but there were never any envelopes left. So, not for the first time in my life, I had to concede defeat to Liverpool, return home and wait another season.

Every time I glanced at the kitchen cupboard, I was reminded that there were only twenty-one Premiership signed footballs and there wouldn't be twenty-two until I gained free entry into Anfield.

I got some funny looks from my wife when visitors called and asked if I would take them into the kitchen and show them my balls.

"Wow," they would all say, "How did you get those?" but then somebody would always spoil it all by asking why I didn't have the Liverpool ball.

I tried pretending it was in the post and it would be here soon. But of course I knew that wasn't the case and as we weren't playing them until the following season, which was still quite a few months away, I decided to stop showing people my balls. I even started avoiding the kitchen myself, so that I wouldn't have to be reminded of the Liverpool ball. Having one ball missing was now keeping me awake most nights; it was so hard not to keep thinking about it.

Eventually the months passed and that week before the Derby at Anfield was building up into a crescendo of nervous excitement. I'd also been having this recurring dream that I was on the TV's *Children in Need* programme and Terry Wogan was shouting at me, demanding to know how much longer they had to wait for the Liverpool ball.

The night before the match had to be the worst dream of all, though; In fact it was more like a nightmare. I turned up at Anfield and waiting there for me was my dad with my old headmaster, Mr Feeney. They were telling me I wasn't getting in here today because I'd been suspended from school. I told them how really sorry I was and could they not forgive me as it was twenty five years ago and I was grown up now with kids of my own.

Just like that time all those years ago, I was being chased around Anfield again by my dad, but this time my old headmaster was also in pursuit. As I was running, I could see huge posters of myself at every turnstile as well as the reception area and the ticket collection windows. They were everywhere. All the staff and stewards were jeering as I ran past, shouting, "You're not getting in here today, lad, and you won't be getting one of our balls either."

My old friend Michael was running after me too, apologizing for giving them a photograph of me. He said he had to do it because he didn't have a ticket for the match. I was crying as I was running and asking, "How could you do this to me Michael? I thought we were friends…"

If all this wasn't bad enough, the man in the suit, who had collected those twenty complimentary tickets and was responsible for me starting this protest in the first place, had now joined the chase. He was laughing at me and said, "You'll always be remembered as the fan who failed to get all twenty-two Premiership footballs."

Even the big ginger-haired security man from the press lounge at Leeds United was there staring at me and, just like before, he didn't say anything. Standing behind him was the Elvis look-alike from our charity gig, shaking his head, in disapproval. I also ran past the two Irish waitresses I met at Wembley when they were looking after the prawn sandwich brigade. They were shaking their heads as well and said how disappointed they were with me for not getting all the balls. I was crying as I told them I was really sorry that I'd failed and I shouldn't have started this protest in the first place.

I was still crying when I woke up, in a cold sweat. My wife was now also awake.

"Are you alright, Peter?"

"No, I'm bloody not alright," I replied and told her what happened and about me being chased.

"It was just a dream," she said.

"This wasn't like a dream, it seemed real. It was horrible. They were all chasing me; my dad, Mr Feeney and that bastard in the suit who ruined football for me. He was laughing at me and saying I'd never get the Liverpool ball and never get into Anfield."

I told her I couldn't wait another season. "I'll go mad. I need to get into Anfield tomorrow. I've got to get their ball and finish this protest."

She told me to stop worrying as she'd had a brainwave.

"Are you kidding?"

"No, I've had this great idea that I'm sure will sort everything out."

"Thank God for that. What is it?"

She said she was going to get on the phone to Anfield in the morning and simply explain to them that her husband had done a marvellous thing for charity by travelling all over the country and had managed to collect twenty-one Premier league signed footballs and would they mind please sending on a signed ball, so that he could complete the set.

"Once they know you have all the others, they're hardly going to refuse, are they? I don't know why I didn't think of it before," she said. "Now go back to sleep and stop worrying. Everything will be okay in the morning."

"Are you serious?" I asked.

"Yes," she said, "I'll phone them first thing in the morning."

"No, I mean are you winding me up?"

"No. Why? Don't you think it's a good idea?"

"Yeah, it's a brilliant idea," I replied. "What a stroke of genius! Why didn't I think of that? There's me been travelling the length and breadth of the country for the past few seasons risking life and limb by sneaking into the FA cup final as well as the World Cup, jumping over and squeezing into turnstiles, walking through countless receptions, dressing up as a footballer in a track suit, pretending to be a journalist, bunking into press lounges, harassing politicians, obtaining tickets inside envelopes that don't even belong to me, and you've just come up with a brilliant idea where I could have avoided all that pain and suffering... now why the hell didn't I think of that?"

"Well alright; there's no need to be sarcastic. I was only trying to help."

"I appreciate you're only trying to help, but the whole point of this protest was to refuse to pay into any more football matches before I could ask them for a signed ball. How could I ever ask Liverpool to send me their ball if I didn't gain free entry into Anfield?" I explained why I couldn't do that; it would be the equivalent of having my photograph taken with a huge fish that somebody else had caught.

"If I'm to successfully acquire a full set of twenty-two signed Premiership balls and end this protest, I'm going to have to get into Anfield tomorrow without paying. It's as simple as that."

"Okay," she said. "I'm certain you won't have a problem getting in, but just remember what your old friend Michael used to say, positive things happen to positive people. Now can we please go back to sleep and talk about it in the morning?"

After another near sleepless night, I got out of bed on match day feeling very tired and nervous. I couldn't understand why I was so worried; I'd got into every other Premier League club, as well as the FA Cup Final at Wembley. I'd even managed to get away with it in the United States, at the World Cup. So why was I so nervous about this one? Was it because I needed one more ball? Maybe it was because it was the last ground to get into? Or was it simply because it was Liverpool Football Club?

I wasn't sure what it was, but I did know that this really was my very last chance, as I had to end this protest. The children were now older and beginning to ask some really awkward questions like, "How come we never pay to get into any football matches, Dad?" They were also asking why I never went in the kitchen any more and why were there only twenty-one autographed footballs on top of the kitchen cupboard and where was the Liverpool ball?

I was also beginning to sense my wife was becoming a bit fed up with it, too. She told me she didn't believe it was a protest any longer, but more of a personal challenge, possibly even an obsession and also a great excuse for not going into the kitchen. She said if I wanted to expose the many injustices faced by football fans, then fine, but she thought I had more than made my point. I could understand what she was saying, because it didn't seem to make much sense any more and I knew it was nearing its end.

Having tried unsuccessfully the season before, I wasn't sure how my day was going to pan out. With it being a Derby match as well, it was an absolute sell-out, with not a single seat left in the house. Even if you wanted to pay, you couldn't.

I travelled to the match with my old mate, Brendan, a big Liverpool fan and the same Brendan who came to the World Cup with me. The first place I tried was reception, but I was recognized immediately and for the second year running, I was turned away. I had been knocked back from every single gate the previous season and I was now suffering the same fate again. Even the ticket window with the envelopes wasn't having any of it. It was all falling apart right at the very end and I had to accept this protest was about to end in failure.

I had exhausted every avenue and with just ten minutes to kick-off it was then that I took the decision to call time on my protest with the football authorities. I sat down on the kerb with my head in my hands and had to concede yet another defeat to Liverpool Football Club. This one, though, without any question was the hardest defeat of all to take; it even felt worse than getting beaten by them at Wembley. I had failed miserably at the final hurdle and just to rub salt in the wound, it had to be at Anfield as well. I realized I couldn't try again next season, I didn't have it in me; the spark had gone now. And even if I did, they'd only be looking out for me again and I knew I'd just be wasting my time.

I was drained mentally and physically and feeling very deflated as I slowly rose to my feet to begin my journey home. I spotted Brendan who didn't have a ticket and as we began walking along Anfield road, just to wind me up even more, I noticed a steward opening one of the large exit gates.

He appeared to be in a bit of a hurry and was also acting rather suspiciously. I continued watching to see what he was doing as they don't usually open these huge gates until after the match, to let the fans out.

As the steward opened the gate, another man, who was obviously a friend of his, appeared from nowhere and then it dawned on me what he was up to. The steward was obviously doing his mate a favour by letting him in for nothing and I couldn't help thinking how unfair it was of them to let their mates in, but wouldn't let me in. But then a sudden thought rushed through my head and I said to myself, hold on a minute; why am I giving up now, when this steward has opened a gate? If it's good enough for his mate, it's good enough for me.

So I grabbed hold of Brendan's arm. "Come on, quick. This is our last chance, mate," as we both sprinted towards the gate. When we got there the steward stopped us going through and made it abundantly clear that we were not part of this invitation.

"Oh, come on mate," I said. "Please let us in. We don't have any tickets and we really want to see the game."

"Fuck off," he said aggressively, trying to close the gate in our faces.

"Hey, hold on mate, you nearly caught my fingers in the gate there," I said.

"Well let go of the fuckin' gate, then," he replied in a very nasty tone.

As he continued in this offensive manner, Brendan and I immediately stood either side of his mate.

"If we can't come in, then your mate's not coming in either," I said.

"What do you mean?" he asked. "Who do you think you two are?"

"We're not here to argue with you," I replied. "But can I be totally honest with you? I'm carrying out a protest of not paying to get into any more football grounds until we fans get some proper respect and I could really do with your he—"

Before I could finish the sentence, he said,"So it's you is it? You're the one, aye. We've all been warned about you. You're definitely not fuckin' comin' in here today without a ticket. No chance!"

My old mate Michael used to say bad attitude is like a flat tyre... it won't take you far unless you change it and this bloke's attitude was terrible. I know I may have been wrong for trying to bunk in, but if he was honest enough to not let anybody in then I would have respected his decision and walked away. The fact that he was corrupt made me even more determined to get past him, if you know what I mean.

He tried closing the gate on my hand once again.

"Wow," I said, pushing the gate with all my

might against his force. "Aren't you brilliant at your job? Your bosses must be delighted with you, keeping dangerous fans like me out of the ground. I wonder what they would say if they saw you letting in your mates without tickets, though?"

"He does have one."

"Well, if you can show me his ticket, we'll leave right now. If we don't see it, we don't budge, right?"

"I don't have to show you fuckin' anything," he said, pushing all his weight against the gate.

We weren't letting go of the gate though and I wasn't going to back down now. I knew this was my absolute final chance to get into the forbidden land and end this protest successfully. I had been given a glimmer of hope and I wasn't letting go.

"Listen mate," I said, "we're either all coming in through this gate, or nobody goes in, including your mate who doesn't have a ticket, so what's it to be?"

He started to get really angry now, but fortunately for me I was with my mate, Brendan, who could look after himself physically and was equal to any minder. Eyeballing Mussolini and squaring his shoulders, he informed him in an equally aggressive manner that we were also coming in with his mate. End of story.

The dictator couldn't afford to stand there arguing a second longer in case one of the senior stewards noticed what he was up to and even if he wanted to argue with us, this certainly wasn't the time or place. He had absolutely no choice but to let us in and I knew at that point there would soon be twenty-two signed Premiership footballs on top of our kitchen cupboard.

The steward was still swearing as we walked

past him and into Anfield.

I couldn't believe it. I'd done it! I'd refused to pay entry into all twenty-two Premiership football clubs and I was becoming quite emotional as I laughed and even cried. I was absolutely ecstatic and although my screams were smothered by the cheers and jeers of about forty-five thousand football supporters, I was shouting at the top of my voice, "Give the fans Sweet F*** A** will you? It's time you gave us respect!" Although nobody could tell what I was shouting, I didn't mind, as at least I knew I was now ready. The protest may have been over, but the campaign had just begun.

Our Jeggsy and I celebrated long into the night, in our kitchen of course and my wife joined in, obviously delighted that I was able to venture into this room once again. For the next few weeks, whenever anybody called to the house, I couldn't help asking them if they wanted to come into the kitchen and see my balls. All twenty-two of them.

Sixteen
The Fans' Final

With the protest now complete, I just had to work out and decide how I was going to expose the many injustices we football fans had to face. When I first spoke to the journalist who gave me the idea for the protest, I knew I needed an arresting story, one that would capture the imagination of the public and grab their attention, but I had no inkling of how difficult this was going to be. I'd achieved my goal and to prove it I also had twenty-two signed Premiership footballs beautifully displayed in prime position on top of our kitchen cupboards. I loved looking up at them with all their different colours and most satisfying of all was that each one had its own story of how it came to be there. It also gave me a warm feeling to know that they would now be going to help raise money for a very worthy cause. I was also very aware I couldn't possibly have carried out this campaign without the help of so many people and I was very grateful to all our clubs who kindly sent me their signed balls, including the many wonderful people at the gates and stewards who allowed me in and supported me during my protest, as well as those who wouldn't let me in.

It wasn't just about having a load of balls in our kitchen, though; it meant much more than that. To me, every one of those balls represented their clubs' fans and with a sense of togetherness, my kitchen with its wall mounted telephone was to become the nerve centre for uniting us fans in our pursuit of proper respect.

Of course, we would always remain rivals competing against each other and that's what makes football so exciting and entertaining; believe me, I wouldn't want to see it any other way. But at the same time I was also very much aware that if we were ever going to achieve the proper respect we deserved, then we fans had to work together.

I also thought it would be a good idea to demonstrate to people inside as well as outside of football, that we weren't all hooligans. I felt this would strengthen our case and having these signed footballs may be the key to helping us to do just that. Although it may not have been understood by the football authorities, the reality was that none of these footballs would exist if it hadn't been for us fans. I kept telling myself that these people in suits, in their privileged positions, wouldn't even have a job without us.

In fact, they had quite a lot to thank us for and we needed to remind ourselves of this. I don't think we realised how important our contribution to football actually was and if things were ever going to change, we really needed to get our act together and up our game.

I thought that raffling off twenty-two signed Premiership footballs for *Children In Need* would be a step in the right direction and a great opportunity to portray football fans in a better light. Surely after something like that, they were going to have to show us a lot more respect? Well, that's what I foolishly thought.

I was now in the process of setting up a telephone auction, inviting callers to phone in to win the ball of their choice by answering a simple question, with the proceeds going to *Children in Need*. I was also receiving requests from quite a few companies who expressed an interest in sponsorship and once they discovered I had the complete set of twenty-two Premiership balls to auction off, a lot more wanted to be involved.

However, there were still some people who didn't quite understand the significance of these footballs and I was absolutely astonished when one particular company telephoned me and asked if they could buy the lot cheaply so that they could sell them on individually for a nice profit. Seriously, I'm still shaking my head in bewilderment at that one.

It seemed everybody wanted a slice and it all appeared to be going exceptionally well, until I mentioned the protest and how I actually obtained the footballs. Once they heard about my protest of refusing to pay into football matches, almost every one of my potential sponsors suddenly developed cold feet.

I was to soon realise this wasn't just a blip, as one company after the other informed me they could no longer be involved. You often hear about sponsors pulling out of deals with clubs over certain matters and I'd heard people say that some of these companies couldn't really care less about these issues, but would just pull out with the sole aim of gaining more publicity than when they went in. In my case though, I'd failed to even get a sponsor to come in.

I tried explaining that this had been a peaceful protest and the only reason I chose this different and unusual method of refusing to pay into football matches, was to hopefully make it stand out so that people would take notice of the disrespectful way football fans were being treated.

I also explained that football fans were often maligned by hooliganism. I told them we were not all hooligans and there were many fans who wanted to support my charity event for *Children In Need*.

However, they'd made their decision. They no

longer wanted to know and I was left feeling somewhat deflated and once again, left wondering what to do with my balls. I didn't want to just raffle them off, as I knew I wouldn't get the opportunity of collecting them all again and I really wanted to use them to bring the fans together. I had to sit down and think very carefully of my next move. I realised that if I was going to raise the fans' profile as well as raising funds for *Children in Need*, then it was probably best not to go public with my illegal entry into football grounds... at least not for the time being.

I was quite frustrated at having to keep quiet, though. After all, the whole point of this protest had been to expose the many injustices we fans were facing. But I did feel quite encouraged by the people who had supported me during my protest as well as staff at some of the clubs who, even when they found out about my protest, still allowed me to enter their grounds in support of what I was doing. It was this more than anything else that made me realise if I was able to collect twenty-two footballs from twenty-two Premier League clubs, then it should be possible to bring fans from all different clubs together as well.

I thought, instead of kicking off on each other, wouldn't it be great for all of us fans to unite and demonstrate to the authorities that we may have supported different teams, but we were not as divided as they liked to think and were no longer prepared to be ripped off and treated so disrespectfully.

I also suspected the authorities wouldn't want us fans getting together, as that could spell problems for them.

I had an exciting idea that could help bring the fans together... a penalty shoot-out before the FA Cup

Final at Wembley. I contacted the Football Association and suggested that instead of some of the hooligan problems that were overshadowing the game, wouldn't it be nice to see fans portrayed in a better light for a change?

I explained that my proposal was for one fan from each Premier League club to take part in a penalty shoot-out competition before the FA Cup Final at Wembley. If this was successful, I would then ask if they could extend this to fans from every other club. It would celebrate the end of the season and had the potential to be a really big and regular event. Knowing they usually have pre-match entertainment, I couldn't think of a more fitting way for us fans to be rewarded for our continued loyal support. It had all the makings of an exciting and completely different event (instead of the usual celebrities), as well as being a very rare opportunity for the FA to show their appreciation towards the fans.

I explained that each club's fan could wear their team's strip in this fun and friendly contest. It would be a marvellous end to the season whereby fans everywhere came together in celebration of the biggest sporting spectacle in the world. To be perfectly honest, though, I did have some serious reservations once I mentioned that word 'together' as I didn't believe the football authorities would actually want us all to get together.

I knew some fans liked to go into Wembley early on cup final day to soak up the atmosphere. I suggested these early arrivals could watch the start of the penalty shoot-out and even if there were fans who didn't go in until about 2.30pm, they could at least watch the climax and see which team's fan would be the winner. He or she could be presented with a small trophy, with the proceeds, as I'd mentioned, going to *Children in Need*.

I went ahead and contacted every Premier club and was delighted that every single one of them thought it was a great idea. I told them it could even become a regular event to promote the fans in a more positive manner as well as raising money for worthwhile causes. I was thrilled to bits when each club agreed to have their own penalty competition that season to decide which fan they would be sending to Wembley to represent their club. All the clubs responded positively and wished me the best of luck with the FA.

I have to say here that one club in particular was very supportive indeed. Whilst phoning round the premiership clubs, I managed to get through to a lovely lady at Manchester United called Lyn Laffin, who happened to be Sir Alex Ferguson's PA at Old Trafford. She was extremely helpful and very easy to talk to. She listened to what I was proposing and she, too, thought it was a brilliant idea. She took my number and said she would get the Gaffer to phone me later.

When I put the phone down, I said to my wife, "I could have sworn she just said she would get the Gaffer to phone me when he gets back." I must confess that although I had no doubt that this lovely lady meant every word, I didn't really expect to receive the following telephone call a little later.

When a strong Scottish accent asked to speak to Peter Farrell, I said, out of habit, "Who's speaking, please?"

"It's Alex Ferguson. I believe you have a few ideas and from what I've heard, they seem very interesting indeed."

I'd be lying if I said I wasn't shocked. I mean, this type of thing doesn't normally happen, well not to ordinary fans like myself.

There had been one or two minor hooligan problems and I told him my idea was all about bringing the fans together before the FA Cup Final.

He told me he thought it was a brilliant idea and he could imagine everybody at Old Trafford watching it and hoping the Man United supporter won. He really did think it would be quite exciting to watch and asked me what he could do to help.

I told him the violinist and passionate Aston Villa supporter, Nigel Kennedy, was helping me as well, but I was hoping for a big name manager to come on board (and they didn't come any bigger than Fergie himself). He just said "count me in" and was really very supportive.

I went on to explain that Aston Villa were playing Tranmere Rovers in the league cup semi-final second leg at Villa Park the following week and as Man United were playing the winners in the final, I assumed he would be on the TV panel at that match.

"Well, it just so happens I am," he said.

"That's great," I told him, "because we're planning to launch this proposal with a press conference at the Copthorne Hotel in Birmingham and I was wondering if you would be able to come to the hotel before the game?"

He told me he would and was looking forward to meeting me in a couple of weeks. I couldn't really believe the conversation that had just taken place and when I put the phone down and told my wife Alex Ferguson was coming to meet us in the hotel to help launch this event, she couldn't believe it either.

I don't know how many Premier League managers would find time not only to phone you at home, but then also offer to go out of their way to visit you at a hotel as well? It was really very kind of him.

I couldn't wait to tell the FA when they asked me if any of the clubs were interested.

"Are they interested?" I asked. Every single one of them, as well as one of the biggest clubs in the world and their manager, who was going out of his way to help!

My wife and I travelled down to Birmingham the night before the game and we began preparing the conference room in the Copthorne Hotel for the arrival of Sir Alex Ferguson, members of the press and the Alliance and Leicester Building Society, who were considering sponsoring the event. I have to say I found it all quite stressful, but it was also very exciting, though it wasn't something I'd want to take on every week.

The next morning we were up bright and early and a couple of reporters and a photographer arrived at the hotel, obviously more interested in finding out what time Sir Alex Ferguson was due to arrive. Quite a few fans had turned up as well, naturally hoping to get a glimpse of Fergie and possibly meet him in person. After a few more stressful hours, his arrival was imminent and I was now beginning to feel very nervous and was worried that I may have got into something I wasn't sure I could handle. At one stage, I even said to my wife, "It's not too late to just get in the car and drive home, you know." She told me to stop worrying and everything would be okay.

As I paced up and down by the hotel entrance, I could sense the press doubted whether he would be coming at all and one or two of them were telling me not to be too disappointed if he didn't make it, as he had hundreds of these functions to attend.

Disappointed? I thought relieved might be a more appropriate word, because I had by now worried myself into hoping he didn't turn up. That way, I had an excuse not to have to go through with it. I could just apologise to everybody for wasting their time and we could all go home.

More and more people began arriving at the hotel and a lot of them were asking where they could put their names down to take a penalty at Wembley before the FA Cup Final. I tried to explain that the FA hadn't even agreed to our proposal yet.

Each time somebody walked into the hotel, all heads turned in anticipation, but there was still no sign of Fergie. (I was half expecting my mate, Ray, to walk in with the commentator, Martin Tyler). It was getting a bit late and I had made up my mind that he wasn't coming. I went outside on my own; I would have to prepare an apology speech for everybody who had turned up, but I was no longer worried because they would all realise that at least I had tried.

Alone, hands in pockets, I rehearsed my short speech of regret. I could hear myself saying, "I would like to apologise to everybody for wasting your time here today," when suddenly a grand silver car pulled up in style right outside the hotel door. The car door opened and out stepped Sir Alex Ferguson, the most successful manager in the history of football, asking me if I was Peter Farrell.

"Yes," I said and just to break the ice, "are you Alex Ferguson?"

How he laughed. "Aye," he replied.

Oh, my God, I thought, there's definitely no

getting out of this now. "Er... thank you for coming," I said and shook his hand.

"Sorry I'm late," he said, "the traffic in Birmingham seems to be getting worse."

I couldn't help thinking to myself, it must be *Fergie Time*.

"Late? Oh, I didn't realise you were, I was just, um... getting some fresh air. Bit stuffy inside, you know..." If only he'd known I was out there preparing my apology speech.

As we walked into the hotel, I felt I should warn him there were a couple of reporters and photographers waiting in the conference room.

"No problem," he said, very calmly, and I knew this was a stroll in the park for him. He was well used to dealing with a room full of them. I, on the other hand, felt like I was on my way to my execution. When I peeked into the room and saw all these people, along with the journalists and photographers with their lights and lenses pointed towards the table where we would be sitting, I caught my wife's eye. She now looked as scared as I did; no words were necessary. My heart pounded; I really was very much regretting what I'd got myself into, as this really was squeaky bum time.

Alex Ferguson must have sensed my fear and before we walked in he asked me if I was okay. "Are ye a wee bit nervous, mebbe?"

A wee bit? I said, "Can I be totally honest with you, Alex? I have never done anything at all like this before in my life and I'm absolutely, one hundred percent terrified."

He grinned. "Och, that's great. Ye'll come across a lot better and much more natural."

I hadn't the faintest idea what he was going on

about, but I knew he meant well.

"Peter, you know what this event is all about," he said. "Ye've spent a lot of time on this, and ye've prepared well for it, haven't ye?"

"Yes, I suppose I have."

He told me if *he* were to talk about it, he wouldn't be as informed as I was and would therefore struggle to explain it properly, but as I knew this event inside out, he didn't believe I'd have a problem.

"Trust me," he said, "ye'll be fine."

I couldn't take it in at all; I was only getting a pep talk from probably the greatest and most successful manager in the history of football.

"Don't worry," he said, "I'll be sitting right beside ye to deflect some of the attention and, like I said, everything will be fine."

Had this been an afternoon or evening event, I would have downed a couple of stiff drinks just to settle the nerves, but it was still morning and the bar hadn't even opened yet.

"Just remember your objective, Peter, which is to bring fans together instead of showing the hatred and hooliganism that crops up in the game today, and your passion for seeing fans respect one another. When you really believe in something in this life and desperately want to see it fulfilled, you're focused so much on your objective that you find you don't worry as much. Listen, when you first spoke to me, I believed in you and your idea of bringing fans together. That's why I'm here today to support you. And remember, the press are also here today to help and they'll publicise the information for you to promote your event."

He knew exactly what to say and it was certainly working, because I was beginning to feel a lot more at ease and definitely more confident.

He went on to say, "This won't be a problem for you; you should see some of the grillings I have to endure."

We both started laughing. "I know," I grinned, "I have seen some of them."

He was very down to earth and made me feel so relaxed, it was as though I had just been hypnotised and somehow, I now felt I could address the United Nations, Parliament... or even read the ten o'clock news.

Then, of course, it dawned on me; making me feel calm and relaxed in front of these journalists and photographers was nothing new to him, but something he did every single week for a living. Because he was a professional; in fact the best professional in the business and his job, week in, week out, was to get the best out of his players. Funny that, really, because I didn't even realise I needed a manager and yet here I was, getting the top man.

It wasn't until this particular day that I fully understood and appreciated why he was so successful as a manager. He was brilliant at getting the best out of people and he was now doing exactly the same thing to me. It's a bit like watching a singer on TV and thinking they're okay, but then you go and see them perform live in a theatre and realise they actually have enormous talent and really can sing.

Well this was exactly how I felt when I saw him in action, first hand, with me that day. Up until then, and I'm sorry to admit this, but I honestly believed that football managers were paid to chew gum and shout encouragement at a team of guys he'd picked who knew how to play football anyway. But Sir Alex Ferguson made me realise that, in a similar way, although I knew how to talk, I still needed to do it to the best of my ability and that was the reason he had been so successful for so many years. He demonstrated very clearly to me that day what management was really all about.

Sir Alex Ferguson helping me launch the Fans Penalty Shootout at Wembley

My wife happened to comment to me later on the significance of having a manager alongside me that day.

She said, "We would probably have been delighted to get a top footballer to help with the campaign, but would they have been able to inspire so much confidence in you?"

How right she was. At the time, we were looking for a big name. Any one of them would have done, but we didn't fully appreciate the benefits of having a manager on board until we saw him in action.

Walking into that conference room with Sir Alex Ferguson alongside me felt like walking into the Colosseum in full armour with a whole army supporting me. I felt absolutely bullet proof... I'd not just had a shot of Dutch courage, but got to drink the whole bottle.

It was quite difficult to comprehend. It had to be one of the most surreal moments of my life, sitting down next to Alex Ferguson, the manager of Manchester United, probably the biggest football club in the world, after Everton, launching this proposal of a fans' penalty prize competition at Wembley.

One of the reporters began asking a few questions such as, did I believe the FA would grant us our wish to stage this event before the Cup Final?

I answered, "We can only try, and with a few big names on board, you never know."

Then he asked me which team I thought would win it, which broke the ice a little and I said, as diplomatically as I could, that I thought Everton would win, with Man United runners up. Everybody laughed and when I looked at Fergie, he had a big smile on his face.

He then asked Sir Alex why he had decided to get involved and I was absolutely thrilled to hear his reply.

"When Peter contacted our club, we all felt it was a great idea and with a minority of fans spoiling it for the majority of decent, well-behaved fans, I agreed it would be nice for football fans to be seen in a better image than the one portrayed."

The way he spoke to the press and made everything sound so professional was very impressive and something he was obviously very experienced in, but the one quality I personally noticed more than anything else that day, was the respect he genuinely held for football fans. Also, every time he mentioned my name to the press, it sounded as if he had known me for years. Although I had only just met him, he had this ability to make me feel he had known me personally for a long time. I am not a person who is afflicted with delusions of grandeur and have no wish to behave in such a way, but I honestly felt, albeit for a very brief moment in my life, that I was one of his players. The way he spoke about me wasn't patronising, either. He was basically telling it like it was: here is an ordinary football fan, hoping to bring his fellow fans together for what promises to be a magnificent and spectacular event and all for a wonderful cause.

My confidence grew and I could have sat there all day answering questions. Once the press conference was over, we had some photos taken with Sir Alex to help launch our campaign and he then went outside to talk to the fans who had waited patiently to meet him. Nothing seemed to be too much trouble for him.

After the press and photographers had left, my wife, Alex and myself had a cup of tea and a private chat. I was relieved it was all over, but extremely happy with the way it went. He told my wife I had done very well and I thanked him very much and told him I couldn't have done it without him. His presence and timely comments had that special effect I could only have dreamt about. When I thought about it, nobody from the press would have come to a hotel that day to meet Peter Farrell and his wife. I was under no illusions; they came to see Sir Alex Ferguson and to this day, I still can't quite believe that he came and helped us out.

Over our cup of tea, he came up with some very good ideas and suggestions to help make this event work. I then asked him which club he thought would win the penalty shoot-out.

"Och, well, Man United, of course," he said as we all laughed together.

I jokingly said, "I'll try and fix it so we can get the Everton and Man United fans in the final." More laughter. It was magic.

We did not talk exclusively about football and Sir Alex asked my wife and I if we had managed to see much of Birmingham the previous night. My wife told him we went to watch the Daniel Day Lewis film, *In The Name Of The Father*, at a cinema not far from the hotel and he said he was planning to watch it himself with his wife. He must have spent a good hour with us in the hotel and seemed in no rush to leave. I imagine he must receive numerous requests from all kinds of people for many different reasons, but I felt he genuinely wanted to help launch this event and clearly demonstrated to me his sincere respect for the fans.

Looking back now, I can think of a lot of other managers who could have done a similar job of talking with ease to the press and bringing the best out of people, but the fact of the matter was that no other manager had telephoned my house offering their help and I knew how very lucky I was to get the best manager, anyway.

It was now time for us all to make our way up to Villa Park, as Sir Alex was on the TV panel to be a pundit at the match between Aston Villa and Tranmere Rovers in the semi-final of the League Cup and as I mentioned, Man United were waiting to play the winners in the final. We had an appointment with the celebrated violinist and fanatical Aston Villa fan, Nigel Kennedy, as well as the Villa Chairman, Doug Ellis. We said our goodbyes and Sir Alex wished us the best of luck with our proposal.

Nigel Kennedy gave us a very warm welcome at Villa Park and said he thought my idea of a fans' penalty shoot-out before the FA Cup Final was brilliant and, naturally, he said he thought the Aston Villa fan would win.

I couldn't resist the temptation of saying, "Well, Nigel, with you being a violinist we'll fiddle it and get the Everton and Villa fans in the final."

Nigel treated me to his enthusiastic trade mark laugh. My wife just looked at me, shaking her head.

Although we were very grateful for Nigel Kennedy's hospitality, I had to tell him that, coming from Merseyside, we would be supporting Tranmere Rovers today. My wife pointed up to the TV screen where Fergie was talking about this match.

"Isn't it funny?" she said, "We were only sitting down having a cup of tea with him half an hour ago."

She was right, it did seem strange. In fact, everything about that day had a rare feel to it, because we were now talking to the Chairman of Aston Villa, (Deadly) Doug Ellis, who was telling my wife and I that he used to play football in the Ellesmere Port league, not far from our house. A lot of people will already know that he got the nickname 'Deadly' for sacking so many Villa managers over the years. And just to add to this rather surreal day, we got to meet Nigel Kennedy's dog. His name? Deadly... what else?

With Deadly Doug Ellis, who didn't appear deadly at all

After the game, Nigel was ecstatic as Villa beat Tranmere on penalties. It was heart breaking for Rovers, but they acquitted themselves very well and almost won.

In the weeks that followed, I was in constant talks with all the other Premier League clubs and I think my wife was getting a bit tired of hearing me telling them all it would be great if Everton and their particular team reached the final.

I went back to Aston Villa a few more times after that and kept in touch with Nigel Kennedy. He was just as you see him on TV, very laid back and with a very dry sense of humour. On one occasion, Roy Wood, the singer with Wizzard and the hit song '*I Wish it Could be Christmas Every Day*' was there with his daughter. I was also with my daughter and I was pleased when Nigel introduced me to my musical equivalent to Alan Ball, but instead of wearing white boots like my old football hero, Roy Wood was renowned for his long wigs and brightly coloured face make-up.

Although I never got the chance to speak to Alan Ball nor get his autograph, at least I was now meeting my musical hero in the flesh. Nigel told me that although Roy Wood was a Birmingham fan, his daughter preferred their rivals, Aston Villa, a bit like my daughter supporting our great rivals, Liverpool.

Frank Sinatra getting in the way of Me and Nigel Kennedy

I told Nigel that the very first record I ever bought just happened to be Wizzard's *See my Baby Jive*, which I bought in 1973, during my school lunch hour. Nigel told me Roy would be honoured and quite pleased to hear this.

"Oh great," I said. So I turned to Roy Wood, "I

know you may have heard this before, Roy, but have a guess what was the very first record I ever bought?"

"I don't know," he replied, looking like he had indeed heard this a thousand times before.

"Well, it was *See My Baby Jive*," I beamed, feeling all made up with myself, though quite unprepared for the uncomfortable silence that followed.

I'm really not sure what I was expecting, but I thought he might possibly give me a big hug and thank me. After all, I did risk getting back to school late after lunch. But there was no hug, big or otherwise. Fair enough, if he preferred to just shake my hand and thank me...I did run all the way to McKenzies record shop in New Ferry and back. But there was no handshake either. I glanced towards Nigel, but he was now looking the other way. I would have accepted anything from Roy now; a smile, a slight nod of the head… surely missing my dinner and helping him get to number one in the pop charts was worth some kind of acknowledgement? But there was nothing. Zilch. I glanced over at Nigel once again, who was now looking at me and laughing his head off.

"Sorry," he said. "I couldn't resist that."

"Bloody hell, what was all that about? "

Nigel Kennedy was in stitches as he told me that Roy Wood happened to be one of the shyest people he'd ever known and he hardly ever spoke to people he didn't know. I'd been set up, hook line and sinker, but I could see the joke and it's something I would definitely do myself.

Strangely enough, I read an article a few years later in which Roy Wood revealed his big secret, that in private he was actually a very shy man and very self-conscious when attending social events. The performer was left in the dressing room with the wild hair and makeup; Mr Roy Wood, the family man, was a very different person.

This made me realise that we can often misjudge people who, for whatever reasons, don't meet all our expectations. I mean if Nigel hadn't mentioned Roy's reticence, I may well have wrongly assumed he was just being rude.

In this article, he was talking about performing. He said it was a weird thing; he had to assume a persona when he was leaping about on the stage in Wizzard; he was a very different person to who he really was. As he put it, 'It's a bit Jekyll & Hyde.'

I know that Roy Wood is not alone in this respect; it appears to be the case with a lot of artists who attract massive media attention when they are performing, but away from the spotlights are surprisingly quiet and reserved. I've heard of people being disappointed when meeting nice, ordinary looking Vincent Furnier, expecting to see his outrageous alter-ego, Alice Cooper, which I imagine was similar to me meeting Roy Wood, who was just another dad, spending the afternoon with his daughter at a football match.

It was the same when Alan Ball drove away and I missed out on his autograph all those years ago. My dad told me then not to worry as he was only Alan Ball when he was wearing his famous white boots. Once he got changed he was just a normal man again on his way home to his family.

Quite often, we build heroes in our own minds, expecting them to be the performer we see on TV and when we meet them and they're not, we can feel let down and disappointed, which is probably why people say, you should never meet your heroes.

And on the other side of the coin, before I wrote to the Football Association, I never really had Sir Alex Ferguson or Nigel Kennedy down as two of my heroes, but I have to say, I will never forget these two genuine people who showed me they really do have the utmost respect for the fans and for that reason, if no other, they will forever be heroes of mine.

Oh, and you, Roy... you're still my hero as well.

Seventeen
Losing my Balls

I was advised and warned by so many different people before approaching the FA to make sure that everything was properly prepared, as their track record of rewarding fans wasn't the best.

This penalty shoot-out idea took up a great deal of time and was probably the busiest period of my whole life. I was talking to anyone who would listen, hoping to gain as much support as possible. I was delighted with all the football clubs, who really liked the idea of their fan taking a penalty before the biggest showpiece of the season. And now, thanks to Sir Alex Ferguson and Nigel Kennedy helping me to launch this campaign publicly in Birmingham, there was suddenly a strong commercial interest once again. It was beginning to capture everyone's imagination. I just hoped the FA would see it in the same light and if it was a success, it could become a regular event every year before the final.

Sir Alex Ferguson, was always on hand to help the fans

I was constantly on the phone and talking to more and more companies who were now expressing their wish to get involved as potential sponsors. When we launched this event, I had to give out my phone number and that meant I was getting calls from all and sundry, far and wide. The phone in our house never stopped ringing and I found it quite amusing when dozens of fans from different clubs were phoning and asking my wife how they could be chosen to take their team's penalty. She just handed me the phone, giving me all kinds of funny looks. It was a good job PPI's hadn't surfaced yet or that would have sent her right over the top, but to be fair, she was very supportive.

Most of these conversations were along the same lines except for one different call I received, which you could say was very much out of the ordinary and seemed a little strange. It was from a man who said he wanted to speak to the person hoping to bring the fans together before the Cup Final.

"Yes, you're through to that person," I said. "Who's speaking please?"

"Look," he replied, "can I be perfectly honest with you? You don't really need to know my name, but I have an idea that may just help you get your Penalty Prize competition granted with the FA."

I was all ears. "Oh, really?"

"First of all, I want to tell you I think your idea is brilliant, having a supporter from every club taking a penalty in their team's kit, before the FA Cup Final. It's a fantastic idea; I can't understand why nobody has ever thought of anything like this before."

"Thank you," I said.

He was very polite and friendly as well as sounding quite professional, possibly somebody working within football, maybe journalism... I wasn't quite sure what, but I was certainly interested in what he had to say.

"Can I tell you something else as well?" he continued, "And I mean this with the greatest respect. I'm sorry to be so pessimistic, but I'm one hundred and ten per cent certain the FA will most certainly not allow this event to take place."

"Wow! That's one hell of a statement you've just come out with," I told him. I wondered at this stage whether to just put the phone down, as I wondered if he was a crank.

"Look, mate," I said, "I don't know who you are, but the way things are going at the moment and with the high profile people we now have involved, it's actually looking very promising to tell you the truth, so..." but then, and I don't know why, something suddenly stopped me in my tracks and I thought to myself, hold on, don't put the phone down yet. How could this complete stranger be so sure that the FA would refuse my request? If I was doing something wrong here, I needed to know what it was, and besides, I was now very curious about what he had to say and maybe he wasn't a nutcase at all.

"Are you listening carefully?" he asked.

I assured him he had my undivided attention and that I was also sitting comfortably.

"Good," he said, "then I shall begin." With that, I detected a little laugh.

"I've seen you in the papers, photographed with a few celebrities, including Alex Ferguson and each time I read your story, it says that you are hoping the FA will go ahead with your idea and allow this magnificent event to take place."

"What's wrong with that?"

"Now, I'm certain the FA do indeed think it would be a magnificent event, as well as being a brilliant idea, but you've overlooked one very important factor here and this is where you've made your big mistake."

"I don't understand," I said. "Is there a problem, then?"

"Yes; a very big problem."

"And what's that?" I asked, mystified.

"It was your idea and not theirs."

I couldn't see what was wrong with that, but had no doubt he was about to enlighten me.

He did.

"Can you imagine the press and everybody else asking the FA why they've never let the fans do anything like this before and why didn't they think about doing it, or something similar, for the fans?"

Even if I could have thought of a reply, he gave me no time to answer.

"Believe me," he continued, "I know how the FA work; they could never leave themselves open to any unwelcome criticism, if you understand what I mean."

My failure to respond must have conveyed to him that I didn't... quite.

"Well, because you have now gone public with it, you've actually put them in an embarrassing situation and they will have to justify their reasons for never doing anything like this for the fans themselves. And the easiest and safest way of doing that would be to decline your proposal, by explaining that they couldn't possibly fit something like this into such a very busy day. So, in a way, what they're saying is, we have already thought of doing something like this for the fans, but unfortunately, we just wouldn't have the time." He added, "You may not have meant to, but you've opened up a real can of worms here for the FA and they're going to have to deal with it as best they can."

"What about all those silly little events they have before the final, with all those so-called celebrities playing five aside and the like, then?" I asked.

"Well, they've come up with those ideas themselves and without anybody putting pressure on them, haven't they?"

I hadn't thought of it like that and it had never been my intention to cause embarrassment to anyone.

"But won't all the publicity help with my request? I asked. "Won't they feel like they will have to do it, especially with some big names involved?"

"No. If anything, you're damaging your chances even more and just putting them in an awkward position, which they will have to get out of and, believe me, they will."

He hadn't finished yet. "Now, if you had phoned them up first and had an informal chat with one of their organisers and diplomatically let them believe it was their idea, they would definitely have gone ahead with it, I'm sure of that. The FA would have come out smelling of roses and everybody would have said what a great idea and a lovely thoughtful gesture that was from the FA. Unfortunately, that's not how it looks and although you never meant it, what you are actually doing is criticising the FA and complaining that fans should be more involved, as if the FA have never included or considered them. That's why your proposal will definitely and without question be rejected. Otherwise, they would be shooting themselves in the foot and admitting they've never really thought about the fans."

I was beginning to understand what he was saying. He was right, because if they agreed to it now, people would question why they didn't do it before. It would certainly be a lot easier for them to explain that they didn't have the time to stage such an event. And If I'm being really honest, I always had my doubts and deep down never believed they would ever allow such an event to take place, but not for the reasons he had just spelled out to me. I was always of the opinion that the FA would never in a million years want to see us fans unite in case we ever stood up to them and complained about the many injustices dished out to us. I always believed it was in their interests to keep us apart and see us kicking off on each other, instead of kicking off on them.

I said to my mystery caller, "Maybe they don't want to see us fans together at Wembley? They may see it as a threat and the start of a fans' revolution."

"Maybe," he said, but he seemed very sure of what he was telling me. "You will then receive the customary response from the FA… 'We would like to thank you for your proposal to stage a penalty shoot-out, which we thought was a marvellous idea, like so many other proposals we receive, but regret to inform you we won't be able to fit this in, due to our heavy schedule and other prearranged commitments on a very busy day, etc, etc.'

I could hardly believe what I was listening to and this was another one of those rare occasions in my life when I was speechless and didn't know what to say next.

"Are you still there?"

"Yes, but I don't know what to say." After a

moment's thought, I said "Earlier, you said you may be able to help me with the FA. How can you do that if you don't even believe they will allow this event to take place anyway?"

"Okay," he said, "the situation is as it is. You've set your stall and there's no going back on that now. It's a tough one, but there still may be a chance for you to make amends."

"How am I going to do that?"

"I won't pretend it's going to be easy, but it's probably the only chance you have left. What you need now is to alter the course of events slightly and gain the sympathy vote."

"The sympathy vote?" I still didn't understand.

"Sometimes in this business, you have to use every tool available to get what you want and if that means resorting to other, premeditated actions, then that's what you have to do. At the end of the day, if you're doing it with the right intentions and the proceeds are going to a worthy cause, like your charity, nobody will really know or even mind."

I told him I hadn't the faintest idea what he was talking about.

"Okay. Look, I've seen the pictures of you in the press, photographed with all those Premier League footballs. Seeing all the balls together makes a pretty colourful picture and symbolises everything you're aiming to do, which is to bring fans together, right?"

"Yes, you're absolutely right."

"It's a lovely thought," he said, "and a really nice story, but the sad reality is, nobody's really interested in reading nice stories about people raising money for worthy causes. It's all very local newspaper stuff, if you don't mind me saying so."

"Okay," I said, feeling deflated.

"Your only chance now is to change this into a national story and get some proper exposure, with a bit of sympathy thrown in."

"And how do I do that?"

"You need to lose your balls," he said.

Excuse me...? "I need to lose my balls?" I repeated. "Is that what you just said?"

"Yes, your balls. You need to lose them, or have them stolen. Either way, they need to go missing."

My mind was in turmoil by now.

"Imagine the headlines," he continued. And they would more than likely hit the nationals as well. "FOOTBALL FAN LOSES HIS BALLS. All that hard work you did for charity and it must have taken you ages to collect them."

"What about another headline?" I said. "FAN TAKES HIS EYE OFF THE BALL."

"That's great," he said. "Can you think of any more?"

"Yes," I said, flatly. "Fan gets phone call from a head the ball and someone who's lost their marbles." My wife popped her head round the door to see what the loud laughing was about.

"Yes, that's another good one," he agreed, before realising I was being sarcastic. "Very funny! Seriously, though, we could have an appeal asking whoever took the balls to please return them, as this charity event is suffering. We could put it on Crimewatch. The whole country could be looking for your balls; it would be a massive story and you could stage a press conference appealing for your balls to be handed in. With all the publicity, the FA would now perhaps look favourably on your proposal and go ahead with the penalty shoot-out as it would show them in a really good light. People's perception of the FA would be sky high and it would be a massive PR success story for them. Everyone's a winner."

My mind suddenly cleared.

"What do you think?" he asked.

I told him I thought it was a brilliant idea and we could ask Match of the Day to mention it. I could also put an ad in the all the papers, asking whoever had hold of my balls to please let them go, as I couldn't stand the pain any longer.

"Now you're thinking right," he said. "Can you think of anything else?

"Yeah," I said, decisive now. "I think I'm either on one of those radio phone-in scams, or you seriously need therapy and for your sake, I sincerely hope I'm on the radio, pal."

But he wasn't laughing and I also realized I wasn't on the radio.

"Look," he said, "I know this sounds absolutely mad, but the reality is if you don't do something like this, you won't have your penalty shoot-out at Wembley."

I thanked him for taking the time to phone and said I'd thoroughly enjoyed our quite extraordinary conversation, even though I privately thought he was talking a load of balls, before I wished him all the best and hung up.

When I told my wife, she laughed her head off.

"You don't 'alf speak to some nutters, you do!"

I said to her later, "I wonder if he really was nuts, or did he actually know what he was talking about?"

After waiting quite some time for an answer, I decided to contact the FA and was told over the phone that my proposal had been rejected. I was very disappointed with their decision and asked them why. They told me there was a letter on its way explaining their decision.

"Does this mean we're going to have to settle for the same old celebrities playing at Wembley, having a great old laugh and a big party after the game?" I asked.

I've often wondered why the FA wouldn't allow the fans to have a penalty shoot-out before the FA Cup Final. I believe it could still be a highly entertaining and exciting spectacle to watch, as well as being a perfect opportunity for the FA to show their appreciation to the fans who travel many miles in all kinds of weather and contribute so much of their hard-earned money towards football and the FA itself. I was disappointed with the FA, but not that surprised, as I've never believed we fitted into their plans, anyway.

Maybe they don't want us fans to have a voice… I don't know, but then again there's a lot of things going on at the FA that we'll never know about.

When the letter arrived, I nearly fainted with shock and I couldn't believe what I read:

We would like to thank you for your proposal to stage a penalty shoot-out, which we thought was a marvellous idea, like so many other proposals we receive, but regret to inform you that we will be unable to fit this in, due to our heavy schedule and other prearranged commitments on a very busy day, etc, etc… '

How very strange indeed.

Eighteen
Pay the Penalty

After the disappointing decision from the FA, I knew it was now going to be difficult to generate the same kind of interest that we once had and like many other stories in the press, we were fast becoming yesterday's news. I put the signed footballs up for telephone auction so that fans could phone in for the ball of their choice and as the proceeds were going to *Children in Need* a phone company was kind enough to waive the cost of setting everything up. However, the lack of publicity didn't do it justice and it didn't really do that well... we were probably way past our sell by date. I sent a few balls around the country to various winners but, sadly, it was a bit of a flop and after a few months I still had a number of balls left, which I ended up donating to local charities. Some people told me I should have listened to the person who suggested I lose the balls, but that never sat comfortably with me.

At least I could now perhaps start explaining and telling people about my protest, as I didn't have to worry about it affecting the charity event any more. I was wondering, though, if some people may have thought I was just complaining because the FA wouldn't grant us our day at Wembley and it may have looked more like sour grapes on my part. Because of this and, as on other occasions, I was advised by many people that it was not the best time to publicise my protest. Keeping quiet once again was really starting to annoy me now. It felt so frustrating, because the whole idea of the protest was to make people aware of the disrespectful way we fans were being treated. I felt I was somehow becoming caught up in some public relations exercise and I wasn't happy that I was still unable to reveal details of my protest.

On a more positive side and unlike the FA who wouldn't allow fans to show the world what they could do for charity, at least our clubs appeared interested in staging a penalty shoot out competition. Not being one to accept defeat easily, I thought, who needs the FA anyway? If they didn't want us fans at Wembley, so what? I'll just approach our clubs. My decision was made and I decided to contact my own club, Everton, first.

My new idea was that two fans would be selected through a raffle, costing £1 a ticket, to come onto the pitch at every home game. The first person chosen would take a penalty and the second person would go in goal and try to save it. If the first person scored, they would win £1,000, but if the keeper saved it, he or she would get the money. If the ball went wide or over the bar, nobody would win and there would be a rollover of £2,000 for the next home game, and so on. I suggested any profits could go to the Youth Academy and I would call this competition *Pay the Penalty*.

When I told my dad about it, he was rather dismissive.

"It's a great idea, son," he agreed, "but if I were you I wouldn't hold my breath; the club must get loads of letters like that all the time."

I didn't hear anything for a while and thought no more about it until one day out of the blue (pardon the pun), I received a phone call from the Everton chairman, Bill Kenwright. I have to say I was quite surprised when he phoned my house and told me he had seen my proposal, in which I had also mentioned that I didn't think the fans were getting a fair deal.

"What exactly do you mean by that?" he asked.

"Well, quite frankly," I replied, "instead of just watching the show, we'd like to be part of the show."

Now being a theatre impresario, Bill Kenwright knew all about shows and, having been a former Coronation Street star, I was hoping he might understand my point. He listened to what I had to say and then told me he understood exactly where I was coming from and although he was the Chairman he was also, just like me, a keen Everton fan and was therefore genuinely interested in what any Evertonian had to say.

"Carry on," he said, "I'm all ears."

So I began to tell him about my proposal for *Pay the Penalty* at half time. "The players, officials and all the coaching staff go down into a nice warm dressing room during the half time interval, which only used to last ten minutes," I reminded him. "Today, in the Premiership, it is fifteen minutes and even the prawn sandwich brigade go into their nice warm executive boxes and lounges, whilst we fans have to wait a quarter of an hour, sometimes in the rain and freezing cold with maybe a cup of Bovril and a pie to keep us warm until the teams come back out for the second half." I paused for a couple of seconds, expecting a comment. No response yet.

"Wouldn't it be nice," I continued, "if the fans could be occupied with something during this interval?"

"Yes; go on," he urged.

"Well, I thought of a competition that would involve fans coming onto the hallowed turf and taking a penalty. This could be quite exciting and also keep the fans warm and entertained during the interval with the possibility of winning a few quid as well. At the same time we could raise a few pounds for the club to reinvest in the Youth Academy. Everyone's a winner."

In fairness to Bill Kenwright, he listened to every word I said without interruption and his reply was quite impressive, too.

Taking my eye off the ball with Bill Kenwright

"I'd like to make three points," he said. "First of all, when I first saw your proposal, I thought it was a great idea with a brilliant name, *Pay the Penalty*." Secondly, listening to the way you just put it to me confirms how good this idea really is."

His third point pleased me no end, coming

from the Chairman of Everton Football Club. He told me how important it was to get this kind of feedback from a fan like me on the terrace.

He said, "Sometimes, you know, without actually realising it, you become engaged in so many other activities and find you are trying to please everybody. Do you think the fans will like it?"

"I believe they will love it and it is certainly well worth trying," I replied.

"Okay, then let's give it a go."

I was delighted when he then said he would be interested in watching it himself. The one thing I would like to say about Bill Kenwright is that he is unlike a few other Chairmen in the game today who don't know the first thing about the new clubs they have just taken over, either as toys, or hoping to make a few quid, or even just for some publicity. I don't know how many other Chairmen would telephone one of their fans and spend an hour talking to them about club issues the way he did with me that day. We have spoken several times since and although there have been occasions when we have disagreed with each other, it's never stopped him from listening to what I had to say and I respect him for that. As I say, he is what I would call a true Everton fan.

I was certain *Pay the Penalty* would make the fans feel welcome and more involved and, if it worked at Everton, I was optimistic that other clubs would also take it on board as well. Even though the FA didn't appear interested, I was pleased with the interest shown by all the other clubs.

A few weeks later, somebody from the marketing department telephoned and invited me to Goodison Park to discuss their new half time competition, *Pay the Penalty*. I was so thrilled... they were even calling it *their* new half time competition. What an honour that the club I'd supported all my life was about to stage an event for us ordinary fans at Goodison Park. I had been to cup finals with Everton, worked there as a steward and even been sacked from my post as a steward, but it now felt like they were listening to one of their fans again. *Pay the Penalty* was born and I couldn't wait to tell my dad the news.

The night before this meeting reminded me of going to my first game in that I could hardly sleep, wondering what questions to ask and what they were going to ask me. My wife accompanied me to the meeting and we were introduced to each member of the marketing team.

My wife was listening intently to everything they were saying, but I was finding it difficult to concentrate, as I was looking around the walls in awe at the pictures of my former heroes.

I was now entering nearly every part of the ground, helping to promote PTP, including the posh lounges once again as I had with my old friend, Michael, who showed me the trick with the envelopes. But this time I didn't have to hide from security as I was now totally official. Most of the corporate hospitality lounges served five-course meals at every home game, with as much to drink as you liked, as well as the best seats in the ground. Although the club sold corporate packages to individuals and companies, I noticed there were still a considerable number of free complimentary tickets being dished out to people who didn't appear to be doing anything for the club.

A lot of these people who didn't pay were called guests and believe me, there were plenty of guests at each game. I couldn't for the life of me see what contribution they were making towards the club or football, for that matter. They just happened to be fortunate enough to have the right contacts and move in the right circles. There seemed to be an awful lot of freeloaders who were not even fans, enjoying this first class hospitality. Whilst these so-called important guests were enjoying the red carpet treatment free of charge, the real fans were expected to cough up even more money, without realising they were actually subsidising this complimentary culture, which seemed to me to be very insulting and disrespectful.

I couldn't wait for my dad to see *Pay the Penalty's* inauguration, as he too thought the fans' involvement was well overdue. From a personal point, I saw it as a bit of a tribute to him for all the times he took me to the match when I was a boy and like me, he always believed the fans had been forgotten. As the day drew nearer, it was like waiting for Christmas Eve or even your very first game.

But nothing could have prepared me for what was about to happen next, as my whole family's world collapsed. Suddenly and quite unexpectedly my dad passed away at the age of sixty-seven, without ever being ill. It was without doubt the biggest shock of my life and as a family, we were all devastated. It was also very upsetting for me that he never got to see *Pay the Penalty* at the ground he took me to as a child. I know he would have been delighted to see the real fans being rewarded for their loyal support.

When they staged *Pay the Penalty* for the first time at Goodison Park, I was invited onto the pitch with my son at half time with two former Everton icons,

Graeme Sharp and Neville Southall, who demonstrated how the competition would take place. The PA man announced to the whole stadium how two fans would be selected to come on to the hallowed turf each week to try their luck and it was very exciting to watch.

Graeme Sharp and Neville Southall launching Pay The Penalty

When the first two supporters' names were drawn out of the hat, they gave it a wonderful build up by announcing, "The winning ticket is sitting in the family enclosure... ticket number... and their name is..." It was especially exciting for the two fans, who were also given free match tickets and a signed Everton shirt to wear on the pitch to take part at the next home match. Talk about looking forward to the next game, they mustn't have been able to sleep for two weeks. I congratulated them both, telling them it was about time we fans were a bit more involved.

I then wrote to other clubs, telling them what Everton were doing and hoping to try and link this concept and encourage all clubs around the country to involve their fans. Most of these clubs were showing quite a lot of interest and I was quite proud that my club was leading the way.

The competition really took off and couldn't have gone any better. In fact it was absolutely fabulous and I couldn't believe how many fans wanted the chance to come onto the pitch, hoping to score a penalty at the club they had supported all their lives.

Whenever I spoke to the lucky contestants of PTP, every one of them told me that although it was great to win a thousand pounds, it was nowhere near as good as walking out onto the hallowed turf in front of all those supporters and taking a penalty. This was like having all their dreams come true and something they would remember for the rest of their lives. I was delighted to see their faces as I knew exactly what it meant to them.

One week, the competition was at serious risk of being stopped when a contestant scored a brilliant penalty, but celebrated in a rather controversial way. Naturally, he was delighted at winning a thousand quid, but even more ecstatic at scoring a goal in front of all those fans in the Gwladys Street end. He celebrated by running over to the fans and lifting up a huge banner, emblazoned with the words, *That's how you do it, Mr Owen,*' referring to Michael Owen who had missed a penalty for Liverpool in the premiership the week before.

The banner could be seen on the giant TV screens and most of the ground was laughing and cheering. It was just as if somebody had scored in a real match. It must have been a brilliant feeling for this fan, even better than when I headed the ball back onto the pitch when I worked as a steward on the TV gantry. The Evertonians found this hilarious and the fan and I were later pictured in the local papers, showing off the banner.

However, not everybody found this amusing and on the Monday morning, I was contacted by the marketing department and summoned to the office immediately. When I reached the office I was still laughing and told them that thousands of other blues thought it was great and, after all, was only a bit of fun. I said it was probably one of the greatest days of the young man's life and besides, the ticket sales for *Pay the Penalty* would soar at the next match with all the publicity.

They didn't agree and said they didn't want that kind of publicity, or Liverpool phoning to make a complaint. They said if any more fans celebrated in this way, they would stop the competition immediately. I was disappointed; it was only a bit of fun and it really was fantastic to see the celebrations.

But this sums up for me what is missing from the game today; there doesn't seem to be a sense of fun any more. When players score a great or important goal, you often see them pulling their shirts off with the excitement and then they are disciplined and punished by the referee. What the hell is all that about… a player being punished for celebrating a beautiful moment in football? That's the FA for you. Anyway, I still thought that what this young man did was priceless, and besides, that *was* how it was done, Mr Owen. One of my mates jokingly asked me if I could fix it for him to win so he could take all his clothes off and do a streak.

SPOT ON: Mike Gavin won £1,000 from a Pay the Penalty event pioneered by Peter Farrell at Goodison Park. PK150404penalty-003

Shooter nets a grand total in penalty drama

After a few more weeks in the executive lounges, I became accustomed to seeing famous celebrities. Another thing that was also quite obvious was the absence of these people at the low-key games or in the cold, wet weather, but the genuine fans would still be out there supporting their team, guaranteed.

One week, one of the girls behind the bar recognised me from when I used to go into these lounges with my good friend, Michael. Although it had been a few years ago, I was pleased that she remembered. She told me she thought *Pay the Penalty* was a brilliant idea and even though they were meant to be serving customers, she and the rest of the bar girls couldn't resist quickly running up the stairs to look out onto the pitch and watch the lucky fan taking the penalty. I was naturally delighted to hear this and was heartened that it really did appear to capture the imagination of everybody, as I already knew the Chairman was watching it as well as most of the stadium. Even the away fans were cheering and enjoying it.

But it was what she said next that absolutely knocked me for six. She asked her friend behind the bar if she remembered me and told her I used to come in with Michael.

"Michael?" her friend asked.

"Yes," she replied, "you know, Michael who used to work on security—"

I looked up straight away, interrupting them. "Did you say Michael who used to work on security?"

"Yes," she said, "Michael from security."

Then her friend remembered him. "Oh, I know who you mean now—"

I interrupted once again. "You definitely said security then, didn't you? I didn't realise Michael worked here."

"Well," she said, "he'd actually retired when you used to come in with him, Peter, but he helped out with security here for years.

Now I had gone really cold.

"Are you okay, Peter? Only you look as if you've seen a ghost."

I thought I was hearing things. In my mind I was now thinking, I used to bunk in here every week with a member of security, in fact, he even showed me how to do it, with the envelopes at the ticket window. I could feel myself beginning to shake.

A million things were now racing through my mind at this point... being a member of the security team, he would know how it could be breached by a member of the public and that's how he was able to show me how to get around it. I was standing there whilst the girls were talking and I was absolutely speechless. As anybody who knows me will tell you, this is something that doesn't happen very often.

It was now becoming very clear why everybody always knew Michael and even more obvious, why he never appeared nervous when collecting the envelopes, yet when I used to collect them, I was always shitting myself. No wonder he looked so happy all the time; he must have been laughing his head off, watching me having to go through that ordeal every other week.

As I've mentioned previously, he was a very funny man with a dry-as-dust sense of humour and I could just imagine him now, looking down at me and having another great laugh at my discovering who he really was. When he was alive, he used to make me laugh so much and he was still doing it, although he was no longer here. The other conclusion I drew, which I was now positive about, was that he really did support my protest, as he had often told me, always agreeing that the fans were no longer treated with any respect.

I walked away, laughing and if I'm honest, also crying to myself at what was a private and extremely funny joke.

I got to meet many top players, managers, soap stars, musicians and other so-called celebrities. Some of them I enjoyed meeting more than others. Although the ordinary fans were only a few yards away in a different part of the ground, they seemed to be a world away from where I was now sitting. I was rapidly becoming bored with all this corporate hospitality. I also found I wasn't watching the match any more either, as there were too many other distractions around me.

As a fan, I was used to sitting amongst the bare-chested fanatics on the terraces and now I was languishing and feeling drawn in with the prawn sandwich brigade in the corporate hospitality lounges. There was no real fan atmosphere in these seats and I've even known of famous footballers who have disguised themselves (yes, really) so that they can sit unnoticed amongst the true fans and experience the real atmosphere.

I was getting really fed up with this false, pretentious environment and for me it wasn't like going to the game any more. There was no passion, just the usual lavish meals and drinks; everything seemed so predictably unnatural and a bit too organised for me and I'd had enough of the same boring routine.

I was missing the raw, natural feeling of being at the game... the unorganised, unpredictable outcome of the day. As a fan, you never really knew how your afternoon would pan out and that's what was so exciting about going to the game. These business people in the lounges knew exactly how their day was planned, right down to the last little detail. A lot of them sat with their diaries open, conducting business meetings as well as entertaining clients, and all this took place during the game. They weren't bothered which football team I supported; they were more interested to know what line of business I was in. These people truly believed that the key to happiness was success, instead of the key to success being happiness. (Yes, another one of Michael's sayings). They were not there to watch football; they were there to see and be seen.

Despite all their wealth, they never seemed to be much fun. I was talking to this bloke at the bar one week, when I asked "What does an accountant and a rhinoceros have in common?"

"I don't know," he replied.

"They're both thick skinned, short sighted and charge a lot."

He just looked at me, not amused.

I said, "You're an accountant, aren't you?"

"Yes," he replied."

"Oh, do you know what... I think that's the match starting," I said, as I made my escape.

Having had the privilege of sitting on both sides of the fence, I knew where I preferred to sit and it wasn't with these people in suits, some of whom couldn't even tell you who was playing.

I also began to sense that the marketing department was losing interest in *Pay the Penalty*. I noticed that ticket sales were decreasing as there were not as many ticket sellers, or as much advertising to keep this event alive. I was beginning to suspect they were neglecting it and planning to drop it.

I was always of the opinion, anyway, that the marketing department, who were already paid a salary, were never that interested in this event and it was probably too much of a headache and an extra job they didn't need on top of their already heavy workload, which when you think about it, is quite understandable. I always felt they only went ahead with it because the Chairman, Bill Kenwright, liked it and wanted to help the fans because he was a fan himself.

Of course, I wasn't sure of this, but I knew there were fewer ticket sellers and less advertising and it did look to me as if it was being run down. I telephoned the marketing department and asked them why there was nobody selling any tickets in certain sections of the ground at the previous game and they replied that the figures were down.

"No wonder," I said, "there were loads of fans near me asking why they couldn't buy tickets as they wanted the opportunity, not just to win a thousand pounds, but most importantly to fulfil their dream of coming onto the pitch."

To be quite honest, I'd had enough of chasing people and it was becoming far too much of a responsibility for me. Believe it or not, I was also fed up with sitting in the Directors' box and the corporate hospitality areas. I wasn't at home in these parts of the ground and I missed that special atmosphere you can only find amongst the real fans. Instead of a football match, it was like going to a business meeting every week.

I also realised I was actually becoming part of the complimentary culture myself and, even worse, I was now a fully paid-up member of the prawn sandwich brigade. I had turned from poacher to gamekeeper; the whole idea of me contacting the club with this competition was to get fans more involved, yet I was feeling more and more isolated and alienated from the people I'd always considered the heart and soul of every club. I didn't feel I was a fan any more and this was something that never sat comfortably with me. I wanted to be a fan again.

Pay the Penalty eventually fizzled out at the end of the season and I think it was fair to say that the marketing department and I had similar thoughts: we'd both had enough. I think what it really needed was for somebody to take on the role full time and, in a way, I was relieved. It felt like a massive weight had been lifted from my shoulders.

I was a bit disappointed for the fans, but I

would never forget those faces who had been lucky enough to come onto the pitch and fulfil a lifetime ambition. I knew how much it meant to those supporters,

A few weeks after *Pay the Penalty* ended, I was making my way into the match and as I walked past one of the hospitality lounges on this really wet and cold winter's day, I noticed some of the prawn sandwich brigade about to go in for a hot five-course meal with as much to drink as they wanted. Shaking my head, I couldn't help feeling so sorry for them as I realised how lucky I was to be queuing up in the cold with the real fans once again.

Nineteen
Never Discuss Football, Religion or Politics

If you liked football, music or even comedy, there was no better place to grow up than Merseyside. We even staged the Grand National at Aintree, the greatest horse race on the planet and for us football aficionados, Saturdays were just out of this world. Sunday mornings, however, for me especially, were always a bit of a come down, as this usually meant going to St John's Catholic Church. Just to make absolutely sure we did actually go, the teachers in St John's junior school would often question us on Monday morning. Which priest gave the sermon? What was it about? What colour vestments was he wearing?

The Protestant kids from nearby Grove Street school must have thought we were nutters and by the same token, we left-footers couldn't understand why they didn't attend. I mean, didn't they want to go to heaven when they died?

Another thing I didn't really pay much attention to at the time was that we never really knew many of those kids from Grove Street, even though their school was only about a mile away from ours. We used to pass them sometimes in the street after school and one or two of us knew some of them by name, but that was about it. We never really saw much of them, apart from getting hammered by their football team twice a year, which in a way had the effect of widening the gulf between us even further. So, although unrecognised at the time, this was just the beginning of some of the separate groups that were mapped out for me in my life.

Although still segregated in secondary school,

there was at least the Beb Youth Club at night, where everybody was welcome and a lot of those Protestant boys were to become some of my best mates.

Enjoying the company of my new mates made me wonder why we ever had to be separated in the first place, until I noticed it wasn't just our school, as the youth club was now competing against other youth clubs. However, I didn't mind too much by then, as some of those great football players from Grove Street were now on my side and I remember thinking, thank God religion didn't exist in football.

As I got older, I saw more and more people separating into many other groups and it wasn't only religion, but also politics, class, nationalism... you name it, we mere mortals were all divided into different groups. Although they differed from religion, they divided people in the same way and the cynical side of me was beginning to wonder if it may have been beneficial for certain people in society to deliberately keep it that way.

I was starting to learn more about this divide and rule strategy and although some other people were calling it divide and conquer, it didn't really matter how it was described, its objective always appeared to be the same. The rich and powerful, it seemed, were enjoying the fruits of our labours and just in case we ever complained or, God forbid, decided to get together and object, they would make absolutely certain we remained divided. That way, with us all neatly separated into our many different groups, we couldn't pose any threat to them. Game, set and match.

I began to wonder if the people in charge of football were thinking this as well, and if they were happy for us football fans to kick off on each other, rather than kicking off on them, as I was becoming more aware of the religious bigotry, the cruel racism and even the bitter hatred and rivalry that existed amongst certain sections of my fellow fans. However sad and upsetting this was, the most troubling aspect for me was that the people in charge were allowing this to happen.

They say you should never discuss football, religion and politics in public, but it's a lot more difficult than you think to go through life without discussing one, if not all of these subjects.

Working on oil rigs off Aberdeen, I've made many great friends from Scotland and I think everybody is aware of the religious issues still prevalent in football north of the border. It's never bothered me, though, which religious side other people belong to and it's something I've never tried to hide. Although I come from a catholic background, I have far too much respect for my mates who support Rangers to ever dismiss them; my respect for them as football fans will always remain equal. I would never attempt or even contemplate interfering with a few hundred years of history of this religious divide, but I would love nothing more than the fans from both Celtic and Rangers to tell the football authorities, 'We may be divided, but we won't be disrespected.'

I suppose there will always be a connection with football, religion and politics. When we were growing up, my mates and I (apart from the odd one or two who couldn't understand what Thatcher was doing to the people of Merseyside) saw ourselves as left wing revolutionaries. We always supported the underdog, the working class as well as the unions and especially the miners' strike in their battle to keep their jobs in the eighties. In our local pub, The Letters, in New Ferry, we staged many different events and collections. Regulars did the same in Luke Lees in nearby Rock Ferry. Incidentally, Rock Ferry happens to be the name of the brilliant singer Duffy's album; her dad comes from there. My mates and I were very much aware of the goings-on in politics, unlike today, when there appears to be a very different agenda and quite an effective and deliberate tactic from the rich establishment, aimed at side-tracking today's generation with the emphasis on race and immigration issues.

With the late Mo Mowlam at her book signing. A lady who knew how to bring people together.

Whether it's football, religion or politics, people will always be divided and that's the way the rich establishment love it. They wouldn't want it any other way as they have had their fingers burnt on too many occasions in history, when ordinary people have stood together and literally changed governments.

Talking of governments, a few years ago I took Tom and his mate, Dave, to watch a match at the Liberty Stadium, Swansea. Inside the ground, we bumped into the former Labour Party leader, Neil Kinnock, who almost beat Margaret Thatcher into government.

Now, for somebody who has always voted Labour and believed in their philosophy of 'the redistribution of wealth' I was particularly pleased to meet him. In fact, being a lot more grown up and with children of my own, you could say I was happier to meet him than a few famous footballers. I had a nice conversation with him and to be fair, he was a very friendly and charismatic kind of person who came across as the gentleman I expected, unlike some other well-known people, who have fallen far short of my expectations, shall we say.

With Neil Kinnock, known as
'The greatest Prime Minister we never had.'

I told Tom and Dave that he was once a left winger, who drifted into the centre later on in his career. Neil Kinnock was quite amused when the boys asked me which team he played for. I had to explain that I wasn't referring to football, but politics, which must have gone right over their heads, bless 'em.

As the boys made their escape to the refreshment bar, he said he doubted very much whether the two young lads would remember him.

"Even if they did," I replied, "you may have already noticed that young people today don't seem to have much interest in politics.

"I have," he said.

"Well, the same thing is about to happen in football, with kids no longer coming through the turnstiles. This will have devastating consequences on the future of football. I mean, when they grow up, who can blame them if they have no interest in the game whatsoever? And if that is the case, they won't be taking their kids, either."

He was listening with interest and while I had his attention, I told him I thought clubs should let children in free of charge, or at the very least for a nominal fee.

"It's hardly rocket science that these kids will then grow up into supporters of the clubs for the rest of their lives. But when we have clubs who know they can fill their stadiums at every game, they obviously feel they don't have to allow our kids to sit in these seats cheaply. Are they not bothered about our kids not being able to afford these very expensive prices in football today? And it seems to me there's far too much greed now, squeezing as much money as possible out of each fan and they actually couldn't care less about football or its future."

I knew he had probably heard it said a million times before, but I mentioned how pleased I was to meet 'the greatest prime minister we never had' referring, of course, to how he almost beat Thatcher and the conservatives in the General Election.

I couldn't resist telling him the story of my wife's Nan, Lil, who was given a lift down to the polling station together with a few other elderly people, by the local Conservatives at the General Election. These Tories were counting on every single vote in a Labour held territory and made sure they took as many people down to vote as possible. Trouble was, when Lil and all her friends got to the polling station, they all voted Labour. Still tickles me, that one. It certainly amused Neil Kinnock.

On the way home in the car, Tom and Dave asked me who exactly this Neil Kinnock bloke was and I told them, amongst many other things, how he was involved in a very well publicised dispute with members of the Liverpool labour party known as the Militant Tendency in the early 1980s. Coming from that part of the world, I tried explaining to the boys what went on.

"The deputy leader of Liverpool Council at that time was Derek Hatton, a big Evertonian like myself, who clashed with Neil Kinnock. On 14 June 1985, Liverpool Council made world headline news when they passed an illegal budget in which spending exceeded income, demanding that the deficit be made up by Thatcher's government down in London. Liverpool City Council adopted the slogan "Better to break the law than break the poor."

I told the boys that Neil Kinnock's argument with Derek Hatton only served to divide the Labour

Party and played right into the hands of Maggie Thatcher and her cronies.

"We working class people had washed our dirty linen in public once again and this was one of the reasons we lost out to the Conservatives and Margaret Thatcher's controversial regime."

"How do you mean?"

"Well, these were very difficult times on Merseyside and it was no secret that, with not that many people voting Conservative from the Liverpool area, it felt like Thatcher was out to punish the people of Merseyside, and even more so if you belonged to a trade union. I mean, I can remember wondering at that time if I was ever going to work again."

I told them about Ricky Tomlinson, who appears as Jim Royle in the very funny TV series, *The Royle Family*.

"He was actually jailed with his colleagues in the early seventies for protesting and fighting for their union beliefs. Yes... I did say the early seventies and not the seventeenth century."

There was no stopping me now. "Our famous shipyard, Cammell Laird, like so many other sources of industry, was hit very hard and Merseyside was in deep decline. We were told by the Conservative Cabinet Minister, Norman Tebbit, that if we wanted work, we should get on our bikes and travel to find it. What a source of inspiration he was, with his vast wealth, telling us to leave our families to find work, when we already had jobs... correction: we did, before they starting closing everything down."

Also at that time the Toxteth riots were wreaking havoc and it appeared that Thatcher and her government had washed their hands of Merseyside.

"A lot of us honestly didn't feel we were part of the UK any more," I told the boys, "and we felt more as if we lived in the People's Republic of Merseyside. Football fans around the country would jokingly mock us with unemployment being so high on Merseyside and hardly any work around, these really were bleak times, you know. But as is so often the case, in the face of adversity, our people of Merseyside refused to lie down and as they have done so often in the past, they fought back. Consequently, the response of our two football teams, Everton and Liverpool, was to dominate English football throughout the eighties."

In fact, they still mock us today with songs like, 'We pay your benefits.' They must be joking; people on benefits were well and truly priced out of going to the game many years ago.

I went on to explain that the city of Liverpool may have been feeling the pain of Margaret Thatcher's premiership, but the rest of the country was now suffering at the hands of the city's two football teams. In a way, it spoke volumes about the heart and soul of our people. Wembley during the eighties was like a second home to the scousers, and local barmen in pubs around Wembley would ask, 'The usual, Sir?'

"So you see, economically and politically, this was probably the worst period on Merseyside since the blitz, yet in a strange contrast, they were probably the most successful times ever for our area's football fans."

I also mentioned that the music coming out of Merseyside was also shaking the world once again with bands like Frankie Goes To Hollywood; my old school mate, Pete Burns's, group Dead or Alive; Icicle Works; China Crisis; OMD; The Lightning Seeds (*Three Lions* with Baddiel and Skinner); Flock of Seagulls; Pete

Wylie; Echo and the Bunnymen; The Teardrop Explodes; The Christians; The Lotus Eaters; The La's; Rick Astley; Sonia and so many more up and coming artists.

"There were also two lovely down to earth people making worldwide news, who personally helped me during one or two charity football matches," I said. "Called Graham and Jan Walton, they were proudly showing off their six daughters, known as the Waltons... the world's first all-female, surviving sextuplets."

"Mm, yeah," one of the boys muttered from the back seat.

I was now in full flow and my soap box offering continued.

"My old school mate, Paul Usher (who played Barry Grant) along with Ricky Tomlinson and Sue Johnston, was keeping Brookside at the top of the soap opera charts and it was a welcome distraction to help us through these difficult times..."

I glanced in the mirror and I could see that the boys were fast asleep on this long journey home from Swansea. I smiled to myself as I wondered if they regretted asking me who this Neil Kinnock bloke was.

Twenty
Lest We Forget

Travelling down to London to watch an all Merseyside FA Cup Final with my dad, brothers and a load of mates, draped in blue and red flags would normally be a fantastic occasion. But, this was 1989 and as everybody who made the journey to Wembley that day will testify, there was a sombre sense of absence. In fact, ninety-six fans were absent and no matter how much we wanted things to be okay, it was achingly obvious that they were far from it.

A few weeks earlier, during the semi-final of the FA Cup, the worst football stadium disaster in British history and possibly the biggest cover up this country has ever seen, took place at Hillsborough. Tragically, ninety-six Liverpool fans would never see another football match, or their families, ever again.

On that same day, our Jeggsy and I were at Villa Park, Birmingham, where Everton were playing Norwich in the other semi-final.

As might be expected, Everton fans were listening to their radios and whereas we usually want Liverpool to lose, most of us were actually hoping they would win their semi-final at Hillsborough. Not because we liked seeing Liverpool win, it was so that we could have an all Merseyside FA cup final at Wembley. In the history of the two clubs, this had only ever happened once before, three seasons previously, in 1986 when Liverpool won 3-1, so it was quite understandable for us to want to meet our fierce rivals in the final once again, to take our revenge.

However, it wasn't long into our match that reports began coming through about crowd problems at Hillsborough and we were hearing that some people were seriously injured in Sheffield. When further news came through that some people had died, it was very difficult to understand. Many of us Evertonians were very worried at this stage, as we had friends and even family who were Liverpool fans and in Sheffield that day.

When we heard there were more fatalities, Jeggsy and I just wanted to get home and find out what was going on; our thoughts were no longer to do with football. Although Everton had beaten Norwich in our semi-final and had made it to Wembley, that didn't really matter any more.

We arrived home at Liverpool's Lime Street train station, still unaware of the full extent of what had happened. We knew it was something dreadful by the bank of TV camera crews interviewing fans on the platform as more supporters from both clubs returned home from Birmingham and Sheffield respectively.

When the magnitude of the disaster was revealed, I couldn't believe it. It didn't seem real that these fans had gone out that morning, just like we did, to watch their team play in a football match, but would never come home, or watch another game again. I couldn't take it in at the time and still find it difficult to comprehend even now.

For a long time, I had been aware of the culture of disrespect shown towards football fans and although it was becoming more and more obvious, I don't think any of us were prepared for what was to happen at Hillsborough. When ninety-six of our fellow fans died on that tragic day, they and their companions were treated with the utmost disrespect. Even worse, it continued long after they were no longer here to defend themselves and the unvarnished truth is now known – that they were treated in a disgusting and despicable manner. I've said it countless times and I will say it again… personally speaking, I am still convinced that those responsible for these fatalities thought they could do what they liked because, after all, they were only dealing with football fans.

This was summed up for me in Brian Reade's article in the *Daily Mirror* in which Trevor Hicks, who tragically lost his two daughters at Hillsborough, sensed about ten minutes before kick-off that there were problems in the central pen area of the Leppings Lane, where he knew his daughters were. He noticed an elderly man who 'looked like he was dying stood up.' He shouted at a policeman to 'do something about it' but was ignored. He shouted at another, that 'people are getting crushed' but was told, 'shut your fucking prattle!'

The engineering company boss remembered thinking at the time: 'If I'd had my MD's suit on, you wouldn't be talking to me like that, but because I'm a football fan in jeans you think you can.'

When I read the book *The Beautiful Game* by the journalist, David Conn, I was very surprised to learn about certain other facts that had not been publicly disclosed. David, who did much to help publicise the corrupt cover-up of Hillsborough, revealed quite a lot that I certainly wasn't aware of. For instance, Tottenham Hotspur fans had also been crushed at Hillsborough only eight years previously when their team played Wolves in another semi-final in 1981 and it was only by good fortune that no one died on that occasion.

I also hadn't realised that Sheffield Wednesday

did not even have a safety certificate in place and the FA, who were aware of this, still went ahead and selected Hillsborough. You would have thought, after this first incident, that the FA would have insisted on a safety certificate at Hillsborough, wouldn't you? Could you imagine a tragedy like this ever occurring in the Directors' box? I don't think so.

From a very early age, I was taught to respect people in authority and institutions like the church, politicians, police, the media and even bankers. Because of my love for football, this respectful attitude also extended to the football authorities such as the FA, UEFA and FIFA. Yet I have so much regret and disappointment that segments of every single one of these groups have sadly let me down.

The Football Association have apologised, and it may well be that they are very sincere in their regret, but I personally don't believe an apology is enough. What the FA should be saying is: we would like to demonstrate to you how sorry we are for what happened and just to prove that we mean it, from now on, we are going to treat fans with a lot more respect and, instead of constantly taking them for granted, we will consult with and include them in the decisions we make.

I am sick to death of the football authorities paying lip service to the Supporters' Federation as well as many of our fans groups. Their contempt for us fans is still there for everybody to see, as they continue to dictate many more disrespectful insults, such as moving the FA cup final to the later time of 5.30pm, knowing full well that fans will struggle to get home, as the last train out of London is 8.30pm.

And this is how sorry they are. They must think

we are absolutely stupid and in a way, we must be, for allowing them to treat us this way. If they are the slightest bit sorry, or have any intention of showing fans proper respect, there can only be one form of action.

They should be announcing that the time has arrived for fans to be invited to sit alongside them in a full time capacity. This is the only way to ensure that we are truly respected, properly represented and to feel part of football, instead of always being the victims. I honestly believe this is the very least they can do, but I am not holding my breath.

The football authorities may have taken down the fences after Hillsborough and stopped treating us like animals when they made all-seater stadiums, but do you know what they did then? They put the price of tickets up and by God, did they put them up!

I also learnt from David Conn's book that football clubs in the top two tiers were given £2m each of public money (oh yes, our money) by the government, to develop all-seater stadiums. They then increased ticket prices... and not by a pound or two, but seven-fold. Imagine a match ticket which cost about £6, suddenly increased to around £42 overnight. How did they justify such a scandalous hike? Well, before these seats were installed, we were packed in like sardines to maximize profits, but because they weren't squeezing us in any more, they had to find another way of relieving us of as much money as possible and now they had the perfect excuse to charge us top dollar. Some clubs tried to justify the increase on pricing out the hooligans. The only people I could see being priced out were the very young, the elderly and, of course, the poorer people in society unable to afford these extortionate price increases.

You have to hand it to them, though; they get a nice hand-out from the government, a top-up from the fans; a windfall from the sponsors and now with an incredible jackpot of £5.14 billion from television… it's as good or better than being in banking.

When my grandchildren ask me what happened that day, I will explain how fans were locked up in cages, like animals, in the Leppings Lane, with virtually no means of escaping the annihilating crush resulting from a catalogue of errors due to the total incompetence of members of the Football Association, Sheffield Wednesday Football Club and the South Yorkshire police force. Not to mention the despicable lies, cover-ups and unforgivable attempts to tarnish the reputations of innocent, respectable people who desired nothing more that day than to watch a football match.

I certainly won't forget to tell them, either, that South Yorkshire Police tried to blame the Liverpool fans by claiming they forced open a gate to gain entry. It has been proved without any doubt that it was actually a senior police officer who ordered it to be opened.

Yes, our police force, the one authority responsible for enforcing the law, yet at times over the years have themselves been caught up in so many miscarriages of justice in the form of corruption, police brutality and numerous other dishonest cover-ups. It's a wonder we have still have any trust in them at all.

Please don't misunderstand me here; I am more than aware there are decent, honest police officers who are genuinely trying to protect the public and striving to prevent crime. But there exists a section who unfortunately believes that, once they don those official uniforms, they are not only the law, but also above the law.

I know it's not just this country that has the bad apples. I'm not sure why, but I always think back to when police in the United States were caught on camera savagely beating a black man, the late Rodney King. Apart from this poor man's horrific ordeal, the incident resonated with me so much because of what Rodney King's lawyer said afterwards... that when his client was lying helpless on the ground being beaten, he instinctively thought to himself that, hopefully, the cops would arrive quickly and rescue him from his terrifying ordeal until, with a fearful sense of foreboding, he realised it was actually the police who were carrying out this vicious, criminal attack. That will always stay in my memory as being one of the most despicable examples of man's inhumanity to man; of literally kicking a person when he is down.

I find a parallel here with what certain members of the South Yorkshire police force did to the victims of Hillsborough and their grieving families, when they were down. In fact, I would go as far as saying that they behaved in a manner even worse than those cowardly American police who kicked the defenceless Rodney King. As callous and shocking as this horrific assault was – and I say this with the greatest respect to Rodney King's family – at least Mr King was still alive. Unlike the innocent victims who died at Hillsborough and no longer had a voice with which to defend themselves.

When you think about the truly abhorrent actions of a so-called responsible police force who altered statements and carried out computer checks on those who had died; who smeared the good names of innocent people as well as intrusively questioning grieving families immediately after identifying their loved ones, you have to wonder just what kind of society allows this kind of behaviour. Certainly not a civilised one.

But they overlooked one very important factor. They seemed to have forgotten that their loving and loyal families were still here, as well as all the other people who knew about the corruption, the dirty lies and massive cover-up that was going on.

I once heard somebody say that a person who does not read a newspaper is uninformed and a person who does, is misinformed. Well this was certainly the case when that filthy so-called newspaper published their disgusting lies about those poor, innocent victims. It was not only an insult to the ninety-six people who died and their heartbroken families, but also to football fans everywhere, who were and still are seen as easy targets.

Another group of people they also didn't care about were the many honest and respectable journalists, who must have felt so let down and embarrassed by certain members of their profession. Fortunately, most of us are all too well aware that the majority of journalists are highly respected professionals who also fought relentlessly for justice in helping to uncover the appalling lies and corrupt behaviour of this questionable newspaper.

These honourable members of the press must feel just as angry as the rest of us at the conduct of so-called professionals who have the nerve to call themselves journalists.

Whilst working in the North Sea, somebody in work once said to me, 'Peter you would still buy the Sun newspaper wouldn't you? I mean you support

Everton, don't you?' The best way I could think of explaining it was to tell him about an article I remembered reading written by Johnny Rotten. The lead singer with the Sex Pistols was expressing his admiration for the people of Liverpool, saying, 'If someone cuts one of you, then you all bleed.' These heartfelt words seemed to sum up exactly how we were all affected on Merseyside, red and blue. Just in case my colleague didn't quite understand my Johnny Rotten analogy, I explained to him that not only was that rag banned from our neck of the woods, I wouldn't urinate on it if it was on fire.

Although our rivalry is well known (and it killed me when I had to sing *You'll Never Walk Alone* that time as my forfeit for charity), I wasn't going to allow anybody to tarnish the reputations of our fellow fans across Stanley Park. I mean, my own two brothers and my daughter support Liverpool and although we may scorn each other on Derby day, deep down, we really do share a unique and special bond.

We must never forget how brutally our fellow fans were handled that day, or the way their distraught families were treated afterwards. The fact that these innocent people supported Liverpool Football Club was a matter of extreme misfortune for those involved because, as I've mentioned, realistically this disaster could have happened to any other clubs' fans. There was certainly a culture of so much disrespect, that we fans had our safety compromised at every single match we went to, which was also sadly apparent when fifty-six of our fellow fans also perished at the Bradford fire disaster.

We should not forget, either, that it would take twenty-three years for the truth to finally come out about Hillsborough – on 12th September 2013 – but it is equally important to remember that this would never have happened, had it not been for the amazing determination of the wonderful families who promised they would never give up on their loved ones and would move heaven and earth to uncover the lies and corruption of the authorities, in their fight for justice.

It was not only important for the families, but also to open the eyes of the general public, so that those who didn't know what to believe could now see the truth for themselves. I never for one second doubted the fans or their devastated families who were treated so contemptibly. Like these special families who had devoted their lives to clearing the names of their loved ones, I was also very gratified and relieved that, at last, everybody knew the truth.

I am delighted to know that schoolchildren will be learning about one of the biggest cover-ups in Britain. I think it's very important that our unfortunate fellow fans are never forgotten, or the contemptible way their grieving families were treated. I also want to see those responsible brought to justice.

When you think about all the other atrocities football fans had to endure over the years from the footballing authorities, it was surely only a matter of time before something like Hillsborough was going to happen. But the sad thing is, this disrespectfulness still continues today. Even with the fences down, there are still those massive psychological barriers in place, which are growing higher every day.

I will certainly not forget to tell my grandchildren, either, how proud I was to witness fans from so many different clubs also paying their respects, as well as two great clubs, who have been arch-rivals for many years, pulling together during that very difficult period in a way that I am never likely to see again.

It was quite strange in a way that one of Liverpool's next fixtures immediately after Hillsborough was to visit Everton at Goodison Park for a league match. Before the game, a delegation of Liverpool fans walked around the pitch parading a banner thanking their neighbours from across Stanley Park. That there wasn't a dry eye in the house is no exaggeration.

If that wasn't strange enough, when Liverpool beat Nottingham Forest in the re-arranged semi-final not long after the tragedy, of all the teams in the whole world waiting to play them in the FA cup final at Wembley it just happened to be Everton... again. I still find that so ironic as they had only ever met once before in the FA cup in over one hundred years, and for them to meet in this particular final was, for me, a perfect tribute to the people of Merseyside who had pulled together magnificently during a very testing time. I believe it was meant to be. I honestly don't think Liverpool could have picked a more fitting opposition than Everton that day as it was an opportunity for all scousers, blue or red, to travel down to dat der London together once more.

I'll never forget watching a TV programme about the tragedy at Hillsborough, when a priest who supported Everton was having a conversation with his friend who supported Liverpool and telling him how great it was to see the city unite during this intensely challenging time. But just ahead of a future derby match, this same priest said to his friend, albeit with the greatest of respect, "Is it okay now for us to hate you lot again?"

I cried my eyes out when I heard him say that and I still become very emotional when I think about the beautiful and respectful context in which it was said, simply because it sums up perfectly the unique rivalry we have on Merseyside.

I have had a couple of moving conversations with the playwright and passionate reds fan, Dave Kirby, who was at Hillsborough. Dave told me the very sad private details of how he was inspired to write a tribute poem called *The Justice Bell*, which are far too personal for me to put into print. Having read his poem many times, I still can't get to the end without filling up. Dave has kindly given me permission to include this exquisite poem as my chosen tribute to those fans who perished and their adoring, wonderful families who have never stopped campaigning for the truth and for justice.

The Justice Bell
A schoolboy holds a leather ball
in a photograph on a bedroom wall.
The bed is made, the curtains drawn
as silence greets the break of dawn.

The dusk gives way to morning light
revealing shades of red and white,
which hang from posters locked in time
of the Liverpool team of 89.

Upon a pale white quilted sheet
a football kit is folded neat
with a yellow scarf trimmed with red
and some football boots beside the bed.

LEST WE FORGET

In hope the room awakes each day
to see the boy who used to play
but once again it wakes alone
for this young boy's not coming home.

Outside, the springtime fills the air,
the smell of life is everywhere.
Violas bloom and tulips grow
while daffodils dance heel to toe.

These should have been such special times
for a boy who'd now be in his prime
but spring forever turned to grey
in the Yorkshire sun, one April day.

The clock was locked on 3.06
as sun shone down upon the pitch
lighting up faces etched in pain
as death descended on Leppings Lane.

Between the bars an arm is raised
a young hand yearning to be saved
grows weak inside this deathly cage.
A boy not barely in his teens
is lost among the dying screams.
A body too frail to fight for breath
is drowned below a sea of death.

His outstretched arm then disappears
to signal thirteen years of tears
as 96 souls of those who fell
await the toll of the justice bell.

GIVE THE FANS SWEET FA

Ever since that disastrous day
a vision often comes my way.
I reach and grab his outstretched arm
then pull him up away from harm.

We both embrace with tear-filled eyes,
I then awake to realise
it's the same old dream I have each week
as I quietly cry myself to sleep.

On April the 15th every year
when all is calm and skies are clear,
beneath a glowing Yorkshire moon
a lone scots piper plays a tune.

The tune rings out the justice cause
then blows due west across the moors.
It passes by the eternal flame
then engulfs a young boy's picture frame.
amidst a human tidal wave,

His room is as it was that day,
for 26 years it's stayed that way
untouched and frozen forever in time
since that tragic day in 89.

And as it plays its haunting sound
tears are heard from miles around.
They're tears from families of those who fell
awaiting the toll of the justice bell.

© Dave Kirby 2002

Twenty-one
The Twelfth Man

Eric Cantona once famously said: 'You can change your wife, your politics and even your religion... but you can never change your favourite football team' (except for our kid, when he changed from Everton to Liverpool in 1971). If you're fortunate enough to own your own club, you can change the colour of your team's strip, the name of the stadium if you fancy and even the club's name.

In fact, you can change almost everything in this life except, as Eric said, the team you support and unfortunately for us fans, that is where the problem lies. This kind of loyalty is an absolutely incredible circumstance and the people making money out of this exceptional, heaven-sent windfall must be kneeling down to thank the Lord every time they hear the *Match of the Day* theme tune.

Ooh aah Cantona...

Yes, we fans are quite unique but unfortunately, this is our biggest downfall. The clubs know only too well that, unlike customers of other businesses, we won't switch our allegiances and take our custom elsewhere. For this reason, they have us over a barrel; it's game, set and match.

It would appear that they are in a brilliant position, reaping the benefits and taking advantage of our sincere love for the beautiful game and you can't really argue with this, because they are. However, in this life there is nearly always a flip side and unfortunately for them, just like the oil in the North Sea, which will eventually dry up, their harvest is also coming to an end.

'Oh, really?' you may ask. 'On what basis?'

The very sad reality is that with hardly any children coming through the turnstiles, there won't be any proper supporters in twenty years' time. I mean, where will the passion be? You can't just become a football fan overnight as an adult; it doesn't work like that. It took years of heartbreak, ecstasy and all those emotions in between for me to evolve into a real, passionate football supporter. As a kid, I was actually there on the terraces, serving my time and going to the match regularly increased my passion tenfold. I was hooked and they had me for life. Well they would have if they hadn't spoilt it.

If we don't let today's kids in to see regular live football and their only experience of the game comes from watching it on TV, then the sad reality is, they won't turn out to be passionate fans. Day-trippers and tourists are what we will be left with. If we allow this trend to continue, football's bubble really is about to go pop. For the future of the beautiful game, we cannot stand by and let this happen.

The most annoying thing of all is that whereas the problem with my job in the North Sea is sadly unavoidable, the problem with football can be rectified. There is a solution. It won't, however, be easy as the people enjoying these benefits simply won't want to listen... well, why would they when they're making an absolute fortune and a lot of them don't even care about the future of our game? The only people who can stop football's well running dry are those who genuinely love the game and that is why we fans must stand together and make it absolutely clear that we want our game back.

But I'm not just talking about the fans here, I'm also appealing to the players, managers, match-day officials and journalists, all of whom must stand alongside us fans and everybody else who wants to see a future in football. We can do it, but we must work together and we must act now.

When teams reach the FA Cup final, they receive 25,000 tickets each. This number is never nearly enough; with the FA keeping back about 40,000. Ironically, though, quite a large proportion of these 40,000 tickets eventually find their way back to the fans, but via ticket touts who are re-selling them on the black market at extortionate prices. Every season, we have the annual mass bellyaching about this huge insult to fans, but as soon as the final is over, it's all forgotten about once again and because the football authorities have got away with it, they think they can repeat this insult the following season. Unsurprisingly, they do... and why? Forgive my parrot-like repetition, but it's because we, the fans, allow them to get away with it.

Then there are the privileged guests sitting

down at Wembley in the warm spring sunshine, watching cup finals and other big games, but at the smaller matches and throughout the cold, wet winter months, these people are nowhere to be seen. The real fans are always there, whatever the weather, which is probably why they're called real fans.

It doesn't have to be this way, though, and we fans could and should put a stop to this selfish behaviour once and for all.

When Liverpool played Chelsea in the FA Cup final in 2012, the FA decided to move the kick-off to 5.15pm. A massive number of fans voiced their concerns, mainly that of being unable to make the last train from London to Liverpool which was due to depart about 8.30 pm.

Their manager at the time, Kenny Dalglish, said: 'I won't support anyone other than the fans. It would be better if they were given greater consideration when the FA are looking at the kick-off time. I don't think anyone's got a voice for them and, let's be honest, it wouldn't be such a special occasion if the fans were not there, would it? Sometimes the problem comes when fans are taken for granted. I don't mean just the fans at this club but fans everywhere. If people have a complaint I'd advise them to complain to the relevant authorities. It hasn't been made easy for them by any means but I'm sure they will get there.'

I know Kenny Dalglish meant every word that he said and although our clubs are great rivals, I respect him for having the courtesy as well as the courage to speak up for the fans.

There are many fans groups as well as the Football Supporters' Federation who are trying their best to fight for fans' rights, but it wasn't until that day when Kenny Dalglish spoke up that I fully realised just how much help we fans actually need. You see, when you think about it, if they are not going to listen to Kenny Dalglish, one of the most respected people in the world of football, well, what chance do you think we fans have of being heard? I rest my case.

In fact, because the FA got away with treating the fans in such a disgusting manner, they decided to repeat this disrespectful kick-off time the following season when Manchester City met Wigan in the final. No matter how many times we allow the football authorities to put the boot in (pun intended), why, oh why do we keep going back for yet another kick up the arse? This is why we need the support of everybody in the game to tell them once and for all, enough is enough and we are not going to accept any more disrespect. I would like to think I am speaking for my fellow fans when I say we would welcome many more people like Kenny Dalglish to speak up and help us fans get the respect we deserve.

A few years ago, a friend of mine queued up at Wembley for about half an hour to buy some pasties and drinks for her children. When she eventually reached the front of the queue, she was told there were none left. Not wanting to return to the kids empty-handed, she asked if there was anything else, only to be told they had sold out of everything, with the attitude of 'Tough luck, missus and go away.' To add to her disappointment, she also missed about twenty minutes of the second half.

Imagine if this had been in a restaurant and after sitting there waiting all that time, you were informed that all the food was finished, there were no more meals and sorry, but you had to leave. At the very least, you would never return to that restaurant again, and who could blame you? But because it's a football match, this kind of disrespect is allowed to continue on a regular basis. I'm not sure whether it's because of the distractions of the game, I really don't know what it is, but so many fans seem to just accept it and most don't even notice that it's happening.

I know this may appear to be a minor issue, but the point I'm trying to make is that outside of football we wouldn't tolerate this kind of disrespect for one moment, yet for some strange reason, as fans collectively, we seem to know our place and just put up with it. In fact, if any other business treated its customers in the same way, they would soon have no customers left.

I think the world and his dog are more than aware that many clubs are now selling not just one, but three or four different football shirts every season to fans in the UK as well as Europe, Asia, Africa and anywhere in the world who will buy them. Now that's fine in a free market where people can choose to buy whatever they want, but not every football fan lives in this free market and can't choose or even afford to pay for these shirts. I personally know a lot of parents who feel pressured into buying them for their children and this can create a huge financial strain.

For parents struggling to find the money to buy these shirts, it can feel very false to hear people constantly calling us fans the Twelfth Man, when they don't really mean it. I know there are genuine players and managers who do appreciate our support and I don't mind them calling us the Twelfth Man, but when the marketing executives patronise us with hype such as, 'the fans have responded very positively to our new strip' it has a very false ring to it for me. It reminds me a bit of certain politicians referring to young soldiers as heroes, whereas in reality there would be absolutely no chance whatsoever of any of their children becoming one of these heroes. It's all clever stuff and they know exactly how to play us, which is why they put those army recruitment adverts on TV at half time… very clever indeed.

Everybody knows that no parent will allow their children to walk out on the street wearing last year's shirt, laying themselves open to mockery and possibly bullying. Despite knowing full well that some families are struggling to find the price of just one of these shirts, they bring out three or four shirts every season, excluding a lot of fans who just don't have the finances to sustain these massive expenses every year.

When I was a youngster, I would save up to buy my Everton shirt, which would last a couple of seasons and I would look after it with pride. If you were to save up today and managed to buy that shirt, you wouldn't have it long before the next one, or should I say the next three or four are brought out and your old one is outdated (and usually discarded by most fans.) This practice by the clubs really does put enormous pressure on a lot of families.

I really hope I misheard that one or two clubs were charging their fans to have a photograph taken alongside a trophy they had just won. Is this their way of thanking them for their loyal support in actually helping them to win that trophy? I cannot believe how any club could do this, when they should actually be inviting those same fans down for a complimentary photograph and a drink in recognition of their devotion and loyalty. Surely I must have heard this one wrong? Please tell me I did.

You may also remember the story of people in charge of a certain club accused of mocking their own fans for buying replica football shirts and calling their female fans dogs. What kind of treatment is this? I mean, how could anybody do this to their own fans?

It was suggested at the time by even the most moderate of people that those fans would have been well within their rights to refuse to return to that stadium until the appropriate disciplinary action was taken. But being the loyal supporters that they are, they still went to the next game and chanting at the top of their voices, 'Sack the board! Sack the board!' which was a bit like throwing out the baby with the bath water.

I don't think we fans actually realise how much respect we could and should command. Many people believed that they should have stood OUTSIDE the stadium and chanted, but because this action wasn't taken, it may have been viewed by future owners that it was okay for them to do just as they liked and the fans would accept anything. This could even allow them to change the name of this magnificent stadium and negotiate sponsorships with certain payday loan companies, who charge massive interest rates.

What I understand about payday loan companies could be written on the back of the replies I've received from the FA. I always think of them as demanding extortionate interest rates of something like 4000% from impoverished and vulnerable people who have poor credit ratings and are therefore unable to take out loans from our rich bangsters... I mean bankers, on the High Street.

It just doesn't seem morally right to me for a club to be endorsing and promoting companies like this. The players may believe they're acting in the best interests of the club by bringing in much needed revenue, but to my mind they are being a little insensitive to the fans from this working class area who are feeling the effects of a painful economic recession, which is one of the main reasons for targeting this particular club in the first place.

I have worked with a good number of these fans, who I know are not too happy. For over one hundred years, these supporters have been one of the most loyal group of fans in the whole of the football league. They are decent, loyal and genuine down to earth people and a lot of them can't understand what's happening at their club. Many people, including myself, believe they deserve a hell of a lot more respect than this and how somebody can suddenly just come in and do whatever they want is simply beyond my comprehension.

Unfortunately, this general trend of disrespect is on the increase and the bad news is, there are more and more people coming into the game who don't really understand football, or even like it. You can't tell me that's a good thing.

To me, a chairman was always the custodian of the club, somebody highly responsible with the honour of leading the club in the traditional and respectable manner expected of his position, up until the point when his successor took over the reins.

It isn't like that any more, when some of them now are changing the names of the grounds, the colours of their teams' shirts and even their clubs' names. And heaven help us if we disagree, or voice our concerns, as they then threaten to leave and take their wealth with them. So what can we do we do about it?

Absolutely nothing, it seems.

But at least we have the football authorities to come to our aid and ensure this type of thing doesn't happen. Don't we?

No, unfortunately, it appears that we don't; *give the fans sweet FA*, once again appears to be the order of the day.

I'm not really sure why this comes to mind and it may seem a silly comparison to make, but whenever I watch shows like *The X Factor* and see a previous winner returning to the show as a successful artist, I notice that instead of being treated with the utmost contempt, as they were when just nervous hopefuls, they are now shown enormous respect with a standing ovation thrown in.

They have obviously crossed over that fence and have been accepted into the exclusive club. Susan Boyle and Paul Potts will understand exactly where I'm coming from here. Perhaps it is a peculiar analogy to make, but that's how I feel the football authorities see us football fans, exactly like those nervous contestants who are ridiculed and belong firmly on the other side of the fence.

On a separate note, I can understand most of our clubs wanting to move to new state of the art training grounds with the best of facilities, but why do they have to be hidden away in the middle of nowhere and secluded from the terrifying prospect of adoring kids waiting outside for autographs? And why do these new training grounds resemble military bases? This only alienates the fans and widens the gap even further between us and the clubs, who enjoy praising us in public, but in private can't get far enough away from us.

Finally, can anybody please explain to me why the football authorities never listen to the fans? Do they think we know nothing about football, or do they not want us involved? Whatever country in the world we happen to come from, why can't we ever have a say in choosing the national manager? We never have a say in any of their decisions. Putting it bluntly, the authorities take it upon themselves to do whatever they like, without any dialogue or consultation with the fans, and I find this extremely insulting, considering how much money we contribute to football.

I don't remember ever voting for them to represent our views and opinions. This, along with so many other reasons, is why I don't believe we fans are the Twelfth Man. More like the Forgotten Man… until they want our money, that is, and then they suddenly remember us once again.

Twenty-two
Life is What Happens When You're Busy Making Other Plans

When *Pay the Penalty* ended, I had no further contact with any officials at Everton. I continued going to the match as a season ticket holder and not overly impressed with seeing the other side of the fence, I felt relieved to be back amongst the fans and my own kind of people once again.

With my other two brothers, sister and daughter all supporting Liverpool, our Jeggsy started taking his young daughter, Rebecca, to Goodison Park, even though she was still only a toddler – just in case, as he used to say – before she was brainwashed by the red half of the family. He knew how important it was for his little girl to become an Evertonian.

He asked me if there was any way I could put in a word for Rebecca to be the match mascot, but even when I was working there, it would have been very difficult and now that I wasn't, would have been impossible.

Never mind, he said, he would contact the club to see if she could be put on some kind of waiting list and even if she had to wait a few years to be a mascot, he didn't mind waiting. He always used to say to me, especially over a few drinks, "Don't worry, our kid; she'll be mascot one day, you wait and see."

"Life is what happens when you're busy making other plans," is a very famous line from a John Lennon song and I lost count of the number of times our kid quoted his former Beatles hero who was taken from us far too prematurely, in New York City in 1980. How significant those words would prove to be, as nothing in this world could have prepared me for what was about to happen in my life.

Whilst relaxing at home one night, I received a phone call from Jeggsy's partner, Andrea. She was crying over the phone and begging me to go round to their house straight away as there was something wrong with Jeggsy. I'm still not sure why I said it, but I instinctively asked her if he was breathing. She told me she wasn't sure, but there was an ambulance on its way. My wife and I rushed round there. My elder brother, Anthony, was already there with his wife. When I got to the top of the stairs, I couldn't believe my own eyes; two paramedics were trying to resuscitate our kid.

Our Jeggsy had stopped breathing and after working on him for what seemed like ages, they decided to take him to hospital. We followed the ambulance to Birkenhead's Arrowe Park hospital. When we arrived, various doctors and nurses were still trying to resuscitate him. Just then my sister, Julie, arrived. It was all extremely distressing and without question, the worst moment of my life. I couldn't watch any longer and waited round the corner, praying that he would be okay. It was horrible, as a part of me knew he wasn't and I was literally just waiting for the screams to start. And then they started... those screams, which, ever since that night have never really stopped.

It is killing me writing this, but when I decided to write a book, I always knew that this bit would come up. Our kid had died of a heart attack at the very young age of forty-two and a part of all of us who loved him also died that night. For the next few hours I sat alone with him in that room, unable to take in what had just happened.

Why is it that one minute in this life, everything

is so beautiful and the next minute your whole world is suddenly turned upside down? I hadn't really understood what John Lennon was talking about until then, but suddenly it all began to make sense. Life really is what happens when you're busy making other plans.

"You know when you asked me that time if Rebecca could be a mascot for Everton?" I said to him, "Well I promise you, our kid, if it's the last thing I do, I give you my word, she will be and you'll be very proud of your little girl, as you've always been."

Jeggsy at Goodison Park watching his beloved Blues

I don't know how I got through the weeks and months that followed. For one thing, Saturdays were never the same again and I found it very hard without him and Rebecca at the match. In fact, life had become very difficult and our whole family was living this nightmare.

Our Jeggsy was a massive Evertonian and loved

taking Rebecca to watch his heroes. I contacted the club a little while after he died and told them the tragic news. I asked if his daughter could be a mascot to help ease the pain and distress she was going through. I mentioned that it had always been his dream for her to walk out as mascot with the team he loved. I spoke to a very pleasant young man who sympathised and promised she could indeed be mascot when she was ready and said he would send me a letter to confirm this. The young man was so understanding when I explained that neither Rebecca nor the rest of us were quite ready for this just yet, but if he could send the letter for now, that would be brilliant to show his daughter.

For the next few months, as people who have loved lost ones will know all too well, we were all in a bit of a daze. One day we would think we were okay and the next, one or all of us would suddenly break down. It hit me really hard and I was unable to work for quite some time.

After a few more months, I contacted the club to inform them that Rebecca was now feeling better and ready to be mascot as agreed earlier. But this time the conversation wasn't as cordial as it had been when I spoke with the young gentleman a few months previously.

I again explained the tragic loss of my brother and told the lady that Jeggsy's daughter had been invited to be a mascot.

She then told me they had tightened things up, as there was quite a long waiting list and asked me if I had anything in writing to substantiate my request.

I replied that I did indeed have a letter and remember thinking to myself at the time, thank God I had that letter sent to me.

There was one small problem, though. Well, I was hoping it was only a small problem. I couldn't for the life of me remember where the letter was and because of the last few months of grief and distress, I hadn't put it away as carefully as I normally would. However, at least I could remember the young man's name and I told this lady that he would certainly confirm this arrangement. I couldn't believe it when she told me he no longer worked at the club and there was nothing in their office to confirm it.

"What, no copy?" I asked. I knew then that I had some serious problems.

I was told in a very business-like way that they were sorry for our loss, but if I didn't have the letter, then she could not be mascot. I appealed once again, even swearing on my mother's life that I had genuinely received the letter, but because of the trauma of my brother's death I wasn't as organised as usual and begged them to try to understand.

I didn't know what else to do. We had searched our house from top to bottom and there was no sign of the letter anywhere. I then began to question my own sanity. Had I even received a letter? Had I actually spoken to that nice young gentleman at the time? I had been going through quite an emotional trauma and was now becoming increasingly concerned that I may have imagined the whole thing.

When I asked my wife, she told me that although she hadn't actually seen the letter, she could remember me speaking to somebody at the club. She recalled me putting the phone down and saying that at least our Becks would have the opportunity to walk out as mascot, taking her mind off things and giving her a little happiness.

But I sensed that my wife now had her doubts as well and I honestly began to wonder if I had indeed undergone some deep emotional crisis and imagined the whole thing. I had heard of people reacting in all kinds of strange ways when they lost a loved one. It had been an extremely difficult time for all the family and I was now really worried that I had got it all terribly wrong.

It was an incredibly frustrating situation that niggled away at me, day and night. By now I couldn't sleep, wondering what had happened to this letter... if there even was a letter and in the absence of a solution, doubting whether it had existed. It was slowly driving me mad, so I did something I hadn't done in years. I began to pray.

"Please, God," I begged, "help me to find this letter. I know I haven't spoken to you for a good while, but please help me find the letter, not just for our kid, or even our little Becks, but also for the sake of my own sanity."

But still there was nothing and I was now reaching the stage where I would have to accept the situation, forget all about it and try to get on with my life. The trouble was, I had already promised our Becks she was going to be mascot. What was I going to tell her? How could I build up the hopes of a young girl like that and then let her down?

After another sleepless night, I began to pray again... but this time to Jeggsy.

"If you're listening to me now, our kid, and you want to see your little girl walk out with your beloved blues at Goodison Park as mascot, then you're going to have to help me find this fucking letter, mate."

I must have dozed off as it was 5.30am when I woke up, my thoughts as usual with Jeggsy and Becks and this whole sorry situation. For some reason, my eyes were drawn to the bedside table. I did a double take, not believing what I could see. Sticking out from between the bed and the side table was what looked like a letter... *the* letter. I checked to make sure it was the letter and to my delight I could see the Everton letter heading, beneath which was neatly typed, 'Dear Mr Farrell...'

I thought for a moment I must be hallucinating from lack of sleep. I had already looked there a thousand times and there was nothing. Our kid must have been listening to me after all. When he was alive, we always used to wind each other up by playing jokes. Was that what he had been doing these last few months and perhaps realised that I'd had enough now?

I woke my wife immediately. There I was, at half past five in the morning, dancing around the bedroom half naked with a piece of paper in my hand, telling her I wasn't mad after all.

I couldn't wait to phone Everton later that morning. When I got through to them, I couldn't resist asking them once more if they would please consider allowing my niece to be mascot.

Their answer, which I knew word for word by now, was the same: "Sorry, if you don't have a letter confirming this, your niece cannot be mascot."

I wanted to make absolutely sure about this, just in case they moved the goalposts by saying Jeggsy had to be present as well. So I asked them once more, if I found the letter, could she be mascot?

"Yes, she can, but only if you have a lett—"

"Guess what? I've found the fucking letter!"

"There's no need to swear, Mr Farrell—"

"Oh yes there fucking is, I've got the fucking letter."

"Good. How did you manage to find it?"

"I found it at half past five this morning, with the help of a little divine intervention, you could say."

I couldn't get round to Rebecca's house quickly enough to give her the news that she was going to be mascot and now we were both dancing round the room, but this time I was fully dressed.

Jeggsy's daughter, Rebecca, as Mascot for Everton

As our Jeggsy's little girl, Rebecca, walked out as mascot with the Everton team against Chelsea, I looked up at the sky, crying my eyes out.

"Doesn't she look beautiful, our kid?" I whispered.

Our Jeggsy must have been very proud of his little girl that day.

Twenty-Three
It's a Funny Old Game

I began taking my kids to the match when they were at an early age and like a few other sad fathers, thought nothing of trying to impress them with my many make-believe talents. Until one day when, sitting at the match, my seven-year-old son quite unexpectedly asked me in a shrill voice, heard by everybody in our section of the ground, "Dad, when you played for Everton, what position did you play?"

If you've never experienced anything like this in your life, trust me, it's not something you want to happen to you. Immediately, it seemed like everybody in the ground had turned around to look at me and I could literally feel the blood rushing to my face.

I tried to whisper, "Ssh, I'll tell you later when we're in the car, son," but unfortunately, it was too late, as he wanted to know there and then and repeated his question. This time, though, it sounded much louder and I thought everybody outside the stadium must have heard it as well as the crowd inside.

There were a lot of heads now turning round and all eyes were looking at me, wondering what position I did play for Everton. How embarrassing and what an idiot I felt; how was I going to get out of this one?

One fan in front of us turned round and said, "So you played for Everton as well, eh? So did I."

Then a bloke behind me joined in and said, "I did as well, y'know... I used to play in goal for 'em."

Another voice from the side shouted, "Ay, I was once their manager!"

From all around us came shouts of, "I once

played for Manchester United... Real Madrid... AC Milan, etc. etc." I was now getting it from everywhere and we were all laughing.

"Okay," I shouted back. "I suppose I asked for that!"

On the way home in the car, I thought it was probably best to confess a few other little porkies, as I didn't want to be in that position ever again. So I began to tell him that Manchester City never really sold me to Everton for a record transfer fee, either... and while we were on the subject, in case we were ever at a concert, I wasn't really on *Top of the Pops* a few years earlier with the Liverpool band, 'Our Kid.'

"So none of those stories are true then, Dad?" he asked.

"Well, not all of them, son, no."

"Is Kevin Keegan your second cousin, then?"

"Well, not quite second cousin... no, sorry son, we're not related."

"So you're not good friends either with Sharon Mcreadie out of the Champions"

"Er.... no, son.

"And I suppose you weren't really on Opportunity Knocks either?

"No."

"And you never won the Donkey Derby in Pontins?"

"Well actually, that one's true."

I think the whole conversation on our way home, consisted of, "No, sorry son, that's not true, either." I'd actually forgotten how many tales I told my kids, but you have my word that I never, ever told them any more made-up stories again after that!

I've always wanted my kids to enjoy the whole

football experience like I did when I was young. But apart from enjoying the match and that real quality time together, we've always enjoyed a good laugh as well, even if it was mostly at my expense.

I love it when I see people enjoying the light hearted moments of football. When Frank Skinner and David Baddiel presented their amusing, alternative fantasy football programme on TV, apart from producing quite an entertaining show, I think they also managed to get people who weren't even that keen on football suddenly interested in the beautiful game. I was even allowed to watch it without my wife saying, "Oh no, not football again," as she would look forward to watching it herself.

Adrian Chiles is another one who, for me, brings a bit of humour into what can sometimes be an all too serious game. James Cordon and a few other people can see the funny side as well and it's people like these who brighten up the game.

Then you've got those people who take it to another level. When the comedy prankster, Simon Brodkin, sneaked onto the pitch at Everton as his alter ego, Jason Bent, to warm up with his beloved Manchester City team, I couldn't help wondering where he found the nerve to do such a thing. You may remember him putting on a Man City strip and pretending he was one of the players, before being sussed and eventually arrested for pitch encroachment. He has also carried out some other stunts like masquerading as a member of the England World Cup squad at Luton Airport, as well as invading the stage of The X Factor, as his other alter ego, Lee Nelson.

There's also Karl Power and Tommy Dunn, two pranksters from Manchester who have carried out some of the most daring and amazing stunts ever at different sporting events. Karl has walked out to bat for England at Headingley, he has played on centre court at Wimbledon, performed the Haka when the English rugby team were playing in Rome and even performed the Riverdance with Tommy on the winner's podium at the British Grand Prix.

You may remember Karl walking onto the pitch in the quarter final of the Champions league against Bayern Munich in Germany, dressed in his Man Utd kit, standing alongside Andy Cole and the rest of the players for a team photograph.

And who can ever forget Conor Cunningham, the cheeky Irish fan who donned an Estonia tracksuit and sat on the Estonia bench in a match against Ireland?

Where did these people get the courage from to do the things they did? I know for sure I would never have had the bottle to do what these pranksters did, never in a million years. Even though I did very similar things when I carried out my protest, I didn't have what these people had, as they did it just for a laugh, which must have taken some nerve.

When I used to walk into football grounds under the guise of player, a member of the press, a steward or anything else for that matter, my motives were completely different. I was fortunate to have the protection of a protest, which provided all the psychological armour I needed to be so daring. In a way, my cause kind of justified what I was doing. The fact that I was also very wound up by all the disrespect shown to football fans provided me with all the tools needed to spur me on. Because I actually believed that what I was doing was right, I managed to do things I would never otherwise have been able to do and this for me, was more effective than any Dutch courage. Without the protest, I simply wouldn't have had the nerve to do what I did.

I also noticed that the longer my protest went on, the more daring and confident I became, which helped me understand how these pranksters could have progressed to go from one event to the next.

I have a theory as to why certain people carry out these pranks. I could be wrong, but I believe that apart from that raw buzz of adrenalin, which I know can be so exciting, they actually do it to help build self-confidence. A good therapist would have an absolute field day with these people.

Take Simon Brodkin, for example, who performs comedy acts as his alter egos Lee Nelson and Jason Bent. Just as I grew in confidence after becoming more and more daring, I believe this could possibly explain why he is now so successful in his stand up comedy act as Lee Nelson. I also believe the same to be true of Karl Power and Tommy Dunn.

In Conor Cunningham's case, he probably felt he could have walked into the White House after his stunt in Estonia.

Well after my protest was over, my confidence was put to the test. I took my son and daughter down to London to watch Chelsea versus Everton. We were waiting outside the Reception area at Stamford Bridge as they were hoping to get some autographs. Unfortunately, there had been a couple of minor scuffles between some Everton and Chelsea fans right beside us and although we were not directly involved, I was still a bit concerned, especially having my kids with me. There were some barriers where Chelsea stewards were stopping people from going any further and one of the stewards who noticed I was with my kids asked me if we would like to wait behind the barrier, out of the way of any trouble. It was extremely kind of him and it was a much safer place to be.

Just then, there was a lot of noise and commotion when three or four big posh cars suddenly screeched to a halt right next to us and out of them jumped several hefty security men with Russian accents and, I think, were armed. Talk about the cavalry arriving in the nick of time.

I remember laughing and telling my kids, "We're okay now, here's the KGB and Russian Secret Service."

Very calmly, out of one of these cars appeared the renowned Chelsea owner, Roman Abramovich, as security and stewards made sure all fans were immediately moved behind the cars.

However, we were on his side of the barrier. I don't think the stewards minded, as I was with my kids. My daughter had her camera with her and I asked one of his minders if he would take our picture alongside Roman.

My smile quickly evaporated when he replied "No!" very sternly.

His terse reply made the position very clear, but after all, he wasn't employed to be taking photographs of Everton fans outside Stamford Bridge; he was a personal bodyguard to Roman Abramovich and had his job to do. I wisely decided not to take it any further, not wanting the kids to have to be travelling home from London without their dad that day.

However, at that point, the owner of Chelsea intervened himself.

"That's okay," he said to his guards, and I was surprised when he came over to stand beside me and my kids and then instructed one of his entourage to take the photograph. Although he didn't say anything to us, he did give us all a very pleasant smile and a pat on the back as he left.

Who needs conversation, when football is the international language of the world?

Outside Chelski with Roman Abramovich

What I really liked about Roman Abramovich was that he could see by our clothing that we were Everton fans. He must have thought to himself, here's a family who have travelled all the way down from Merseyside to London, which I thought was very considerate of him and more importantly to me, he showed great respect towards football fans, as he obviously knew we didn't support his team, Chelsea.

I told my children how unusual this was, as

there couldn't be that many people who had their photographs taken with Roman Abramovich. He is not what you would call the flamboyant type and I've never even seen him give an interview. Anyway, quite a lot more people had now noticed him and came over, also hoping to get a photo with Chelsea's rich owner. Unfortunately for them, it was too late. The Chelsea stewards made certain that nobody else crossed the barrier to where we were.

To this day, I'm still not sure how it happened. It may have been because Roman Abramovich had his arms around us, but as we were still on the same side of the barrier as him and his entourage, one of the Chelsea stewards began escorting us towards this very swish lounge. When I carried out my personal protest a few years before, I could only have dreamt of having an opportunity like this.

We were within touching distance of the lounge, when my kids asked me why I had stopped. I told them we couldn't go any further as we were not supposed to be there.

"What about all those times, Dad, when you walked into every Premiership club, Wembley stadium and even the World Cup in America?"

"That was different as I was protesting, but the protest is now over and it wouldn't be right to walk into a place we're not supposed to," I said.

"Aw, come on, we'll get to see the players… and the stewards did say walk this way."

"You've lost your bottle, haven't you, Dad?"

"Can I be very honest with you both? I never even had it in the first place."

I explained to them that I was only able to do what I did because I really believed in the protest and without that belief; I wouldn't have had the courage or the audacity to do such a thing.

"Sorry, kids, but we won't be walking into this lounge today. Those days are over."

For a few moments, I stood outside that lounge and all those memories of the protest came flooding back and I couldn't help asking myself, did I *really* walk into these stadiums free of charge?

Once inside the ground and sitting in our more humble seats, which we paid for, one of the Chelsea stewards came over.

"Didn't I see you outside having your photo taken with Roman Abramovich earlier?"

"Yes, you did," I replied.

"Well, that's most unusual."

"What is?"

"I've never seen anything like that before."

"I don't understand. What do you mean?"

"He never has his photograph taken with members of the public."

"Well," I said, "he just happened to be very lucky to catch us on a good day," as we all burst out laughing.

Twenty-four
The International Language of Football

Isn't it amazing how you can communicate with somebody from another country, without even speaking their language or them knowing yours? I've been lucky in my job as a welder to travel to many places around the world and it's never long before the topic of football shoots up, if you'll pardon the pun. Once it does, the next important bit of business that needs to be established is which team we support. Let me explain.

When Steve, Robbie, Neil and I arrived in Jeddah to carry out welding repairs in Saudi Arabia, we were met at the airport by Ali who, for the next few weeks, was our driver, minder, babysitter and very good friend.

When he asked us our names, my old mate Robbie Clement, one of the funniest people I've ever had the pleasure of working with, who has since sadly passed away, told him we were John, George, Paul and Ringo. This, surprisingly, went right over his head because on the way to the hotel he kept calling me Mr Ringo and I remember complaining to Robbie, why did I have to be the drummer?

It wasn't the easiest of conversations, due to our complete lack of Arabic, compounded by the fact that it was a tiny bit better than his English. When I pointed at myself and mentioned the word Everton, he did the same and said Arsenal. How amazing that we couldn't understand a single word we were saying to each other and knew nothing else about each other for that matter, apart from the fact that he now knew I was a toffee and I knew he was a gunner.

The following day, whilst driving us to our place of work, he suddenly and unexpectedly blurted out, "Thierry Henry, Arsenal." Sitting beside him in the front, I just looked at him and smiled. Then he said, "Frank Lampard," paused for a few seconds and said, "Chelsea." I smiled at him again. I thought he wanted to show us how much he knew about the English Premier league. As we drove on, he said, "Wayne Rooney," and just looked at me.

I kept on smiling.

He looked at me again. "Wayne Rooney."

"Yes," I replied, nodding my head. "A great player."

I think it was my boss, Steve, who cottoned on to it.

"Peter, do you not notice what he's doing?"

"What do you mean, Steve?"

"He never mentioned Wayne Rooney's team."

I still didn't understand. "What do you mean?" I repeated.

"Well, when he mentioned Thierry Henry and Frank Lampard, he told you who they played for, but when he mentioned Wayne Rooney, he didn't, he just kept looking at you. I think he wants you to join in and play a quiz with him. Unless I'm mistaken, Peter, I think he wants you to tell him who Wayne Rooney plays for."

When the penny eventually dropped, I looked at Ali and said, "Manchester United."

He cheered and started laughing.

Robbie was shouting from the back, "Once a blue, always a blue!"

Steve was absolutely spot on. Ali and I had managed to strike up some kind of dialogue, even though neither of us could understand a single word of the other's native language.

"Bloody hell, Steve, you're right!" It was amazing. Charles Darwin would have been in his seventh heaven with all this. Well, maybe not quite heaven in Charles Darwin's case, but he would have been very intrigued all the same with this social science interaction.

This guy must have known everything there was to know about the EPL. As soon as I said a player, he would immediately tell me his team. He loved this game and it did shorten our journeys to and from work. I've got to be honest, he put me in my place a few times and I even found myself looking up players' names on the hotel's Wi-Fi the night before in the hotel, hoping to catch him out in the car the following morning, but he was far too good.

I was now becoming even more determined to get him and the following morning on our way to our job, I began reeling off players names.

"Stephen Ireland."

"Manchester City," he replied.

"Aaron Lennon."

"Tottenham Hotspur."

"Gabriel Agbonlahor."

"Aston Villa." he quickly replied, laughing. He was too good.

This went on for the next few weeks. Even if our conversation for the remainder of the job was in broken biscuits, our little game continued. But because he knew them all, it was now becoming a bit tedious. One day, we had a bit of an argument when I asked him a player and he gave me the wrong answer. I was delighted to have caught him out at last but he was having none of it.

"No, no… Internet, Mr Ringo, Internet," he insisted.

When I got back to the hotel and checked it on the computer, I couldn't believe it. He was only right; this player had been transferred to another club without me realising it and I just laughed to myself, thinking our friend Ali really did know the lot.

Each time, when I didn't know, he would say to me, "Internet, Mr Ringo. Internet."

I was now becoming obsessed with trying to get him. The job didn't seem to matter any more and I was more interested in getting him before I went home. As I said, he was far too good for me and knew absolutely everything there was to know about the premiership.

We were coming to the end of our job and we contractors had to start looking for the next. This is so often the case in what is a very insecure industry at times. Anyway, I'd managed to get another job in the North Sea on one of the gas platforms and as they needed me immediately, Steve allowed me to leave Saudi Arabia early.

Our good friend Ali took me to the airport and when I got out of the car, I thanked him for looking after us and for his great company during the last few weeks. It was then that I came out with it and I couldn't wait to see the look on his face.

"Frank Spencer," I said.

He looked at me, but this time, he wasn't smiling. For the first time in a few weeks, he looked puzzled.

"Frank Spencer…" he repeated, as his whole expression changed and looked very worried. He was fucked.

"Get out of that one," I said to him and, as I

waved him goodbye, "Internet, Ali, Internet!"

Call it sour grapes if you want and I know it was bang out of order, but I still laugh today when I think of him swearing as he's looking at Frank Spencer on the Internet telling Betty that the dog's done a whoopsie on the carpet.

In our hotel in Jeddah, Saudi Arabia

With so many talented players, a lot of countries around the world look with envy on the EPL and when I worked in South Africa, I found they were no exception. Almost every single person I met loved football and as soon as they found out where I was from, it seemed to be the only thing they wanted to talk about.

They have some great clubs, like Orlando Pirates and the Kaiser Chiefs, both from Soweto, Johannesburg whose rivalry, I understand, is just intense as our own Derbys at home.

I was pleased to have work mates both white and black in Port Elizabeth. I asked Joe, one of my black friends, if he'd heard of the Kaiser Chiefs, the Indie music band from England.

He just looked at me and started laughing. "Is that the best you can do, Peter? Yes, I know they come from Leeds in England. I also know that's how they got their name – from their former Leeds United captain, Lucas Radebe, who came from Soweto and who used to play for the Kaiser Chiefs."

I had thought there for a minute I could catch Joe out, but not only do these people know their football, they obviously know their music as well.

I had a bit of an eye-opening moment one day when I mentioned to Joe that I wouldn't mind going to watch one of their football games. However, Dave, another mate who was white, pulled me over to one side and quietly told me that you don't really see white football fans at these matches. This not only surprised me, but also disappointed me.

"I thought Apartheid was over," I said.

"It may well be," he replied, "but there are deep-rooted traditions that will take years to sort out."

I was learning more about this country and he was absolutely right; football in South Africa is for the black people and rugby and cricket is for whites. I was saddened to hear that South Africa was still divided, especially in sport. However, one thing they all agreed on was their passion and love for the English Premiership League.

Our local pub during our stay in Port Elizabeth was The Beer Shack and the proprietors, Matt and Gabby, made myself, Graham, Stevie and Ali all very welcome. With Matt being a big Liverpool fan, the craic was more than guaranteed between us. I brought a smile to his face one night when he asked if I'd ever seen real animals in a game reserve before. I told him I hadn't, but I'd seen a lot of dirty players in reserve games.

Matt and Gabby introduced us to their mates and most of the locals and it was great talking with so many people who all supported so many different teams in the EPL. When I spoke to the white people, they were in no doubt the Premiership was the best thing since sliced bread and absolutely loved it. The black people did as well, but I did notice that some of them expressed a few concerns about the EPL having a detrimental effect on their own domestic football leagues. One of them told me that with some of their best players being exported to England and the huge interest in the EPL, there were serious consequences, such as reduced attendances. He said it wasn't just in South Africa, but the rest of Africa as well.

I understood what he meant and agreed that although the EPL was such an exciting phenomenon, there were also many losers and people were definitely affected by it. I told him that our clubs in the lower leagues in England, who had for many years stayed afloat by selling their best players to the top teams, were also struggling to survive, as the big boys in the Premier league were now shopping abroad.

I also told him that the same thing was happening with the development of our own young players in these lower leagues, who now have next to no chance of playing in the Premiership due to its global success and attracting players from further afield.

He asked me what would happen to our clubs if the TV companies decided one day to pull out. Or what would happen if the rich owners decided they'd had enough. He said all of these were possibilities that would cripple our game.

'The people in charge would have to increase ticket prices by a substantial amount to maintain the big money they had become accustomed to. Although they have always been loyal, even your fans in England have their limits, Peter.'

When we finished our work in Port Elizabeth, we flew to Cape Town before flying back to the UK. I was so excited, as this was a lifetime opportunity to pay my respects to one of the greatest people that ever walked this earth. I was looking forward to visiting Robben Island where Nelson Mandela spent many years of his life fighting for basic humanitarian rights which we take for granted everyday of our lives.

We all have heroes and I have often asked people in my company over a few drinks to name their favourite person in history. The interesting thing about this conversation is that it's a personal thing and I always respect everybody's view, as long as they don't say Thatcher.

I've heard Martin Luther King, Muhammad Ali and Gandhi. Jesus Christ often gets a mention and our Jeggsy's favourite was always John Lennon. All of these people have left their mark on history and as I said, it is a personal thing but mine, without any question, has always been Nelson Mandela. What an amazing man. To give up his liberty, which for me was as good as giving up his life, for others, went way beyond the call of duty.

I asked the receptionist at the hotel about directions to Robben Island and she told me it was not somewhere where you can just pay to get into on the day. As thousands of people who visit the Island every year will confirm, it has to be booked in advance. When she looked at the bookings, she told me the next available date was in a few weeks' time.

"Are you joking?" I asked her. "I'm flying home to the UK tomorrow afternoon."

She told me I could take a chance and go down to the pier in the morning and see if there were any cancellations, but she couldn't guarantee that there would be any available.

I was up about six o'clock the next morning and with Graham, Steve and Ali still not down, I decided to head down to the pier by myself. When I got there, the queues resembled those outside a Premiership match back in England. I then found out that the next boat wasn't due to leave until about nine o'clock, with another leaving about midday. The later one wouldn't have given me enough time to get back to my hotel, change and travel to the airport, so it had to be the nine o'clock sailing.

I waited in the queue and when I eventually reached the front, a lady asked me if I was picking up tickets.

"No, I'm not, but I was wondering if there were any tickets left over for this morning's visit, please?"

"I'm afraid there are none whatsoever. I'm sorry," she said, "but they've all gone."

Where was my old friend Michael with those envelopes when I needed him?

I wasn't sure what to do now. Not only had I travelled all the way to South Africa, but I just happened to be in Cape Town, in this vast country, where Robben Island just happened to be. In fact, I was actually at the boat terminal that went to Robben

Island.

This was now becoming a bit of moral dilemma for me. Although my football protest of gaining free admission was well and truly over, I kept thinking to myself, you can't leave South Africa without seeing Robben Island, especially being this close to it. I was also thinking, if I can walk into every Premier league club, Wembley stadium and the World Cup without paying, then surely a boat to Robben Island shouldn't be too much of a problem? That was it. I decided there and then that I was going to pay my respects to Nelson Mandela. I wasn't sure how, but I was getting on that boat by hook or by crook.

I tell you honestly, this is something I wouldn't normally do, but I had a little bit of experience in this sort of thing and I was more than aware I would never get this opportunity ever again.

During my protest, I was always looking to my old friend Michael to help me get past these people, but the person I was hoping would inspire me today was somebody who knew all about security and was something of an expert in protesting. The way I looked at it was, if my hero could spend all those years behind bars, then I should be able to breach security by walking onto this boat and I did have form. I made up my mind I wasn't leaving South Africa without paying my respects to one of the greatest men who ever lived.

When it was time to board the boat, everybody began walking on. It resembled the ferry boats that cross the River Mersey from Birkenhead to Liverpool. Security was tight and with bags being scanned, I was hoping this may work to my advantage and that they'd be more interested in security than somebody not having a ticket. However, my worst fears were confirmed when these big and brawny members of security began shouting very loudly, informing people to have their tickets ready and reminding everybody that if they didn't have their ticket, they wouldn't be getting on the boat.

Oh my God, I'm too old for all this, I thought. It was okay years ago when I was younger and had the bottle to do it, but I don't need all this now. Graham, Steve and Ali were peacefully sound asleep in the comfort of the hotel and here was I about to relive yet another one of those nerve racking moments that belong to the Midnight Express movie.

Everything was going through my head at this moment. I was trying to think of as many ways as possible to help me out and I kept reminding myself what Nelson must have gone through.

For many years, countless people must have thought up millions of different ways of trying to escape and get off this island and here I was, trying to think of a way of getting on it. I could just picture my mum, Josie, saying to me, "Why do you always have to do things the hard way, Peter?"

When we reached the front, I was asked for my ticket and I told them my friend had just gone ahead and he had the tickets. They wanted a description of my friend so that they could go and find him and bring him back with my ticket.

What a shit excuse! How on earth had I managed to carry out my football protest? I had definitely lost my touch and this excuse just sounded pathetic. I knew then I was in big trouble.

"Can I tell you the gospel truth?" I blurted out to this person. "I don't have a ticket. I did try to buy one but they're all booked up, until a few weeks' time and I'm going back to England today. I'll probably never be in Cape Town or even South Africa ever again and I just wanted to pay my respects to one of the greatest men that ever lived."

The man laughed and said, "Well, you got it wrong, didn't you?"

"Yes, I did. I'm sorry," I said, turning to walk away.

"Oh no, you misunderstood me… when I said you got it wrong, I meant he wasn't one of the greatest, he was *the* greatest person that ever lived." Then he winked at me and said, "Enjoy Robben Island."

Visiting Robben Island, Cape Town, with the beautiful Table Mountain in the background.

Paying my respects to one of the greatest men that ever lived

Twenty-Five
The Premier League's Bitter Taste

When I worked in Jamnagar, in the state of Gujarat in India, like every other place I visited, everybody knew of the English Premier League and just like everywhere else, the very first thing they wanted to know was, who was my team.

But I was also beginning to see another side... it seemed not everybody loved the EPL. One day, I was talking to an Indian colleague, when he asked a most unusual question.

"What do the Premier League and a gin and tonic have in common, Peter?"

"I haven't the faintest idea," I said.

"They are both very important weapons used by the British to rule the world," he told me.

If you seem a bit confused, so was I. They say that travel broadens the mind, and it was here that I discovered that gin and tonic first originated in India with the British, during the Empire days, to fight the deadly disease of malaria.

He explained that the British officers consumed their daily dose of quinine from the Indian tonic water that they drank, and later added gin to disguise its bitter taste... oh, and to get drunk as well. Quinine was found in the bark of the Cinchona tree, which grew in South America and for most European imperialists, it was one of their greatest weapons. He added that a slice of lime in their G&T was also used to prevent disease, when it was discovered that a lack of Vitamin C caused scurvy. The Royal Navy handed out limes to sailors to fight the disease, which is how the British ended up with the nickname, Limeys.

I knew that one about the Limeys, I told him, but where did the Premier League come into this?

"Well, you see, just like the old British Empire, the football authorities in England, armed with the greatest league on earth, look like they are returning to those colonial days of conquering the world once again."

God, I loved this travelling. "This is better than being back in school," I told him.

"Before you all start patting yourselves on the back about how strong your league is, be careful and remember how the Empire finished up. Believe me, Peter, this great league of yours will come back to bite you with a vengeance."

I listened with interest as he continued.

"On the surface, the Premiership looks like the best thing since sliced naan bread, (*He didn't really say naan. Sorry, I threw that one in…*) and who can argue? You do have a truly exciting league to football lovers all over the world. But all this action sold around the globe by the marketing experts comes at a very expensive price and not just financially."

He made the point that, like everything else in this life, there was always a flip side and in the case of the EPL, there were many losers.

"Unfortunately, this exciting phenomenon is not to everybody's liking and is having a very damaging and detrimental effect. If you look at Africa, who have produced so many brilliant players and even here in India, we are both in direct competition with the EPL.

"There is a growing fear that fans in the subcontinent and Africa will lose interest in their own local teams, instead preferring to spend their money watching the EPL on TV and it isn't just in India or Africa. Fans from many countries around the globe are becoming hooked on the EPL, but the football authorities in these countries cannot stand by and watch their own football leagues suffer greatly at the expense of the Premiership. How can they? And, you know, it won't be long before they may even pursue a case for compensation. You will then be left with other nations resenting your country and its EPL. In fact, this seems to be already happening, as they no longer want to vote for England whilst bidding for the World Cup."

I told him it was already happening in the Eurovision Song Contest, but I don't think that one registered.

"They may not have realised it, Peter, but they have created a Premiership monster and a huge one at that, which is becoming hungrier and growing bigger by the day, consuming everything in its path. The Premiership will continue taking the best players from countries around the world at an increasing rate to feed this hunger, thus leaving others with sub-standard leagues. This will have drastic consequences on their own domestic football, with reduced attendances, as well as damaging their own World Cup chances. And, you know, in a strange ironic twist, this is exactly the same reason why England will never win the World Cup ever again."

I was beginning to understand what he was saying because, just like other countries, the success of the Premiership did seem to have a detrimental effect on England's standing in international football.

I had to agree with him that the Premiership wasn't all a bed of roses and explained that we fans in England were now paying through the nose, whether we actually went to the game or stayed at home to watch it on TV. Either way, it was now costing us an absolute fortune and it was becoming more difficult to go to every game like we used to.

I was somewhat bemused when another Indian colleague asked me, "Peter, why would you want to go to every game?"

I tried explaining that it wasn't like going to a show every now and again but that we were football fans who supported our teams, which meant going week in, week out, in all kinds of weather.

I also pointed out that people watching the match on TV today no longer felt like fans, but more like customers and although we may not be like normal customers that will choose to shop elsewhere, we could just decide to stop shopping at our clubs altogether. After all, there is only so much we can take.

Gujarat was a dry state where alcohol was banned since Indian independence in 1947. It was imposed out of respect to Mahatma Gandhi, father of their nation, who was from here. Some of my Indian colleagues told me it was also a protest gesture as a constant reminder of English Imperialism, when the British would sit there drinking their gin and tonics.

Unofficially, of course, we were told that if we respected their culture and didn't get too drunk, they would respect ours and allow us to travel over the border into the next state and buy some beer. After a few bottles of kingfisher, we were in another state alright and it wasn't long before I had my Indian mates singing *Everton, Everton, Everton.*

In India with my newly converted Evertonian colleagues.

Another thing that surprised me was when one of them said how great it must be to walk down the street, meeting and speaking to all those famous players. He seemed a bit surprised when I told him it wasn't quite like that, as the players lived in a totally different world and to be perfectly honest, we never really saw them.

That is not intended as a dig at the players, but in today's society, we do seem to live in completely different worlds. Although some people may be envious of them, I say good luck to them. I really mean that, because my own personal interpretation of a footballer is a person who genuinely loves the game and has made sacrifices in life to fulfil his dream. I am more than aware that player status hasn't just been handed to them on a plate, but has taken years of commitment to get to where they are and not all of them make it to the top, of course. The ones who do, though, are handsomely rewarded and if people are a little resentful of their salary or lifestyle, we must remember that these players are, after all, just like us fans, who eat, breathe, live and love the game. They will always have my respect because, again, just like us fans, football runs through their blood.

I want to be absolutely clear on this; the people I don't respect are the ones in suits who have never played, supported, or even liked football, but have suddenly developed a very keen interest purely for their own personal gain. These are the people who are destroying our game.

The former player turned soccer pundit, Robbie Savage, gave a very frank interview when he said that most footballers wouldn't have a clue how much it costs to go to a football match and they don't worry about ticket prices. He was responding to the BBC Sport's Price of Football study, which revealed that the price of the cheapest tickets across English football had increased at almost twice the rate of the cost of living since 2011.

You would have to read his whole interview to understand that he wasn't being rude, but merely pointing out that it just wasn't something people in football spoke about. Apart from his honesty, the way that he spoke up for the fans was particularly heart-warming.

He said he understood why there was concern over the rising cost of watching football in this country but, for most Premier League players, it was not something they were ever going to worry about. Below is the full interview:

'To be completely honest, during my twenty-year

playing career, I never once thought about how much it was costing fans to go to games. Other players might have been different, but I did not meet any.

I never discussed the issue with any of my team mates at any of my clubs and, whoever I was playing for, ticket prices did not cross my mind once, let alone how much the pies or the programme were costing.

I cannot imagine things have changed much in the last few years.

The truth is that most Premier League players live in a bubble. If you ask most of them what a ticket costs, they would not have a clue.

Players get the best deal they can.

Even if you told them that a fan has to pay £100 to get in, players are more likely to say, 'only £100?' than think it is expensive.

You have to remember that most of them would not know what a pint of milk costs, either.

The big stars at the top clubs will have their own executive boxes for their family and friends to watch them, but no Premier League players ever have to buy tickets in the same way that fans do.

At the teams I played for, if I was in the match-day squad then I got between four and six complimentary tickets. If, for whatever reason, I needed more, I could always get some from the players who would not be using theirs.

I appreciate I was in a fortunate position, but, if someone had come up to me when I was a player and said that ticket prices were too high, I would not have been bothered at all.

There is a link between players' wages and the price of tickets but I cannot think of any player, myself included, who thought about that when they were negotiating a contract. I was always thinking of myself.

I don't feel guilty about saying that because I don't think you can blame anybody for getting the best deal that he can. Outside of football, it would not be seen as a problem and, even knowing what I do now, I have no regrets about the wages I was on.

An individual player is always going to take what a club is prepared to pay him and I think the only time he should feel bad about it is when he has not given one hundred percent in a game.

That was never an issue for me. I might have been a bit flash and drove expensive cars but my relationship with the fans mattered to me at all of my clubs and I loved feeding off their support and passion, and giving everything I could.

The atmosphere they created made such a difference and I always appreciated that, but I never made the connection between the size of the crowd and what they were being asked to pay. None of my team mates did either.

Not once when I ran out on to the pitch before a game did I think, oh, only twenty thousand here today – if it wasn't for ticket prices, there might be more in the ground.

I had no idea what it was like for the working-class man with a family to go to a match once or twice a week, put petrol in the car to get to the stadium and buy food for his kids when he was there.

Players do not automatically consider that there might be a financial reason for not going to games, because they themselves never have to pay.

Because of my media work, I still do not do that very often now I have retired from playing. The last time I paid for a ticket was to watch Wrexham play at Macclesfield in the Conference last season.

But I now understand more about how the prices have hit the man on the street, especially the next generation of football fans who have never been to a Premier League game.

There is more TV money coming into the top level of the English game than ever before but the Premier League seems to be more interested in taking their 'brand' overseas rather than looking after the supporters in this country, who should be the priority.

They are talking about playing one game a season abroad but if you are going to do something different then why not have a game where you charge a knockdown price so that families can get in for next to nothing and watch a game live?

For me, that would be much more beneficial.

I respect Robbie Savage for having the courage to be very open and upfront when he needn't have been, as well as speaking up and saying that the Premier league should be looking after their fans, especially the kids, who are football's future.

It is also refreshingly welcome to see other people in the game like Joey Barton, who is constantly sticking up for the fans, as well as Gary Lineker, who tweeted, 'The game is awash with money, cut ticket prices and make it affordable for real fans to attend.' It's also great to see Gary Neville and Jamie Carragher joining forces and asking for sensible ticket pricing and grass roots football to benefit.

There is certainly not enough done, either, to

re-invest in grass roots. Too many of our children are still playing on farmers' fields, with no proper changing facilities and a lot of them are unable to even have a shower after the game. No wonder the England football team regularly struggle against other countries on the international stage. Our big clubs have scouts and representatives attending these matches on a Sunday morning, snapping up any potential young star, but they don't appear to be returning the compliment with much needed financial support. There can be no excuse for substandard facilities in the most lucrative footballing country in the world. None whatsoever.

Smaller clubs down the lower leagues are also struggling to stay in business and how can this be right when there is so much money in football today? Surely some of this money could be passed down from the bigger clubs as well as The Football Association and The Premier league?

There are many more well-known people in the world of football, as well as politicians now fighting our corner. We fans appreciate their genuine support, we really do, but the fact that they feel the need to speak up for us just confirms my point, that we don't have a voice to speak up for ourselves.

Twenty-Six
Divide and Conquer

When the offer of working on a three week contract in Toronto came along, there wasn't really much to consider and it was, as they say on both sides of the Atlantic, an absolute no-brainer. It was also a great chance to find out a bit more about Major League Soccer, which has really taken off in the United States and Canada, as well as a brilliant opportunity to meet Canadian and American football (or should I say soccer) fans.

No matter where I travelled, everybody wanted to know straight away who my team in England was and Toronto was no different. They obviously knew all about the English Premiership, but with the meteoric rise of the MLS, there seemed to be an extra buzz of excitement here and you could really sense their passion for soccer, which has now finally gripped our cousins across the pond.

When you consider that MLS in Canada and the United States is only about twenty years old and with the United States now virtually a fully paid up member at the World Cup finals, it is really quite amazing how far this league has come in a very short space of time. In fact, I can actually see the USA winning the World Cup within twenty years.

On one of our days off, my colleague, Phil, and I decided to get the train to downtown Toronto to have a look around the city.

We took the escalator up to the street, to be met by an incredible sight that will quite literally stay with me for the rest of my life.

We couldn't believe our eyes. Thousands of

people, almost all of them dressed in blue, appeared to have taken over the city centre. They were everywhere; in bars, restaurants, shops… you name it, downtown Toronto, for reasons unknown to us, had been invaded. It was obvious there was some huge event going on and if I hadn't known better, it looked just like a football match back home. It reminded me of England and my team Everton, especially with all those beautiful blue shirts. There were, however, two very noticeable differences. First of all, you would never get weather like this back in England, as Toronto was absolutely sweltering in a heat wave and secondly, which was a lot more apparent than the first, I couldn't see one single police officer in this crowded and very friendly atmosphere.

We still didn't have a clue what was going on, until somebody explained that Toronto's Blue Jays baseball team were playing at home to America's Detroit Tigers.

"Just imagine," I remarked to Phil, "a crowd like this before a match back home. There would be police everywhere."

I had to laugh at Phil's reply. "Well, it has to be the equivalent of a couple of Canadians, not into football, innocently coming up the escalator at Wembley Park train station on cup final day and wondering why thousands of people were walking around with blue shirts on."

It certainly felt like that for us. It was also one of those occasions of when in Rome, do as the Romans do. Okay, it was Toronto and not Rome, but take it from me, for the next few hours we were definitely Blue Jay baseball fans. We were treated to some great Canadian hospitality and it's at times like this when I can't help wondering why football hooligans behave the way they do. I just wish they could see how truly wonderful it is to meet fans from different places. Why anybody would want to spoil something special like this is really beyond me.

You will have gathered by now that I love talking to people and I was so interested in speaking to as many fans as possible. We weren't that far from Niagara Falls, either, and when I spoke to an American from New York, he told me you can actually look over from this iconic waterfall and see the state of New York.

"I know what you mean," I told him. "You can also stand on the pier in Liverpool and see the state of Birkenhead."

The great thing I've always found about talking to so many different people is that you never know what you're going to hear next and the conversation that was about to take place between me and my American friend in the next few minutes was to be another one of those defining moments in my life. Unbeknown to me, it would prove to be even more significant than when I met that man in the suit.

As has always been the case in my life, it wasn't long before the topic of football came up and our friend from the Big Apple asked me who my team was. I told him it was Everton and he told me his team was New York City FC, who incidentally are the latest club to join the MLS. He said he loved the English Premier League, but was so excited about his home city of New York now having their own team, as they were preparing to kick off their first ever match at the Yankee Stadium in the Bronx. It was great talking to him and his passion for football... oops, sorry done it again, I mean soccer, was so obvious to see.

Five minutes ago, we didn't know a single thing about each other, but because of our shared affection for the beautiful game, we could easily have known each other for years. We had so much in common, I could have spent all day talking to him. But it was what he said next that would prove to be another major turning point in my life.

He told me his team had a supporters' group called the Third Rail, which is aptly named after the third rail that powers New York City's subway system. We both agreed how important it was for fans to have a voice, especially with the many injustices we constantly face in today's money rules all game.

But as he was telling me about the Third Rail, something I had never experienced before in my life suddenly hit me smack in the face. It was that flash of insight – that epiphany moment when I realised for the very first time in my life why we fans suffered such appalling disrespect – and not just the fans of a few clubs, but supporters of every club in the land.

It was difficult to comprehend why this had never occurred to me before and it really was a very strange and surreal moment that I swear I will remember for the rest of my life and where I was when it happened.

I just looked at my friend, shaking my head.

"Say, are you okay?" he asked.

"Have you ever had one of those eureka moments in your life?" I replied.

"All the Goddam time."

"Well, I've just had one myself… a monumental one at that," I told him. "I've had one or two others over the years, but never before like this. If I hadn't spoken to you today, I don't think I'd have ever worked out why the football authorities have always got away with being so disrespectful to us fans." Again I shook my head, astounded that my realisation should have been so long in coming. I couldn't believe how strange it was - after all those years of following my team all around the UK and Europe, why was it that here, in Canada, I would discover why we fans have always been ripped off? I mean, of all the places I've travelled to, why Canada?

"Wow!" he exclaimed. "What did I say that was so important?"

"You just told me about your team, New York City, the latest team to be launched in Major Soccer league, right?"

"That's right," he agreed.

"Well, it was only when you mentioned your supporters' group, the Third Rail, that the penny dropped," I began. "We have different supporters' groups in the UK as well. In fact, we have loads of them. My own team, Everton, have The Blue Union, Liverpool have one called The Spirit of Shankly, and nearly every team I know has their own fans' group. I don't know why it's never really registered with me before... maybe it was the way you mentioned that your new club is born and the most natural thing in the world to do next is to create another fans' group."

"Yeah, I think I know now where you're going with this one, Buddy," he said.

"I've no doubt that every single one of these fans' groups works tirelessly to protect their fans, but the sad thing is, no matter who we support or which group we belong to, we fans are still being treated with the utmost disrespect and the very fact that we need to have a fans' group at all just confirms how vulnerable we fans really are, even your team, New York City, with your fans group, the Third Rail. Without any intention of doing so, you have just brought home to me why football fans all over the world have been and always will be treated like mugs and left to rot in our multiple, tiny groups." I wondered how I could have missed seeing something so obvious.

"Without putting too fine a point on it," I continued, "because we're all split up and so divided, we'll never be strong enough or loud enough to be heard and from where I'm standing right now, the Third Rail, much to the delight of the football authorities, have just become the latest division."

"I can see what you mean," he agreed.

In England, we have the National Supporters' Federation and Supporters Direct who both work relentlessly to represent the fans. But as I say, with so many injustices still happening to fans all over the world, it really seems to me we have far too many groups. I think everybody knows that, unlike other customers, we have one massive, unique disadvantage and major weakness, which they are fully aware of – that we won't take our support elsewhere and support another team.

The football authorities have stood by for years and watched us all, isolated and separated. They have publicly criticised hooligans at matches... well they would, wouldn't they? But privately, I'll bet they're delighted to see fans kicking the hell out of each other instead of venting their anger at them. I mean what a brilliant deflection for them. Talk about us fans taking our eye off the ball!

I told my American buddy that from a very early age and throughout my whole life, all I've ever known is division and segregation. From as far back as when I started in St. John's Catholic infants school and not knowing one single kid from Grove Street Protestant school, which was only about a mile up the road.

"Throughout my whole life, I have witnessed splits and divisions, just like meeting you today, with our two separate fans groups, The Blue Union and The Third Rail," I said. "And although we have a lot in common with our love for soccer, we are after all, very much divided. Each team's competitive rivalry is what makes soccer so exciting and is the whole point of competing against each other, but the unfortunate thing for fans like you and me is that the footballing authorities have always used it as a stick to beat us with."

I told him I sincerely wished his new club, New York City FC, the very best of luck and many years of success.

"I pay the Third Rail the greatest of respect, but

what you just told me has brought it all home to me why we fans have never really had a proper voice. As long as we remain divided, we will always be disrespected."

"I have to admit, I never really thought of it like that before," he said.

"And I have to confess," I replied, "that until I met you, neither did I."

It was time for my pal to make his way to the game, as we shook hands and wished each other all the best.

"Up the Toffees, man; I'll keep an eye out for Everton," he said.

I also wished New York City FC many years of success and promised him that from now on, I would always look out for their results.

When he left, I couldn't stop thinking about our conversation. For the remainder of my stay in Canada, I kept thinking back to all those years I'd witnessed at first-hand, football supporters being treated disrespectfully. We had kick-off times changed at the last minute to suit...well everybody except us fans. We had huge numbers of tickets taken away from us for cup finals and other big games. Even when we could get tickets, they put the price up dramatically to exploit us even more, even though they were making a fortune from TV revenues. They even changed our club shirts every season and with some clubs having as many as four or five strips, this was so unfair to fans who had always been loyal to their clubs.

There were so many more injustices, I could write another book on that subject alone. I was always amazed that the football authorities could get away with treating fans like this and I never even realised how they could... until I travelled to Canada. One would have thought I could have worked out the answer in Liverpool, London or even Manchester. Or perhaps travelling in Europe, but Canada? The last place I would have imagined having that light bulb moment.

The powers that be have enjoyed the benefits of divide and conquer for centuries and the footballing authorities, watching the fans split into many different groups, are apparently no different.

Imagine if we had an international body of supporters and were not separated. We could still remain fierce rivals competing against each other, but we could at least say to the authorities, disrespect us at your peril.

Why would you want to fight these fans?

Niagara Falls

Once a Blue, always a Blue

Rogers Centre, with the famous CN Tower. What a stadium!

Outside the Rogers Centre, home of the Blue Jays, Toronto, Canada.

Twenty-seven
SING Your Hearts Out for the Fans

Have you ever noticed the number of people who say, "I don't like football, but my team is…"

It is quite amazing when you think about it, but although they have stated quite clearly that they have absolutely no interest in the sport, for some reason they still feel this certain affinity towards one particular football team. It's something I've always found difficult to get my head round and to try and find out the reason for this, I conducted an experiment a few years ago in work, when I asked about ten colleagues that I knew hated football, who their football team was.

Now, instead of saying they didn't like football and therefore couldn't pick one, the strange thing was that they all picked a team and I mean every single one of them. There were a few different reasons for this, such as most of them coming from that particular area, or members of their family who followed that team and I suspected there were one or two who just picked a team to be part of the crowd.

It doesn't matter where I travel, whenever I meet somebody who allegedly has no interest in football, I still can't resist asking them who their team is. Up to now, I've never had one person say they don't have a team. You can carry this experiment out yourself, anywhere.

As for the rest of us, these non-football people would never in a million years understand what makes us fans fall passionately in love with our clubs and when you think of the lengths we go to demonstrate our loyalty… well, no wonder they think we're nuts.

Because of my protest and one or two other things, I know I've had an absolutely crazy life as a football fan and I really have lost count of the number of times I've asked myself how different it would have been if I hadn't queued up that day and encountered that man in the suit obtaining those complimentary tickets.

The man in the suit has become more than just a distant memory to me. It was without any doubt his red rag presence which lit the blue touch paper that day and which was the catalyst for my protest of refusing to pay into any more football grounds.

There was never a shadow of doubt in my mind that what I witnessed that day was an insult to football fans everywhere who were struggling to afford these ever increasing ticket prices. I know I could have just turned a blind eye and forgotten what I'd seen, but people who know me will confirm that walking away and saying nothing was never an option.

I am not overly proud of having to resort to entering football grounds without paying and if I could have worked out a better way of publicising this protest, believe me, I would have taken it. I knew if I was to have any chance of highlighting the many injustices we face, then I had to do something quite outlandish. I mean, who was going to listen to a nobody like me trying to stop us fans being ripped off? Certainly not the football authorities.

I still can't believe what I put myself through and still tremble when I think of some of those terrifying moments. Even though there are some amusing memories that still make me laugh, I would be very disappointed if people didn't see the serious significance of my protest, which I sincerely hope they understand.

I felt passionately that somebody had to do something and even though I took the risk of making a complete and utter fool of myself, if it helped to reveal just some of the disrespect shown to us football fans then, to me, it was justifiable and a risk well worth taking.

I am fully aware that many people will have considered my protest a futile exercise, as it didn't seem to make the slightest bit of difference. I've even asked myself, numerous times, if it really was a total waste of time, as football fans are still being treated disgracefully. But as I've said, I was so incensed by it all that I felt I had to protest in some way.

Even when the protest was finished, countless other disrespectful issues began to emerge and, just as I stumbled across the man in the suit, I started tripping over many more forms of disrespect, as each injustice began to unravel. There were now some very serious issues and with fans becoming angry and boycotting football matches as well as carrying out other various protests, this was definitely not the same game I grew up loving. For the first time in my life, I could see how much trouble football was actually in and although it wasn't the fans' fault, we did have to accept some of the blame for allowing these people in charge to get away with it. If that sounds a bit over the top, ask the supporters of every club whose existence has been seriously threatened, from the giants of Glasgow Rangers. To FA cup giant killers, Hereford United.

Many more unscrupulous people are looking to capitalise on all the money coming into the game. Their interests are more about their own personal greed rather than the future of football and on that basis alone, no club is safe. I mean, how can any football club be in financial trouble, when there has never been so much money in the game? It is glaringly obvious that something is not right.

It can't just be a coincidence that during those halcyon days of 1966 when England won the World Cup, football fans were not expected to take out a mortgage to buy a season ticket. We didn't have to buy three or four shirts every season and club owners would never have been allowed to disrespect their fans by changing the colour of their teams' strips, not to mention renaming their once proud old stadiums with tacky new sponsored names.

TV companies and the football authorities didn't try to seduce fans across the world by changing the kick-off times just to fit in with their time zones. They never instructed us what time we had to turn up to watch our teams, or how much extra we had to pay to watch it on TV... and without any of this diktat, England were the champions of the world. Makes you think, doesn't it?

If all this isn't bad enough, for me, the most despicable injustice of them all has to be that we are no longer seeing our kids coming through the turnstiles. A lot of people in football don't seem to care about the kids any more and even a lot of our bigger clubs now seem to be more interested in day-trippers and tourists, who are willing to pay top dollar for admission, with the added bonus of visiting their souvenir shops.

But they are making a huge mistake, as there won't be any proper fans left in twenty years' time and the football fan that we have come to know will simply become extinct. I foolishly and naively thought I was just complaining and publicising the point about supporters being ripped off, but the whole world and his dog already knew this. It was no longer just about the sheer contempt shown to us fans, it was now a very serious case of whether the football fan could possibly survive and still be around for the next generation.

It doesn't take a soccer statistician to work out that without any fans there won't be any game. The powers that be are either unable to see the dangerous consequences that lie in store for our game, or even worse, maybe they can, but just don't care. What a lot of people don't realise is that, with the average age of Premier League supporters now being over forty, not inviting kids to grow into football fans will sadly prove to be the final nail in the coffin of our beautiful game.

When I was young, my admittance fee wasn't that expensive and I really felt I was welcome. With clubs today making an absolute fortune from television and sponsorship, there can be no justifiable reason whatsoever to charge these extortionate prices. Excluding the ordinary fans like children and the elderly from the game they love can only be summed up in one word... greed.

You may have seen the banner at various football grounds around the country, *Don't let your kids grow up thinking that football is a TV show*. But that's exactly what it is turning into. Football really is fast becoming just another TV show, and we all know that TV shows can be switched over. They can also be switched off.

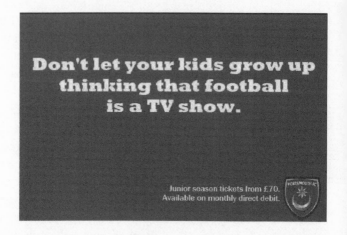

Don't let your kids grow up thinking that football is a TV show.

Junior season tickets from £70.
Available on monthly direct debit.

There may be more bums on seats, but the real fans can no longer afford to get into the most expensive league in the world and, as many Premier league games are nearly always sold out, the sad reality is that while there is such a massive demand for tickets from tourists and day trippers, clubs can and will charge whatever they want. Just like we see in the West End or on Broadway, it won't be long before there is a different audience every week. You may not believe this could happen, but it is already happening at some of the big grounds.

What we have now is a very dangerous scenario, believing that football fans will always be there and these people are deliberately ignoring the prospect of there not being any proper fans in twenty years' time, or even less, the way the situation is escalating. Inevitably, the people running football will become victims of their own success, as the younger generation of fans they have killed off will no longer be interested in football and pursue other interests. Biting the hand that feeds them is unwise when there is no back up in place… and we all know the idiom of the goose that was killed with the golden egg.

The really scary thing about it all is that the people running football are not stupid and are fully aware of the real dangers that lie ahead. Honestly, this has me more fearful about the future of the game than anything else, because these people in suits don't usually make mistakes. It's a very sad fact of life, but there will always be individuals who are making so much money today that they couldn't care less about football's existence tomorrow.

If I hadn't travelled with my job and met so many fans in other parts of the world, I may never have noticed that it wasn't just football supporters in Britain being taken for a ride. Oh no, it was happening to decent, loyal fans everywhere across the globe. The English Premier League has become such a major financial commodity that it doesn't matter where in this world you are, there are countless business people using this global enterprise to extract as much money as possible from those of us who love the game. These opportunists see us as easy prey and this will only stop happening when we decide enough is enough.

Is it any wonder that everywhere you look, fans' groups are being set up at every club and who can blame them? Apart from being treated so disrespectfully from the authorities, many fans are now even feeling a lack of transparency at their own clubs and no longer feel so involved or as welcome as they once did.

When I last counted, there were only fourteen clubs throughout the whole football league who had any kind of fan involvement on the board of directors, with Swansea City being the only club in the Premiership.

Full credit must go to co-owned Swansea City for asking the Premier league to cut ticket prices. Their vice-chairman, Leigh Dineen, made a very important point when he said it couldn't just be his club making this stand, as it would give every other club an unfair advantage. For reasons known only to them, not every club is willing to allow ordinary fans onto their board, but even if they did, there is a feeling amongst some that these fans would then become ingrained in their new, comfortable status and instead of fighting the problem, there is the danger of them becoming part of it.

In Britain, The National Supporters Federation and Supporters Direct are working relentlessly to represent and protect the fans, but why do I constantly feel that the footballing authorities are merely paying them lip service? Even with hundreds of different fans' groups now operating and constantly striving for fans' rights, we are still being treated appallingly.

Everybody is calling on FIFA and many of their employees to stand down, myself included, but why is there never any mention of the fans in any of this? If it was up to me, I would have a body consisting of people who truly love the game and care about its future, like former players, managers, referees, football journalists and the most important component of all, ordinary football supporters. I wouldn't hold my breath though, because these people in suits don't want to relinquish their power and it looks like we're going to have to put up with these cronies for many years to come.

As supporters of the beautiful game, who needs FIFA anyway? We have it within ourselves to ensure football's future and it will be football fans all over the world and not a posse of suits in Zurich that will save the game. We can only do this by gaining everybody's respect, but before we can achieve this, we must learn to respect each other. Of course we can still compete and remain fierce rivals; that is one of the most exciting things about football, but the fighting, hooliganism, racism and hatred... all that has to stop.

We really do need to move the goalposts, before there are no goalposts left to move. If we are to succeed, we have to up our game and show the world that football fans are not all thugs. Otherwise, the football authorities will make sure we remain in our separate groups, achieving nothing. They must love it when they see fans despising each other, as they can pick us off one by one. As custodians, we have an obligation to future generations to wake up and smell the coffee before it is too late and to stop falling for the clever tricks designed by these people in suits to keep us apart.

Believe me, it is no coincidence that everywhere you look, people are divided, whether it be politics, religion, class, nationalism or – yes, even football fans. You name it, we're all separated and the only groups that aren't divided are the ones in charge of every one of these institutions.

Football fans have fought against each other for far too long and the footballing authorities have always stood back, watching us remain divided. Of course they condemn this behaviour and just to assure everyone that they are doing something about it, they issue an occasional fine or a ban. They even employ people who are handsomely paid to deal with these incidents, which, to me, suggests acceptance that problems will continue. If this was to occur in the directors' box, you can bet your bottom dollar that it would be nipped in the bud once and for all.

They say there are none so blind as those who will not see and football hooligans definitely do not see that they are playing right into the hands of the footballing authorities with their thuggish behaviour. Instead of fighting each other, we fans should all be pulling together to stop them making us extinct. Apart from the obvious pain and suffering they inflict on others, they are also responsible for tarnishing the good reputation of the majority of football supporters, who are decent and respectable and who just want to follow their team. If these hooligans haven't the nous to see that these people in suits will end up killing us off, then we're better off without them anyway.

There are many fans' groups now fighting for more respect and saying enough is enough. I sincerely wish every one of these groups the best of luck, but I really believe that if we are to achieve this, then we have to stand together. By showing mutual respect for each other, we would be demonstrating to the authorities that this is what we expect from them as well. We need to show them that we may all hail from different clubs, but we are not prepared to stand by and watch football fans become extinct.

It would be great to see fans groups like New York City's Third Rail, Everton's Blue Union and Liverpool's Spirit of Shankly, as well as every other group from across the globe working together to safeguard the future of the football fan and the beautiful game for generations to come.

It wouldn't be the first time that great rivals have come together and a great example of this was when the two Newcastle United fans, John Alder and Liam Sweeney, were tragically killed in the Malaysian Airways plane crash on 17 July 2014. Their fierce arch-rivals, Sunderland, reminded everybody just how close football supporters really are when people hurt us.

You may recall that John and Liam were on their way to see their beloved Magpies play a pre-season tour match in New Zealand, when their plane was shot down over the Ukraine. Gary Ferguson, a staunch Sunderland fan, created a fund, hoping to raise £100 for a floral tribute.

He said, "We may be Sunderland fans who traditionally have deep rivalry with Newcastle, but there are things far more important than any football games."

His fellow fans from the Stadium of Light responded, not by raising £100, but an unbelievable £30,000 and this was from their bitterest and fiercest rivals. But that's football fans for you... I mean *real* football fans proving they can come together when they have to.

If we could follow the example of the Hillsborough families by never giving up, as well as the way the people of Newcastle and Sunderland put aside their differences for two of our fellow supporters, then we may just be able to help our kids grow into fans and enjoy the beautiful game as we did. If we don't, the football fan will simply not survive.

I am sick to death of hearing that the reason for fans always being treated disgracefully is because they always accept everything thrown at them and never do anything about it. I'm even more sickened by the fact that it is actually true. It has never been so important for fans to do *something* about it and this really is our last chance... not just to save the football fan from becoming extinct, but by saving football as well. Because, and I make no apology for repeating this, without fans, there is no game.

I have never regretted carrying out my protest, but I now know, deep down in my heart of hearts, that trying to do something like that single-handedly was a huge mistake.

With football fans still being treated like second class citizens, I don't need anybody telling me that I didn't achieve anything. The people paying to get into football matches are now actually paying even more money and as for the rest of us, meaning the real fans, including children and the elderly, I am not exaggerating when I say that we feel totally excluded from the game we love. It saddens me to say there is even more disrespect shown towards fans today, than when I began my protest.

As you know, it was only when I spoke to the New York City supporter whilst working in Canada, that the penny finally dropped and I saw so clearly the reason why we have always been treated so appallingly. *Because we have always been separated.* That moment of enlightenment really brought home to me that we needed to try something different. That is why I honestly believe the only way for football to survive is for fans to stand together in one group. I would love to see, for the very first time in history, football fans from all over the world sing together in a Supporters InterNational Group (SING).

SING would welcome fans from clubs in every corner of the earth and ensure that the people who truly care about the future of football have a voice loud enough to be heard.

We really are an endangered species which

urgently needs protecting and if we are to save the football fan from extinction as well as the beautiful game itself, we need to all SING our hearts out for the fans.

Who knows? This time, I may not be alone.

The End

14687338R00209

Printed in Great Britain
by Amazon.co.uk, Ltd.,
Marston Gate.